Introduction to China's S&T Innovation focuses on China's economic development, medical and health care, digitalization construction and other hot spots of China's livelihood, and showcases the fruits of reform and development that have benefited all Chinese people.

In recent decades, with the wave of economic globalization, China's economy has taken off rapidly, and at the same time, China has also made great achievements in science and technology, education and culture, which have attracted the world's attention. This series is a classic work that helps overseas readers understand China's economic and social development in all aspects. Each book in the series is edited by authoritative experts and scholars in the relevant fields. By elaborating on the development history, technological innovation, policy evolution, underlying logic, and international cooperation in their respective fields, the series comprehensively introduces the quality and speed of China's modernization, and shares the experience of Chinese-style modernization, which will help people around the world better understand China, promote the exchanges and mutual understanding among different civilizations, and advance common development.

Zhanchun Feng · Juyang Xiong · Xiaofeng Zhao
Editors

China's Health System

華中科技大學出版社
Huazhong University of Science and Technology Press

Springer

Editors
Zhanchun Feng
Huazhong University of Science
and Technology
Wuhan, Hubei, China

Juyang Xiong
Huazhong University of Science
and Technology
Wuhan, Hubei, China

Xiaofeng Zhao
Huazhong University of Science
and Technology
Wuhan, Hubei, China

Translated by
Tao Hong
Huazhong University of Science
and Technology
Wuhan, Hubei, China

Introduction to China's S&T Innovation
ISBN 978-981-95-1204-1 ISBN 978-981-95-1205-8 (eBook)
https://doi.org/10.1007/978-981-95-1205-8

Jointly published with Huazhong University of Science and Technology Press

This Springer imprint is published by the registered company Springer Nature Singapore Pte Ltd.
The registered company address is: 152 Beach Road, #21-01/04 Gateway East, Singapore 189721, Singapore

Editorial Board

Series Editor's Preface

Throughout the history of mankind, when education in a country thrives, the country will thrive, and strong education makes a strong nation. Today, as economic globalization continues to deepen, the opening-up of education has become an essential strategy for national development. Since the 18th National Congress of the Communist Party of China, numerous important documents concerning the internationalization of higher education have been issued, with international exchange and cooperation now being one of the five major functions of universities. Huazhong University of Science and Technology (HUST) has actively responded to this call by releasing a series of guiding documents to promote the internationalization of education, and placing significant emphasis on the education of international students in China. The "Introduction to China's S&T Innovation" is a classic collection of works created for international students in China in this context, which can be said to be both a need of the times and a responsibility.

We live in an era characterized by advanced transportation, frequent interpersonal exchanges, and increasingly dynamic cultural interactions. In this era, how to tell China's stories well and let the world understand China better has become an important issue for us. We are fully aware that international students in China possess the unique advantage of being "bridges between China and the world," serving as special envoys of friendship between China and the world and important connectors between China and the world. By providing international students with a comprehensive understanding of China's economic and social development, we can empower them to tell China's stories well, thereby enhancing the international dissemination of Chinese civilization.

In recent years, Xi Jinping, General Secretary of the Central Committee of the Communist Party of China, has written numerous heartfelt letters to overseas students, returning scholars, and international students in China. Studying these letters has deeply inspired and encouraged me. On the one hand, as a former overseas student who studied abroad in Germany and the United States for over six years starting in 1995, I have gained a deep understanding of the academic and living needs of international students in China. On the other hand, since returning from studying abroad over 20 years ago, I have been engaged in research, teaching, and administrative work at universities. During my tenure as Vice President of Huazhong University of Science and Technology, I was responsible for international exchange and cooperation for many years, with international student education being one of my primary responsibilities. I have witnessed and experienced the rapid development of China's higher education and scientific research. As the number of international students in China continues to grow, I feel proud and honored, and at the same time, I also feel a great sense of responsibility.

At present, China is in a new phase of high-quality development, where promoting high-quality development through high-level opening-up has become a requirement of the times, both in the economic and educational fields. I believe that high-level opening-up of education is not only a driving force for the "Double First-Class" initiative in Chinese universities, but also an opportunity to explore new areas of international cooperation for universities. Therefore, in our internationalization efforts, we have consistently adopted an international perspective, positioning ourselves within a global framework, benchmarking against world-class universities, and actively expanding substantial cooperation with top international institutions. While expanding the scale of international students in China, we have also worked to further improve the quality of their education.

The "Introduction to China's S&T Innovation" selects key topics related to China's economic development, medical and health care, digitalization construction and other hot spots of China's livelihood. By explaining the development process, technological innovations, policy evolution, underlying logic, and international cooperation in these fields, the series provides a comprehensive introduction to the quality and speed of China's modernization efforts. It not only serves as a vivid record of China's modernization, but also highlights the spiritual symbols and cultural essence of Chinese civilization.

Each book in this series is edited by authoritative experts in the relevant field. Here, I would like to extend my heartfelt gratitude to the chief editors for their strong support and hard work. They are leading scholars deeply engaged in scientific research, with keen insights into the trends of economic and technological development in China and internationally. They possess rich experience in book compilation and a profound understanding of the content. Furthermore, they are front-line educators with extensive teaching experience, who understand the needs of international students in China, know the ways of teaching, and have unique insights into talent cultivation. I am confident that this series, which fits the background of the times, carefully selects hot topics, and understands readers' needs, will be able to present a comprehensive, multidimensional, and authentic China to international students. It will empower them to tell a good story about China, act as good envoys of friendship, and build bridges of cooperation.

Looking ahead, the "Introduction to China's S&T Innovation" will continue to be developed and published, laying a solid foundation for the education of international students in China. We will continue to advance the internationalization of our university step by step. I look forward to seeing international students and overseas readers get to know, understand, and fall in love with China through the "Introduction to

China's S&T Innovation." I also hope that this series will become a beautiful landscape of cultural exchange between China and the world, contributing our wisdom and strength to the building of a community with a shared future for mankind.

Jianguo Chen
Former Vice President of Huazhong
University of Science and Technology

Preface

When you open *China's Health System* of "Introduction to China's S&T Innovation," you might be pondering a profound question: How can a developing country with a population of over 1.4 billion achieve universal access to basic health care services under limited resources? This is precisely the Chinese wisdom that China's medical and health system reform has contributed to the world. As witnesses and participants in this reform, we are honored to share our practices and reflections with global peers, especially those from developing countries, through this book.

China's medical and health system reform is not an ideal model conceived in a laboratory but a practical endeavor unfolding across a vast land. When the new medical reform was launched in 2009, China faced typical challenges of developing countries, such as significant urban-rural disparities, uneven resource distribution, and the dual burden of infectious and chronic diseases. However, through over a decade of exploration, China has built the world's largest basic medical insurance network. The proportion of personal health expenditure dropped from 34.34% in 2012 to 27.60% in 2021, and the average life expectancy increased from 74.8 years in 2011 to 78.2 years in 2021. Behind these figures lie five key experiences.

Prioritizing equity in system design China's medical and health system reform has vigorously addressed the urban-rural dual structure by integrating the new rural cooperative medical care system with the basic medical insurance system for non-working urban residents into a unified basic medical insurance system for rural and non-working urban residents. By the end of 2023, the number of people covered by basic medical insurance reached approximately 1.33 billion, with a coverage rate stable at over 95%. Central government subsidies to central and western regions ensure that even the most remote villages have access to basic medical services. This "bottom-line equity" approach has made the right to health a universal benefit.

Strengthening health defenses with grassroots networks By the end of 2021, 90% of urban and rural residents in China could reach the nearest medical facility within 15 minutes. This was achieved not by building super hospitals but through a "county-township-village integration" mechanism, turning 35000 township health centers and 599000 village clinics into "health gatekeepers." The hierarchical diagnosis and treatment model, featuring primary care first diagnosis and two-way referrals, has reduced outpatient visits to large hospitals, with over 90% of patients treated within their counties.

Making prevention a national priority China has established the world's largest direct reporting system for infectious disease epidemics and a monitoring network for diseases and health risk factors. Chronic diseases such as hypertension, diabetes, and chronic obstructive pulmonary disease have been incorporated into the national basic public health services. The Patriotic Health Campaign has evolved from the Elimination of the Four Pests to the creation of healthy cities. For example, this initiative has effectively reduced the incidence of liver cancer in Qidong, Jiangsu Province—a region previously known as a high-risk area for liver cancer.

Breaking resource bottlenecks with technological innovation Through "Internet + Healthcare," experts from Grade-A tertiary hospitals can guide rural doctors in Xinjiang, 5000 kilometers away, in real time. China has actively promoted AI-assisted diagnostic systems, and piloted their use in some impoverished counties, effectively reducing misdiagnosis rates at the grassroots level. Traditional Chinese medicine formula granule technology has brought ancient prescriptions into modern pharmacies, benefiting a vast number of chronic disease patients.

Inspiring systemic vitality through institutional innovation The "Triple Linkage" reform in Sanming, Fujian Province, demonstrates that coordinated reforms in health care, medical insurance, and medicine can improve service quality without increasing financial burdens. This reform wisdom is now being translated into national-level payment reforms and centralized drug bulk-buying systems, saving patients over 100 billion yuan.

Of course, China's medical and health system reform is still ongoing. The "silver wave" of an aging society, profound changes in disease patterns, and higher public expectations for quality health care are all driving new transformations. However, we firmly believe that as long as we adhere to the principle of "putting people's health at the center," any challenge can become a stepping stone to progress.

For our peers in developing countries, the core lesson from China's experience is that there is no one-size-fits-all template for health governance, but there are universal values: treating health as a social investment rather than a consumptive expense, transforming institutional advantages into resource integration capabilities, and bridging ideals and reality with appropriate technologies. For example, the Chinese Brightness Action in Africa has been carried out in Zimbabwe, Malawi, Mozambique, and other countries, restoring sight to over 2000 African cataract patients. Meanwhile, the first AI cooperation and innovation platform between China and ASEAN countries has been established in Laos. These practices vividly demonstrate the Eastern wisdom in global health governance.

We hope this book will serve as a key to unlocking the door to understanding China's medical and health system reform for its readers. Furthermore, we hope that readers from around the world will gain inspiration from it and work together to write a new chapter in the advancement of global health and well-being.

Wuhan, China
February 2025

Zhanchun Feng
Juyang Xiong
Xiaofeng Zhao

Contents

Chapter 1
Overview of China's Health System

China's basic political systems include the system of multi-party cooperation and political consultation under the leadership of the Communist Party of China (CPC), the system of regional ethnic autonomy, and the system of community-level self-governance. China's administrative organs are composed of the State Council of the People's Republic of China and local people's governments at all levels under its leadership. Local health administrative departments are under the leadership of the people's governments at the same level and accept the guidance of the health administrative departments at higher levels. Since the early 1980s, with the rapid growth of China's economy, the rapid advancement of urbanization, the rapid development of industrialization, the large-scale flow of population, and the deepening of the aging of the population, diseases related to lifestyle and aging have become one of the most important health problems in China.

1.1 Background of China's Health System

1.1.1 Geographical and Demographic Background

The People's Republic of China was founded on October 1, 1949, with a total land area of about 9.6 million square kilometers, ranking third in the world, and a total sea area of about 4.73 million square kilometers. As of 2022, China has a total of 34 provincial-level administrative units, including 4 municipalities directly under the central government (Beijing, Shanghai, Tianjin, Chongqing), 23 provinces (including Taiwan), 5 autonomous regions and 2 special administrative regions (Hong Kong Special Administrative Region and Macao Special Administrative Region). At the sub-provincial level, there are 333 prefecture-level administrative units, 2843 county-level administrative units, and 38,602 township-level administrative units.

Z. Feng et al. (eds.), *China's Health System*, Introduction to China's S&T Innovation,
https://doi.org/10.1007/978-981-95-1205-8_1

China has a large population. In 2020, the Chinese population (excluding Hong Kong, Macao, and Taiwan) reached 1.41 billion, accounting for about 18% of the world's total population; 48.8% of the population was female; from 2010 to 2020, the average annual population growth rate was about 0.5%. According to the standards of the World Health Organization, China has entered an aging society in 1999, and the population aged 65 and above accounted for 14.2% of the total population in 2021. In recent decades, the education level of the Chinese population has increased significantly. The proportion of the Chinese population with high school (including technical secondary school) education or above increased from 9.4% in 1990 to 30.6% in 2020, while the illiteracy rate decreased from 15.9% in 1990 to 2.7% in 2020.

Since the mid-1980s, China's urbanization has been advancing rapidly, and the population flow has become more active. In 2011, China's urban population reached 691 million, surpassing the rural population for the first time. In 2020, China's urban population reached 902 million, accounting for 63. 9% of the country's population. In the same year, China's floating population reached 376 million, accounting for 26.6% of the country's population, and the direction of population flow was mainly from rural areas to cities. The distribution of the Chinese population is very uneven, with dense populations in the eastern and central regions and sparse populations in the western plateaus. In 2020, the density of the Chinese population was 147 people per square kilometer.

1.1.2 Health Status of the Population

Like most other countries in the world, China's population and disease patterns have shifted from one dominated by high birth rates, high mortality rates, infectious diseases and malnutrition to one dominated by low birth rates, low mortality rates and chronic diseases. This is highlighted in the following aspects.

Average life expectancy. The average life expectancy of Chinese residents has increased significantly, from 35 years in 1949 to 70.8 years in 1996 and 78.2 years in 2021.

Child mortality rate. The infant mortality rate decreased from 46.9‰ in 1980 to 5.0‰ in 2021, and the mortality rate of children under five decreased from 62.7‰ in 1980 to 7.1‰ in 2021. The gap between urban and rural child mortality rates is narrowing, but it still exists. In 1995, the rural infant mortality rate was 2.9 times higher than the urban infant mortality rate, while in 2021 it was 0.8 times higher; the mortality rate of children under five in rural areas was 3.1 times higher than that in urban areas in 1995 and 1.1 times higher in 2021.

Maternal mortality rate. China's maternal mortality rate dropped from 88.8 per 100,000 in 1990 to 16.1 per 100,000 in 2021. The gap between urban and rural maternal mortality rates has gradually narrowed. In 1990, the maternal mortality rate in rural areas of China was 2.5 times higher than that in urban areas, while in 2021, the two were basically equal, with the maternal mortality rate in rural areas (16.5 per 100,000) slightly higher than that in urban areas (15.4 per 100,000).

Composition of the causes of death. Since the 1990s, the biggest change in the composition of the causes of death in the Chinese population is that the proportion of malignant tumors, cerebrovascular diseases and heart diseases has been increasing, while the proportion of infectious diseases, chronic respiratory diseases and digestive diseases has been decreasing. Along with this shift, non-communicable chronic diseases have become the major disease burden in China. Among the deaths caused by various diseases each year, malignant tumors, heart diseases, and cerebrovascular diseases are the top three contributors, and the number of deaths caused by them accounts for nearly 70% of the total deaths.

Infectious diseases. Infectious diseases, including cholera, leprosy, tuberculosis, schistosomiasis and malaria, used to be the most important diseases affecting the health of Chinese residents. Through the establishment of a disease prevention and control system and the implementation of vaccination programs and patriotic health campaigns, China has successfully reduced the incidence of infectious diseases and effectively controlled key infectious diseases, such as severe acute respiratory syndrome (SARS), human infection with highly pathogenic avian influenza, hand, foot and mouth disease, imported polio, and human infection with H7N9 avian influenza. In 2019, China reported a total of 21 cases of Class A infectious diseases with 1 death. Among these, there were 5 cases of plague with 1 death and 16 cases of cholera with no death. At present, the main infectious diseases in China include viral hepatitis, tuberculosis, acquired immunodeficiency syndrome (AIDS), etc. In 2021, the incidence of viral hepatitis in China was 87 per 100,000, the incidence of tuberculosis was 45.4 per 100,000, and the incidence of AIDS was 4.27 per 100,000. In 2021, the number of deaths due to AIDS, tuberculosis, and viral hepatitis in China were 19,623, 1763 and 520, respectively.

1.2 The Basic Composition of China's Health System

In 2009, the "Opinions of the Central Committee of the Communist Party of China and the State Council on Deepening the Reform of the Medical and Health System" was promulgated. It is a programmatic document for a new round of medical and health system reform (referred to as the new medical reform) in China. Under the guidance of this document, China has built a framework for China's health system in recent years based on the principle of "one goal, four beams and eight pillars" (Fig. 1.1). Among them, "one goal" is to establish a basic medical and health service system. The "four beams" refers to the public health service system, medical service system, medical security system, and drug supply guarantee system that cover both urban and rural residents. The "eight pillars" refer to the medical and health management system, the operation mechanism of medical and health institutions, the mechanism of diversified health investment, the mechanism of pharmaceutical price formation, the medical and health supervision system, the mechanism of medical

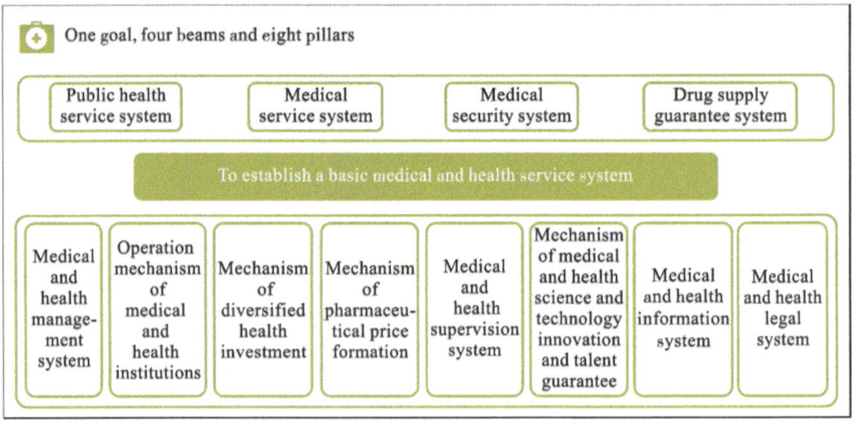

Fig. 1.1 "One goal, four beams and eight pillars" in the construction of China's health system

and health science and technology innovation and talent guarantee, the medical and health information system, and the medical and health legal system.

1.2.1 Main Component Systems

1.2.1.1 The Public Health Service System

In China, public health services are mainly provided by primary medical and health institutions and professional public health institutions. China has established a public health service system based on community health service centers (stations), township health centers, village clinics, and other urban and rural primary medical and health service networks, with disease control and prevention, health education, maternal and child health care, mental health, emergency treatment, blood collection and supply, health supervision and other professional public health institutions responsible for specific professional guidance. The National Health Commission of the People's Republic of China has 19 internal institutions, including the Department of Medical Administration, the Department of Primary Health and the Department of Medical Emergency Response, as well as the CPC Committee and the Bureau of Retired Officials. It is mainly responsible for the supervision and administration of public health, medical services, health emergencies, etc. Local health administrative departments set up relevant institutions to take charge of local public health management.

1.2.1.2 The Medical Service System

In China, the medical service system consists of medical and health institutions such as second-level and third-level general hospitals, specialized hospitals and primary medical and health institutions. Among them, the second-level and third-level general hospitals mainly provide outpatient and inpatient medical services, specialized hospitals can provide medical services related to mental diseases and oral diseases, and community health service centers (stations), township health centers, village clinics and other primary medical and health institutions are responsible for providing basic medical services for residents in their jurisdictions. Both urban and rural residents can choose to go to various medical and health institutions.

1.2.1.3 The Medical Security System

China implements a multi-level medical security system with basic medical insurance as the mainstay, medical assistance as the foundation, and supplementary medical insurance, commercial medical insurance, charitable donations, mutual medical assistance and other forms of support developing together. Among them, the basic medical insurance includes the basic medical insurance for urban employees and the basic medical insurance for rural and non-working urban residents. The former covers the urban employed population, while the latter covers the urban non-employed population and the rural population. In recent years, the basic medical insurance has basically achieved population coverage (the coverage rate is stable at more than 95%), but its reimbursement ratio for expenses still needs to be improved.

Medical assistance is the foundation of China's multi-level medical security system. The medical assistance system raises funds through various channels such as government appropriations and social donations, mainly to provide financial assistance to urban and rural households eligible for subsistence allowances, households enjoying five guarantees (the elderly people, disabled individuals, and minors under the age of 16 in rural areas who are unable to work, have no means of livelihood, no legal guardians or supporters, or whose legal guardians or supporters are incapable of fulfilling their duties are guaranteed by the government to provide food, clothing, medical care, housing and burial) and other families with financial difficulties. This ensures that impoverished populations have access to basic medical services. Medical assistance primarily focuses on inpatient assistance while also considering outpatient assistance.

Critical illness insurance for urban and rural residents is an institutional arrangement that further guarantee the high medical expenses incurred by seriously ill patients on the basis of basic medical security, and is an expansion and extension of the basic medical security system. In order to avoid catastrophic family medical expenses for urban and rural residents, it is stipulated that the actual payment ratio of the critical illness insurance compensation policy shall not be less than 50%. The payment ratio is determined according to the level of medical expenses, and in principle, the higher the medical expenses, the higher the payment ratio.

With the further improvement of China's socialist market economy system and the increase of residents' income, the demand for medical and health services of residents is increasing, and the role of commercial medical insurance in the medical security system is becoming more and more important. In the current commercial medical insurance market, student medical insurance, supplementary medical insurance, and comprehensive insurance including medical insurance, accident insurance, property insurance, and life insurance are more common.

1.2.1.4 The Drug Supply Guarantee System

Since the 1980s, after more than 40 years of legal construction, China has established a relatively complete legal and regulatory system for drug management consisting of laws and regulations, departmental rules and other normative documents, including the Drug Administration Law of the People's Republic of China, the Law of the People's Republic of China on Traditional Chinese Medicine, the "Provisions for Drug Registration," the "Good Manufacturing Practice" (GMP), and the "Good Supply Practice" (GSP). Since 1995, China has successively implemented certification systems such as GMP, GSP and "Good Agricultural Practice for Chinese Crude Drugs" (GAP), and in 2006, the unannounced inspection system was implemented to strengthen the supervision and management of the quality of pharmaceutical production and operation. In addition, the National Medical Products Administration (NMPA) is the administrative institution for drug supervision and management in China. The drug regulatory departments of the people's governments of provinces, autonomous regions and municipalities directly under the central government are responsible for the drug supervision and management within their respective administrative regions. They implement unified supervision and management of drugs and their production, circulation and consumption. The National Administration of Traditional Chinese Medicine is responsible for the supervision and control of Chinese crude drugs.

In the process of solving the problem of drug accessibility, China has taken a series of measures to establish and improve the pharmaceutical management system and medical security system, which have reduced drug prices, stimulated the research and development of new drugs, and improved drug accessibility to a certain extent. In recent years, China has taken major measures to ensure access to drugs, including the establishment of a national essential medicine system, the improvement of the selection and adjustment mechanism of the National Essential Medicine List, the reform of the drug procurement mechanism, and the promotion of government-run primary medical and health institutions to implement zero-margin sales of essential medicines at purchase prices. As of 2013, all provinces in China had achieved full coverage of the essential medicine system in government-run primary medical and health institutions. In order to solve the problem of insufficient or unstable supply in the market, the implementation of fixed-point production of essential medicine varieties with small dosage and clinical necessity also ensures the supply of drugs to a certain extent.

Traditionally, the circulation of drugs in China has mainly flowed from manufacturers to wholesale enterprises, then to hospital pharmacies or retail enterprises, and finally to consumers. However, since the establishment of a national essential medicine system was officially implemented in 2009, China has begun to implement centralized bidding and procurement of essential medicines at the provincial level, which has changed the original drug circulation mode of primary medical and health institutions. In addition, since the pilot program of state-organized centralized procurement and use of drugs (also known as the "4 + 7" pilot program) was launched at the end of 2018, China has carried out 10 batches of state-organized centralized drug procurement. At the same time, various localities have also actively carried out centralized drug procurement in the form of provincial or inter-provincial alliances. In China, almost all medical institutions have pharmacies, which are responsible for the sale of drugs; hospitals are the main channel for drug sales.

1.2.2 Support Systems

1.2.2.1 The Medical and Health Management System

The National People's Congress (NPC) of the People's Republic of China is the highest organ of state power in China, and its permanent organ is the Standing Committee of the NPC (NPCSC). The main functions and powers exercised by the NPC include amending the Constitution, supervising the implementation of the Constitution, formulating and amending fundamental laws in criminal, civil, state institutional and other areas, etc. The Education, Science, Culture and Health Committee of the NPC was established in 1983. It is mainly responsible for deliberating bills, draft laws and interrogatories on education, science, culture and health assigned by the Presidium of the NPC session or the NPC, submitting to the Presidium of the NPC session or the NPCSC proposals related to the Education, Science, Culture and Health Committee within the scope of the NPC's powers, participating in the legislative work of education, science, culture, health, sports, and population, and inspecting and supervising laws in the fields of education, science, culture, and health in accordance with the law under the leadership of the NPCSC, and so on.

The National Health Commission is subordinate to the State Council and is the highest health administrative organ in China. The National Health Commission and the National Administration of Traditional Chinese Medicine and the National Disease Control and Prevention Administration are the most important health administrative agencies in China. According to the division of responsibilities, among the other departments of the State Council, the National Development and Reform Commission, the Ministry of Civil Affairs, the Ministry of Finance, the Ministry of Human Resources and Social Security and other departments of the People's Republic of China also assume corresponding responsibilities in China's health governance, such as planning, financing, and insurance management. Among the national bureaus managed by the ministries and commissions of the State Council, the NMPA and other institutions are also involved in China's health governance.

In health governance, the specific responsibilities of administrative institutions at various levels in China differ, forming a top-down hierarchical management system. Each work department of a local government is under the unified leadership of the people's government at the same level, and is subject to the operational guidance or leadership of the competent department at the level above in accordance with the provisions of laws or administrative regulations. The health administrative organs at the provincial, municipal and county levels are the health administrative functional departments of the people's governments at the same level. Under the direct leadership of the people's governments at the same level, they are responsible for the health administration and management within their respective administrative areas, and accept the operational guidance of the health administrative organs at the higher levels. China's health management organization system is divided into four levels: national, provincial, municipal, and county. Townships (towns) generally do not have independent health administrative departments.

In China, non-governmental organizations (NGOs) are also involved in various areas of the health system, including philanthropic organizations, foundations, and professional associations. Professional associations, such as the Chinese Medical Association, the China Association of Chinese Medicine, the Chinese Preventive Medicine Association, the Chinese Medical Doctor Association, and the Chinese Nursing Association, play a certain role in health governance. Their main responsibilities include organizing on-the-job training or continuing education, reflecting the opinions, suggestions and requirements of medical workers to the government and relevant departments, and organizing experts to assist the government in demonstrating relevant laws and policies, etc.

1.2.2.2 The Operation Mechanism of Medical and Health Institutions

This section primarily introduces two key components: hospitals and primary medical and health institutions. Among them, public hospitals account for the vast majority of health resources, providing major outpatient and inpatient services. As early as over a decade ago, China began implementing pilot hospital reforms and gradually established corresponding institutional operating mechanisms. In 2010, China launched a pilot project to carry out a comprehensive reform of public hospitals, including exploring the separation of medical services from pharmaceuticals, eliminating the hospital compensation mechanism of "using drug sales to supplement medical income," and the updating of the wage distribution system for medical staff and the drug procurement system, etc. In 2012, China began to promote a pilot comprehensive reform of county-level public hospitals. The main content of it include reforming the compensation mechanism, such as changing the compensation of public hospitals from three channels of service charges, drug markup income and government subsidies to two channels of service charges and government subsidies, and eliminating the practice of "using drug sales to supplement medical income."

After 2012, in order to accelerate the formation of a diversified medical pattern, China further proposed to vigorously promote the development of non-public medical institutions. Specific policies include requiring local governments to issue implementation rules to encourage social capital to run medical institutions, and encouraging areas with abundant public hospital resources to use social capital to participate in the transformation of some public hospitals. China is also further exploring and establishing mechanisms for the operation of hospitals. At present, there is a lack of objective evaluation of the impact of these operating mechanisms on hospital behavior.

In addition, in 2009, China began to reform the operational system of primary medical and health institutions, and implement systems such as the two-way referral system and the primary care first diagnosis system, as well as mechanisms such as the performance appraisal mechanism of primary medical and health institutions and personnel, and the income distribution mechanism of primary medical and health institutions. In 2012, it was clearly proposed that the income distribution of personnel in primary medical and health institutions should be based on the quantity and quality of services and be tilted in favor of the core and backbone health technicians.

In recent years, the facilities of primary medical and health institutions in China have been improved, but there are still problems of shortage and insufficient capacity of health technicians at the primary level. To this end, China has implemented strategies such as building a primary medical and health team, training health personnel for rural primary medical and health institutions, and introduced measures such as establishing a general practitioner system.

1.2.2.3 The Mechanism of Diversified Health Investment

In China, government health expenditure, social health expenditure, and personal health expenditure are the main sources of health financing and input. In terms of the sources of financing for total health expenditure, the proportion of government health expenditure to GDP decreased from 1980 to 1995 and nearly doubled from 2005 to 2012. However, the share of government health expenditure in the total government expenditure declined from 5.7% in 1995 to 4.5% in 2000, and although it began to rise slowly to 4.6% in 2005 and further to 6.7% in 2012, it remained at a low level. China's personal health expenditure as a proportion of total health expenditure is relatively high, reaching a peak of 60% in 2001 and then begin to decline gradually, falling to 34.3% in 2012, the lowest level since 1990. Personal health expenditure is also one of the main components of private health expenditure, and its share has declined year by year, from 95.6% in 2000 to 78.0% in 2012.

1.2.2.4 The Mechanism of Pharmaceutical Price Formation

In China, there are three forms of drug price management: government pricing, government-guided pricing and market-regulated pricing. Drugs included in the national drug catalog for basic medical insurance and drugs with monopoly production and operation characteristics outside the national drug catalog for basic medical insurance are subject to government pricing or government-guided pricing. Other drugs are subject to market-regulated pricing. The Drug Administration Law of the People's Republic of China has formulated a more detailed pricing method for the above three pricing forms. The drug pricing authority of the State Council and the drug pricing authorities of the provincial government formulate and publish the drug pricing catalog at the same level respectively in accordance with the central and local pricing catalogs. The government drug pricing department is responsible for monitoring the changes in the actual purchase and sale price and distribution price differential rate of drugs that are subject to government-guided pricing and market-regulated pricing. In 2009, the new medical reform began to study the abolition of drug markups, improve the public welfare of medical institutions, and reduce the burden of drug costs. The "Interim Measures for the Management of Prices in Drug Circulation," which came into effect in July 2012, controls the price differential rate (amount) at the wholesale stage and the sales stage of non-profit medical institutions, stipulates that the actual price difference in the wholesale stage shall be controlled in accordance with the method of "low price with high differential rate, high price with low differential rate," and gradually abolish the markups of drug sales by medical institutions.

In addition, medical institutions can apply to the health administrative department for practice registration of for-profit or non-profit medical institutions, and non-profit medical institutions enjoy certain preferential policies in terms of taxes and fees. China implements government-guided pricing for basic medical services provided by non-profit medical institutions and market-regulated pricing for for-profit medical institutions. For non-profit medical institutions, the National Development and Reform Commission, the Ministry of Health and the National Administration of Traditional Chinese Medicine issued the "Notice on Regulating the Management of Medical Service Prices and Related Issues," and officially promulgated the "National Medical Service Price Items Specification (2012 Edition)" to comprehensively regulate the management of medical service prices in 2012.

1.2.2.5 The Medical and Health Supervision System

China's medical and health supervision system usually includes three forms: first, set standards and enforce them; second, provide advice and policy guidance; third, set up prohibited matters. Health supervision is mainly carried out by the restrictions (regulations) set up (promulgated) by the government, that is, the specific regulatory activities are carried out by the relevant government departments, and their subordinate institutions can also undertake some regulatory activities, but they needs government authorization. The Central People's Government is mainly responsible for the overall design and arrangement of the development of public health undertakings at the national level, and local governments at all levels exercise the health supervision functions conferred by laws and regulations within their jurisdictions.

The National Health Commission, the Ministry of Finance, the Ministry of Human Resources and Social Security, the Ministry of Civil Affairs, the National Development and Reform Commission, and the NMPA are the main state agencies involved in health supervision. Local governments have also set up corresponding departments. These agencies and departments carry out corresponding health supervision activities according to their respective functions, which provide guarantees for clarifying the scope and level of medical security, standardizing medical and health service behaviors, and ensuring the quality and safety of medical services.

For the supervision function with high professional and technical requirements, the Chinese government will also entrust relevant professional and technical associations and industry associations to formulate standards, participate in the implementation of the standards, and supervise the implementation of the standards. For example, in addition to carrying out relevant technical training for physicians, the Chinese Medical Doctor Association will also organize regular examinations of physicians, promote professional self-discipline and rights protection, and provide relevant information for the government to formulate policies, laws and regulations. These industry associations have also set up branches in various places to ensure coordination and joint interaction between the top and bottom of the work. Each industry association formulates the relevant articles, membership management regulations and other regulations within the association. All organizations or individuals participating in the work of the association must abide by relevant regulations, which also play a monitoring role in industry supervision.

1.2.2.6 The Mechanism of Medical and Health Science and Technology Innovation and Talent Guarantee

The Chinese government attaches great importance to the progress of medical and health science and technology, regards medical and health science and technology innovation as the focus of the country's scientific and technological development, strives to overcome difficulties in medical and health science and technology, and provides technical support for the people's health. In recent years, China has continuously increased its investment in medical scientific research, integrated superior medical research resources, implemented major special programs for medical and health science and technology, encouraged independent innovation, and strengthened research on major disease prevention and treatment technologies and key technologies for the development of new drugs. There have been significant breakthroughs in areas such as basic and applied medical research, high-tech research, traditional Chinese medicine (TCM) and integrated traditional Chinese and Western medicine research.

In terms of talent security, since 1949, China has gradually established a continuous and unified medical education system, including medical school education, post-graduation medical education and continuing medical education.

In China, medical school education includes undergraduate education, junior college education and other levels of education. After taking the national college entrance exam, the high school graduates will enter different levels of schools to receive different medical education according to their test scores. In addition to training clinicians, medical education also trains other types of health technicians, including nurses, health administrators, pharmacists, and medical laboratory personnel. Medical school education in China also includes postgraduate education. Undergraduate graduates are qualified for postgraduate studies by recommendation or by taking the national graduate school entrance examination. The duration of master's and doctoral studies ranges from 2 to 4 years, and they are awarded master's and doctoral degrees respectively after graduation.

Standardized training for residents belongs to post-graduation medical education, which refers to the systematic and standardized training that medical students receive as residents at recognized training centers with a focus on improving their clinical skills after completing their medical school education. Standardized training for residents is a unique and necessary educational stage of clinician training, which is of irreplaceable significance for improving medical quality and ensuring medical safety.

Continuing medical education refers to on-the-job continuing education after completing medical school education and post-graduation medical education. It aims to ensure that working health professionals keep abreast of new knowledge and technologies related to their profession and the development of medical science. Continuing medical education in China is subject to a credit system. Working health professionals are required to participate in continuing education activities each year and complete a certain number of credits.

In 1998, China promulgated the Law of the People's Republic of China on Medical Practitioners, announcing the implementation of a medical practice registration system. Health technicians need to pass the national unified physician qualification examination, and obtain the physician qualification certificate issued by the National Health Commission. Only those who have obtained the physician qualification certificate and have been registered to obtain the physician practice license are qualified to engage in medical activities independently. Institutions entrusted by the administrative departments of health of the people's governments at or above the county level shall, in accordance with the practice standards of physicians, conduct regular evaluations of physicians' professional level, work performance, and professional ethics. Currently, physicians can only practice medicine in the medical institutions where they are registered, but China is developing and implementing a multi-site practice system for physicians. There are three levels of health technician titles in China: junior, intermediate and senior.

1.2.2.7 The Medical and Health Information System

The medical and health information system is an important part of the health system, and China's new medical reform regards health informatization as an important task and an important support and guarantee. From the perspective of business fields, China's medical and health information system mainly includes hospital information system, public health information system, medical security information system, comprehensive health management information platform and regional health information platform. Among the above-mentioned medical and health information systems, except for the basic medical insurance information system for urban employees and urban residents in the medical security information system, which is mainly managed by the human resources and social security departments, all of the rest are mainly managed by the health administrative departments.

The management of China's medical and health information system mainly includes the formulation of medical and health information management policies and regulations and the development plan of medical and health information, the establishment of a comprehensive and systematic information resource development and sharing mechanism, the promotion of the standardization and unification of medical and health information standards, the strengthening of medical and health information infrastructure and network construction, and the enhancing of medical and health information security. At present, China's business application-based information system has played an important role in improving business efficiency and decision-making. With the popularization of information technology, the development of extended networks and advanced data mining technology, more and more data and information are rapidly accumulating.

1.2.2.8 The Medical and Health Legal System

The socialist legal system with Chinese characteristics is an organic and unified whole composed of multiple legal laws such as Constitution and related laws, civil and commercial law, administrative law, economic law, social law, criminal law, litigation and non-litigation procedure law, with the Constitution as the commander, the laws as the backbone, and the administrative regulations and local regulations as important components.

The Constitution of the People's Republic of China clearly stipulates the health rights and interests of residents: "Citizens of the People's Republic of China have the right to receive material assistance from the state and society in the event of old age, illness or loss of ability to work. The state develops social insurance, social assistance and medical and health services for citizens to enjoy these rights." According to the adjustment object of the health law, China's medical and health legal system is divided into the legal system of medical and health institutions, the legal system of medical and health professions, the legal system of medical and health services and so on. These systems mainly regulate and guide a specific field. China currently lacks a comprehensive law that can govern the health legal system and link the Constitution with specific health laws and regulations.

At present, China does not have a specific health law, and has only a relatively complete system of health laws and regulations composed of individual laws and regulations focusing on public health and medical administration. In terms of medical aspects, it mainly includes the Law of the People's Republic of China on Basic Medical and Health Care and the Promotion of Health, the "Implementation Measures of the Law of the People's Republic of China on Prevention and Treatment of Infectious Diseases," the Mental Health Law of the People's Republic of China, the Drug Administration Law of the People's Republic of China and others. In addition, there are a large number of local regulations, ministerial and local government rules and normative documents, etc.

1.3 Development of China's Health System

Since the founding of the People's Republic of China in 1949, China's health system has gone through different stages of development, culminating in the formation of the current health system. The establishment and development of China's health system, especially the reform of organizational and governance models, is closely related to the reform of China's political, economic, and administrative systems. China's socio-economic development and reform can be divided into different stages, and the development of the health system presents different characteristics at different stages. From the founding of the People's Republic of China to the period before the reform and opening-up, China's health system was based on a planned economy and mainly relied on public financing for development. During this period, there were prominent issues such as a shortage of health services and insufficient service providing capacity. From the beginning of the reform and opening-up to 2002, China's health system gradually transitioned to being primarily based on a market economy. Governments at all levels mobilized all sectors of society to raise funds for the development of health services, health resources continued to increase, and the ability to provide health services was rapidly improved, but in the same period, the government's investment responsibility was weakened, and the personal health expenditure accounted for nearly 60% of the total health expenditure around 2000. Since 2003, China has continuously strengthened the responsibility of governments at all levels to invest in health. By 2021, the proportion of personal health expenditure in total health expenditure dropped to 27.6%.

1.3.1 The First Stage: From the Founding of the People's Republic of China to the Period Before the Reform and Opening-Up (1949–1978)

At the beginning of the founding of the People's Republic of China, China's economic development level was low. The government took the realization of social equity as one of its core values and ran social equity through the design process of the socialist political system, economic system, and distribution system, gradually forming a planned economic system characterized by a high degree of centralization with the administrative management as the main means. The state managed social and economic affairs through administrative means, and in terms of income distribution, a system of "distribution according to work" was implemented. Under the strong unified planning and organization of the government, the top-down health administrative organization system had been formed, and the health system had also been established and developed rapidly: a relatively complete health system including medical treatment, prevention, health care, rehabilitation, teaching, and scientific research had been formed, especially the rural health service system represented by the rural cooperative medical care and the rural three-level medical and health service network, which had been highly praised by the World Health Organization. The basic framework of China's medical and health service system was largely formed during this period. Due to the constraints of the level of socio-economic development at the time, China's health system was characterized by "low level, wide coverage," the financing and reimbursement levels were low, and the overall planning unit was usually a city or county. Overall, health workers had a low level of education, poor capacity to provide health services, and provided poor quality of services. Publicly-financed health insurance covered the majority of urban dwellers, but the level of compensation was very low, especially in the case of rural cooperative health care. At that time, the situation of "lack of medical care and medicine" was more serious. It was partly because there was an overall shortage of health personnel at that time, and partly because although a large number of primary health personnel (such as barefoot doctors) could be trained through short-term training and other means, their service capacity was relatively low, and there was a shortage of high-quality health personnel. At the same time, since there was no direct relationship between the income of health technicians and the quality of medical service under the conditions of planned economy, the enthusiasm of health technicians to provide medical and health services was low, and the service efficiency was not high. In the period leading up to the reform and opening-up, various contradictions within China's health system became increasingly prominent.

1.3.2 The Second Stage: The Initial Stage of the Reform and Opening-Up (1979–2002)

The Third Plenary Session of the 11th Central Committee of the Communist Party of China held in 1978 ushered in China's transition from a planned economy to a socialist market economy, and made a historic decision to shift the emphasis in the work of the party and the country to economic construction and to carry out reform and opening-up. During this period, China's political, administrative, economic, and fiscal systems underwent tremendous changes, which had a profound impact on the health system.

First, reform of the political system. The Constitution of the People's Republic of China promulgated in 1982 established the program for China's political system and economic development in the new period, and the 13th National Congress of the

Communist Party of China held in 1987 proposed establishing a highly democratic, well-regulated, efficient, and dynamic socialist political system as the long-term goal of political system reform. From 1979 to 2002, the reform of China's political system was mainly based on the separation of the functions of the party and the government, decentralization, and streamlining of institutions.

Second, reform of the administrative system. The reform of China's administrative system was carried out simultaneously with the transformation of the planned economic system to the socialist market economic system. With the development of China's economic and social undertakings, the Chinese government had begun to streamline administration and delegate powers. Local governments had begun to take on more health responsibilities, which was reflected in the fact that most medical institutions had begun to become independent operating entities that "operate independently and are responsible for their own profits and losses."

Third, reform of the economic system. From 1979 to 2002, the core of China's economic system reform was the gradual transition of resource allocation from administrative allocation to the basic role of the market. In the field of medical and health services, many health elements had been becoming more and more market-oriented, mainly regulated by the market, but the price of medical services was mainly in the form of government pricing.

Fourth, reform of the fiscal system. In 1994, China initiated the tax-sharing system reform, and the concentration of financial resources of the central government increased, while local government revenues declined, and the pressure on fiscal expenditure increased significantly. There was a contradiction between the continuous upward transfer of government financial power and the decentralization of government power in the field of health, and the government's investment in health had been greatly affected.

In order to solve the contradiction between the people's health needs and the efficiency of medical and health services during the period of planned economy, after the reform and opening-up, with reference to the practice of economic system reform, the health field has also begun to introduce more market mechanisms, including changing the income distribution method of medical institutions, adjusting the drug price policy and charging standards, etc. Medical and health services mainly focus on the needs of residents. In addition, private capital began to be allowed to open clinics and other medical institutions and provide medical and health services. At the same time, some public medical institutions were privatized. From 1979 to 2002, China's health service developed rapidly, with a rapid increase in the number of health institutions, health personnel, medical beds and equipment, and a significant increase in the capacity of health service delivery. However, due to the lack of institutional reform, the tendency of medical institutions to seek profits was becoming more and more serious, resulting in problems such as the rapid rise of medical costs and the escalation of the conflict between doctors and patients. In 2001, the proportion of the personal health expenditure in total health expenditure reached 60%, hitting a record high, while the proportion of government health expenditure was less than 16%. At the same time, the problems such as the lack of government investment in public health and the lag in the construction of rural health service system and medical security system were becoming more and more prominent. The emergence of these problems had made the reform of the medical and health system and the development of health undertakings included in the important agenda of the Central People's Government.

1.3.3 The Third Stage: The Deepening Stage of the Reform and Opening-Up (2003 to Present)

During this period, China's political, economic, and fiscal reforms entered a critical stage, and the economy continued to maintain a relatively high growth rate, but it faced some uncoordinated problems, such as the gap between the rich and the poor, the dual system between urban and rural areas, and the low social security coverage rate. In 2003, the Third Plenary Session of the 16th Central Committee of the Communist Party of China put forward the Scientific Outlook on Development, emphasizing people-oriented and balanced economic and social development. In 2007, the 17th National Congress of the Communist Party of China proposed to "continue to emancipate the mind, persist in reform and opening-up, pursue development in a scientific way, promote social harmony, and strive for new victories in building a moderately prosperous society in an all-round way," of which the promotion of health development is one of the most important elements.

In 2003, the SARS epidemic spread throughout China, and China's health system experienced severe challenges. After the outbreak of SARS, the Chinese government began to reflect on the problems existing in China's health system, make efforts to solve the shortcomings of "emphasizing medical treatment over prevention" and "emphasizing urban areas over rural areas" in health work, strengthen the construction of public health service system, and vigorously promote the construction of rural health and urban community health. After 2003, the new rural cooperative medical care system has entered a period of accelerated development, but the positioning of the market and government functions in the medical and health system has not been fully clarified. There are still problems such as medical institutions relying too much on market competition to maintain their own development and the prominent situation of "difficult and expensive medical treatment", and the multi-level needs of the masses have not been well met.

In order to solve the contradictions and problems in the field of health and achieve the goal of everyone enjoying basic medical and health services, the new medical reform was officially launched in 2009, and the long-term goal was clarified: by 2020, a medical and health system covering urban and rural residents will be basically established. The new medical reform further clarified the responsibilities of the government in the field of health, and clearly proposed that the growth rate of government health investment should be higher than that of recurrent fiscal expenditure. For example, the per capita expenditure standard for basic public health services should be no less than 15 yuan in 2009 and no less than 20 yuan by 2011. Besides, the pilot reform of public hospitals has been implemented in some cities and the level of financing and compensation for basic medical insurance has continued to increase. In 2021, the per capita financial subsidy standard for basic medical insurance for rural and non-working urban residents reached no less than 580 yuan per person per year, 7.25 times that of 2009. In 2021, the proportion of government health expenditure in total health expenditure reached 26.91%. In addition, China has also stepped up efforts to encourage private capital to run medical institutions, relaxed the access scope for medical institutions run by social capital, and improved the practice environment for medical institutions run by private capital, resulting in an increase in the number of private hospitals from 6240 in 2009 to 24,766 in 2021. Compared with the second stage of reform (1979–2002), which encourages social capital, the third stage mainly emphasizes encouraging social capital and private capital to enter the medical and health field on the premise of ensuring the public welfare and non-profit nature of government-run medical institutions, so as to meet the multi-level needs of the masses, and at the same time pays more attention to the improvement of the policy environment.

In 2018, the State Council embarked on its eighth institutional reform since the reform and opening-up, integrating the responsibilities of the National Health and Family Planning Commission and other institutions to form the National Health Commission. The National Working Commission on Ageing would be retained, and its daily work would be undertaken by the National Health Commission. The China National Committee on Ageing, which was managed by the Ministry of Civil Affairs, was transferred to the National Health Commission. The National Administration of Traditional Chinese Medicine would be managed by the National Health Commission.

Case Study: Rural Three-Level Medical and Health Service Network

From the 1950s to the 1970s, China established a relatively systematic rural three-level medical and health service network through the construction of three-level medical and health institutions with county-level medical and health institutions as the leader, township health centers as the main body, and village clinics as the basis, which effectively guaranteed the health level of farmers. This measure was praised by the World Health Organization as a model for developing countries to solve medical and health problems. The rural three-level medical and health service network mainly undertakes the tasks of preventive health care, basic medical care, health supervision, health education, etc., providing guarantee for farmers to obtain basic medical and health services, alleviating the problem of "difficult and expensive medical treatment," promoting the realization of rural medical and health development goals, and allowing farmers to receive treatment for minor illnesses within their villages, for common illnesses within their townships, and for major illnesses within their counties.

At present, the rural three-level medical and health service network in China is basically sound. By the end of 2021, China had established 17,000 county-level hospitals, 35,000 township health centers, and 599,000 village clinics across counties (districts, cities), townships, and administrative villages nationwide. Improving the rural medical and health system is the "first line of defense" to ensure the health of hundreds of millions of farmers, and it is the due meaning of comprehensively promoting rural revitalization. At present, China requires further deepening reforms to promote the healthy development of the rural medical and health system, including upholding and strengthening the overall leadership of the Communist Party of China over rural medical and health work, strengthening the overall planning and optimization of medical and health resources in counties, developing and expanding the rural medical and health workforce, and improving the level of medical and health security in rural areas. The goal is to achieve the following objectives by 2025: the functional layout of rural medical and health institutions will be more balanced and reasonable, the infrastructure conditions will be significantly improved, the rural medical and health personnel team will be developed and expanded, the personnel quality and structure will be significantly optimized, the operation mechanism of the rural medical and health system will be further improved, the reform and development of the rural medical and health system will make significant progress and so on.

Chapter 2
China's Health Work Guidelines and the Healthy China Initiative

In China, health work guidelines serve as the guiding ideology for the development of health undertakings, possessing a comprehensive and overarching nature. They represent the fundamental guidelines for the Communist Party of China and the Central People's Government in leading health work. The Healthy China Initiative is a key task under China's health work guidelines during specific periods, aiming to promote public health and comprehensive development. Understanding and mastering the basic content of health work guidelines and the Healthy China Initiative, as well as the fundamental principles of formulating health work guidelines and health development strategies, are of paramount importance for guiding the reform and development of the health system.

2.1 China's Health Work Guidelines

A work guideline is a program that guides a job or career forward. Health work guidelines are the basic principles for the development of China's health undertakings. They are also the main basis for formulating various health systems and health policies.

2.1.1 Development and Content of China's Health Work Guidelines

Since the founding of the People's Republic of China, the Chinese government has formulated health work guidelines for different periods based on the country's fundamental conditions, the basic laws of the development of health undertakings, and the health needs of the people. These health work guidelines have been proven to adapt

Z. Feng et al. (eds.), *China's Health System*, Introduction to China's S&T Innovation,
https://doi.org/10.1007/978-981-95-1205-8_2

to the health development situation of specific periods, guide the development direction and path of health undertakings in different historical periods, and promote the sound development of China's health undertakings.

2.1.1.1 The Four Major Health Work Guidelines in the Early Years of the People's Republic of China (1949–1977)

1. Formation of the Four Major Health Work Guidelines

From September to October 1949, the National Health Administration Conference was held. Given the severe shortage of medical resources, extremely poor medical and health conditions, and the prevalence of infectious diseases at the time, a preliminary health construction guideline was established, which is "putting disease prevention first, focusing on ensuring production and national defense construction, serving rural areas, factories, and mines, relying on the masses, and developing health care work." In August 1950, the Ministry of Health of the Central People's Government and the Ministry of Health of People's Revolutionary Military Commission of the Central People's Government jointly held the first National Health Conference, discussing and determining the general policy and tasks of China's health work. They established three major principles of health work: serving workers, peasants, and soldiers, putting disease prevention first, and uniting TCM and Western medicine. In September 1950, the 49th Executive Meeting of the Government Administration Council of the Central People's Government officially approved these three major principles. In December 1952, the second National Health Conference included "integrating health work with mass movements" into the principles, forming the four major principles of health work. These four principles are also known as the four major health work guidelines.

2. Basic Content of the Four Major Health Work Guidelines

Serving workers, peasants, and soldiers. This guideline clarified the direction and service objects of health work, emphasizing that the health work must serve the people, which is a major issue of principle. Workers and peasants, as the main population of China, formed the foundation of the people's democratic regime and were the backbone of production construction in the People's Republic of China. The health challenges they face were particularly acute, yet the support they receive in terms of health security was relatively limited. Soldiers, as the core members of the national armed forces under the leadership of the Communist Party of China, were the cornerstone of national defense construction. Without the participation of the military, China's construction and development and the peaceful life of its people would not be fully guaranteed.

Putting disease prevention first. This guideline represented an economical, humane, proactive, and effective disease prevention and treatment strategy aligned with the fundamental interests of the masses. All medical, preventive and health care institutions, as well as all practitioners, should make prevention one of their primary responsibilities to ensure that the goals of disease prevention and health promotion are achieved.

Uniting TCM and Western medicine. This guideline aimed to unite practitioners of TCM and Western medicine to jointly provide health services. By giving full play to the respective professional advantages of TCM and Western medicine and promoting mutual learning and common development between them, the optimal allocation of medical resources and the overall improvement of the quality of medical services will be realized.

Integrating health work with mass movements. This guideline emphasized relying on and mobilizing the masses to participate in health work. Such mass participation not only promotes the popularization of health awareness and the development of healthy habits, but also accelerates the development of health undertakings, especially in the establishment of primary medical and health institutions and the training of health personnel.

These guidelines fully reflected the nature and characteristics of the socialist health service with Chinese characteristics, fitting China's basic conditions, the health needs of Chinese people, and the laws of the development of China's health undertakings. Under the guidance of these guidelines, China's health work achieved significant accomplishments.

2.1.1.2 The Health Work Guideline in the New Period (1978–2015)

1. Formation of the Health Work Guideline in the New Period

The Third Plenary Session of the 11th Central Committee of the Communist Party of China held in 1978 marked the beginning of China's reform and opening-up period. With the steady establishment of the socialist market economy system and the deepening reforms and developments in social, economic, cultural, and scientific and technological fields, the health work guidelines established in the early years of the People's Republic of China faced the challenge of misalignment with the development trends of health work in the new period. To address this challenge, the "Decision of the Central Committee of the Communist Party of China and the State Council on Health Reform and Development" issued in 1997 clearly proposed the health work guideline that meets the requirements of the new period.

2. Basic Content of the Health Work Guideline in the New Period

The health work guideline in the new period is "making rural areas the focus of our work, putting disease prevention first, supporting both TCM and Western medicine, relying on science, technology and education, mobilizing the whole society to join the efforts, improving the people's health and serving socialist modernization." This guideline reflects China's special attention to rural health work, emphasizes the central role of prevention in health work, and stresses the development philosophy of supporting both TCM and Western medicine. It also highlights the critical role of science and education in enhancing the professionalism of health services and calls for broad societal participation to achieve broader health service goals, thereby providing a solid health guarantee for socialist modernization. The strategic focus of this guideline includes making rural areas the focus of our work, putting disease prevention first, and supporting both TCM and Western medicine; the basic strategies are to rely on science, technology and education, and mobilize the whole society to join the efforts; the fundamental purpose is to improve the people's health and serve socialist modernization.

Making rural areas the focus of our work. Rural health work has always been a key area of high concern in China. Although China's rural health work has made great progress since the reform and opening-up—with the construction of medical and preventive health care network at the county, township, and village levels further strengthened, and the rural health teams gradually adjusted and enriched—it still faces many difficulties and problems. Therefore, it is imperative to significantly strengthen rural health work to curb the constraints on rural economic and social development caused by poverty due to illness and poverty returning due to illness.

Putting disease prevention first. The health work guideline in the new period continues to prioritize disease prevention. Medical, preventive, and health care institutions at all levels should implement the approach of putting disease prevention first and effectively carry out three-level prevention work.

Supporting both TCM and Western medicine. Supporting both TCM and Western medicine in the new period is an inheritance and development of the guideline of uniting TCM and Western medicine. It is also a policy guarantee for revitalizing TCM and promoting it globally. It requires TCM and Western medicine to strengthen their unity, learn from each other, jointly improve themselves, and actively explore ways and methods for the integrated development of them.

Relying on science, technology and education. Relying on science, technology and education reflects the implementation of the idea that science and technology are the primary productive forces and the strategy for invigorating China through science and education. It also summarizes the basic experience of significant development in health work since the founding of the People's Republic of China.

Mobilizing the whole society to join the efforts. Mobilizing the whole society to join the efforts is the further development and improvement of the guideline of integrating health work with mass movements. It involves the attention of party and government leaders at all levels, the collaboration of various social departments, and the active participation of the broad masses.

Improving the people's health and serving socialist modernization. The health undertakings is a public enterprise that benefits all members of society. Its development must always adhere to two core directions: one is to ensure and enhance the health level of the broad masses, and the other is to actively support and promote the process of socialist modernization. Improving the people's health means continuously meeting the growing health needs of the people and ensuring their right to health by providing comprehensive and high-quality medical services. Meanwhile, serving socialist modernization requires that the development of the health undertakings be coordinated with China's overall development strategy. By improving the people's health level, it contributes to China's economic development, social progress, and cultural prosperity.

The health work guideline in the new period effectively addressed many difficulties and problems in China's health undertakings, guiding the correct path for health development under the socialist market economy system. By clarifying strategic priorities, basic strategies, and fundamental purposes, health work can better serve the people, promote socialist modernization, improve public health, and foster social harmony and stability.

2.1.1.3 The Health and Wellness Work Guideline in the New Era (2016 to Present)

1. Formation of the Health and Wellness Work Guideline in the New Era

Since the 18th National Congress of the Communist Party of China, the Central Committee of the Communist Party of China has identified universal health as a fundamental foundation for a moderately prosperous society and has emphasized prioritizing health in strategic development. The focus of China's health work has gradually shifted to managing and promoting health, as well as formulating and implementing the Healthy China Initiative. From August 19 to 20, 2016, the National Health and Wellness Conference was held in Beijing, where General Secretary Xi Jinping profoundly elucidated the significant importance of building a Healthy China. He also clarified the health and wellness work guideline in the new era, stating "focusing on the grassroots, taking reform and innovation as the driving force, putting disease prevention first, supporting both TCM and Western medicine, incorporating health into all policies, and promoting co-construction and sharing by the people." Subsequently, on October 25, 2016, the Central Committee of the Communist Party of China and the State Council issued the "Outline of the Healthy China 2030 Plan," calling for the construction of a Healthy China and outlining the major policies and action plans.

2. Basic Content of the Health and Wellness Work Guideline in the New Era

Focusing on the grassroots. Focusing on the grassroots is a significant reflection of the health and wellness work guideline in the new Era adapting to the new socio-economic development landscape in China. As urbanization progresses, traditional rural areas are gradually transitioning to urban settings, and farmers' identities are shifting to residents. In this context, shifting the focus of health work from "rural" to "grassroots" more accurately reflects the current social structure and population distribution and better meets the new demands of the public for medical and health services. Focusing on the grassroots means that the allocation of health resources, the provision of medical and health services, and health promotion activities should all pay more attention to the grassroots. This requires strengthening the service capabilities of grassroots medical and health institutions, improving the professional skills of grassroots health personnel, and enhancing the grassroots medical service network to ensure that grassroots people can enjoy convenient, efficient, and high-quality medical services. Simultaneously, focusing on the grassroots also emphasizes integrating health work with grassroots social governance, mobilizing and relying on grassroots people to participate in health work, and forming a beneficial situation where the government leads, society participates, and the public benefits.

Taking reform and innovation as the driving force. Taking reform and innovation as the driving force marks an important evolution of health and wellness work guideline in the new era. It transcends the traditional scope of "relying on science, technology and education," incorporating cultural and institutional innovation as core driving forces for health work. This reflects the comprehensive implementation of the five major development concepts: innovation, coordination, green development, openness, and sharing, and it is the only way to promote the sustained development of China's health undertakings.

Putting disease prevention first and supporting both TCM and Western Medicine. Putting disease prevention first and supporting both TCM and Western medicine are crucial principles of China's health work. Currently, the situation of infectious disease prevention and treatment remains severe, and the mortality rate of non-communicable chronic diseases is rising. Cardiovascular diseases, malignant tumors, and other chronic diseases have become the main causes of death among urban and rural residents. In health work, comprehensive prevention strategies must be implemented to effectively reduce the incidence and mortality rate of chronic diseases. The implementation of these strategies aims to build a more comprehensive medical and health system, improve the health level of the public, and lay a solid foundation for achieving the goals of Healthy China. China will leverage the advantages of TCM in prevention and treatment, accelerate the modernization and industrialization of TCM, promote the complementary and coordinated development of TCM and Western medicine, advance the high-quality development of the TCM industry, and promote TCM globally.

Incorporating health into all policies. Incorporating health into all policies is a concrete action to realize China's comprehensive health concept, reflecting a comprehensive understanding of and response to health impact factors. Globally, there is a consensus that health status is closely linked to multiple social factors such as poverty, education, environment, and employment. To ensure the sustainability of health outcomes, China must integrate the comprehensive health concept into all government policies, establishing the idea that maintaining health is a shared responsibility of all government departments and implementing comprehensive health management.

Promoting co-construction and sharing by the people. Promoting co-construction and sharing by the people further improves the guidelines of integrating health work with mass movements and mobilizing the whole society to join the efforts, reinforcing the concept of "sharing." Health and wellness involves all aspects of society, relates to every household, and is a systematic project. Only with active cooperation from various social sectors and widespread participation from the public can the goals of universal participation, shared responsibility, and universal benefit be achieved. Party committees and governments at all levels bear significant responsibilities. Only by adhering to co-construction and sharing by the people can the sustainability of health outcomes be ensured.

2.1.2 Basic Principles for Formulating Health Work Guidelines

In China, the formulation of health work guidelines adheres to the following fundamental principles:

Adhering to the comprehensive leadership of the Communist Party of China in health work. This principle reflects China's firm commitment to the development of its health undertakings and the fundamental purpose of the Communist Party of China to serve the people wholeheartedly. Only by adhering to the comprehensive leadership of the Communist Party of China in health work can effectively progress and implementation of health work be ensured.

Maintaining the welfare and public nature of health undertakings. China's health undertakings is characterized by its welfare and public nature. The welfare nature emphasizes the government's responsibility for the development of health undertakings and the health of the people, particularly the protection of vulnerable groups. The public nature stresses the shared responsibility of the government, society, and individuals in developing health undertakings and safeguarding public health. Under different economic systems, the nature of China's health undertakings varies. During the planned economy period, the health undertakings was a welfare one. However, with the establishment of the socialist market economy system, the health undertakings has evolved into a public welfare one with a certain welfare nature that does not aimed at profit.

Ensuring the fundamental position of health undertakings in economic and social development. Health departments protect people's lives and physical and mental health through the provision of medical, preventive, health care, and rehabilitation services. They participate in the enhancement of productivity and the restoration of labor force, thereby promoting economic and social development. This function cannot be replaced by any other department. Health, education, culture, science, and sports hold equally important positions as they are different aspects of the superstructure. The fundamental position of the health undertakings in economic and social development must be guaranteed, and sufficient support and attention should be given to it.

Adhering to a plan-led health reform orientation. This principle reflects the Chinese government's responsibility and commitment to health undertakings, emphasizing China's macro-control and management of the health field. Health reforms led by the plans ensure balanced development of basic health services and prevent neglect of underserved regions and vulnerable populations, while market-driven health reforms might overlook these aspects, leading to disparities in access to basic health services. In the health field, market forces cannot entirely replace the government's duties and functions. The government should ensure and improve the quality of public health services and expand service coverage, as well as guide the rational allocation and flow of health resources through the implementation of the plans to meet the basic health service needs of the people.

Prioritizing the protection of people's health in strategic development. This principle is very important. It underscores the importance of safeguarding people's health, placing it at the forefront of economic, social, and national defense development to ensure the comprehensive attention and protection of people's health rights. This principle promotes the steady development of health undertakings, helps improve overall health levels and national quality, and contributes to the sustained development of society and the economy. Therefore, it is crucial to understand the significant importance of "prosperity for all is impossible without health for all" and "striving to ensure people's health throughout the life cycle."

2.2 The Healthy China Initiative

2.2.1 The Health Development Strategy

The health development strategy is a long-term plan designed to meet the health needs of the population. It is a crucial area of economic and social development strategy, which must be coordinated with the overall economic and social development strategy. The core focus of China's health development strategy is to improve the health level of the population by strengthening the construction of basic medical and health services and achieving a combination of both qualitative and quantitative development. The guiding principle of this strategy is to maintain a balance between equity and efficiency, ensuring that all people have access to basic health services.

2.2.1.1 The Significance of the Health Development Strategy

Promoting economic development and social progress. One of the primary objectives of the health development strategy is to promote economic development and social progress. By improving the health level of the population and strengthening the construction of basic medical and health services, health work can restore workforce and enhance labor productivity, thus providing strong support for economic development. Additionally, health work can reduce the negative impacts of diseases and health issues on society, improve the quality of life for the population, and enhance social stability and sustainability of social development.

Guiding the scientific development of health undertakings. The formulation and implementation of a scientific health development strategy ensures that the health undertakings progresses in the right direction, and enhances the scientific, targeted, and effective aspects of health work, thus better serving the population and improving overall health levels. A scientific health development strategy also stimulates more innovative researches in the health field, and elevates the development level and international competitiveness of health undertakings, laying a solid foundation for its long-term development.

Facilitating the achievement of health goals. The formulation of the health development strategy allows managers to align with objective laws and circumstances, seize opportunities presented by the environment, shift from reactive response to proactive action, and facilitate the achievement of health goals.

Highlighting the development priorities of health undertakings. The formulation of the health development strategy can make the development of health undertakings more targeted and efficient. It focuses on the most pressing current and future health issues, prioritizing the development and improvement of health service quality and levels to meet the health needs of the population. By clarifying the development priorities of health undertakings, the health development strategy can guide the rational allocation and use of resources and promote substantial progress in health undertakings.

Improving national health quality. China faces both traditional health problems common to developing countries and health issues typical of developed countries, along with significant health disparities between urban and rural areas, regions, and populations. The health development strategy focuses on addressing major health problems affecting urban and rural residents and strengthens effective interventions for long-term health issues by formulating practical national health action plans to maintain and enhance national health.

2.2.1.2 Characteristics of the Health Development Strategy

The health development strategy has the characteristics of comprehensiveness, long-term perspective, leadership, programmatic nature, adaptability, and foresight. These characteristics collectively form the theoretical foundation and practical guide for the scientific development of China's health undertakings.

Comprehensiveness. The health development strategy needs to adopt a macro perspective, comprehensively considering key elements such as the formulation of health policies, resource input, and talent cultivation. It should cover various aspects of the health field, including medical services, health education, and disease prevention and control, with a focus on the future to lay a solid foundation for the sustainable development of health undertakings.

Long-term perspective. The health development strategy should be a medium- to long-term plan, focusing on the overall survival and development of health undertakings. It requires the establishment of long-term goals, continuous strengthening of infrastructure construction and talent cultivation, and the promotion of sustained progress in health undertakings through scientific development concept.

Leadership. The health administrative departments play a leading role in the development of health undertakings. They are responsible for defining the development direction, setting strategic goals, formulating relevant policies and plans, and organizing and supervising the implementation of various tasks to ensure coordinated and stable development of health undertakings.

Programmatic nature. As a programmatic document guiding the development of health undertakings, the health development strategy provides comprehensive guidance for setting health development goals and policies, as well as resource allocation, management and service planning.

Adaptability. The health development strategy should possess flexibility and adaptability to meet the changing and diverse health needs of society. Health departments need to timely adjust health service models, improve health service levels, continuously innovate and promote highly adaptable health technologies and policies, expand health service coverage, and improve health service quality.

Foresight. The formulators of the health development strategy should have foresight, anticipating potential new problems, situations, and challenges that may arise in the future and formulating corresponding coping strategies. This helps guide health undertakings towards a more targeted and sustainable development path, avoid blind following, and ensure smoother and healthier development of health undertakings.

2.2.1.3 Basic Principles for Formulating the Health Development Strategy

The core of China's health development strategy is to uphold the purpose of serving the people's health and comprehensively improve the health level of the population. The formulation of the health development strategy should adhere to the following fundamental principles:

People-centered principle. The goal of enhancing the health level of the population should be a core objective of national development and should be fully integrated into economic and social development planning. Health is not only the foundation for individual and family happiness but also a crucial cornerstone for the development of the nation and its different ethnic groups. By prioritizing the development of health undertakings and comprehensively safeguarding the health of the people, society's emphasis on health can be elevated, and the achievement of strategic goals of economic and social development can be ensured.

Equity first, balancing efficiency. It should be ensured that different groups have equitable access to basic health services while emphasizing the efficient use of health resources to achieve the greatest health outcomes with the least resource input. Additionally, there should be a focus on combining government responsibilities with market mechanisms, mobilizing the participation of the entire society, forming an orderly competition mechanism, and meeting the diverse health needs of the population.

Overall planning, focusing on key areas. When formulating the health development strategy, it is essential to consider all aspects comprehensively, balance various interests, focus on key areas, strengthen collaborative efforts, and enhance the overall coordination and coherence of the development of health undertakings. By creating comprehensive and systematic plans, the rational allocation and utilization of health resources can be achieved, thereby addressing fundamental contradictions in the health field.

Prevention-oriented, combining prevention with treatment. It is essential to emphasize the prevention and control of diseases at the source to reduce the waste of medical resources. Simultaneously, it is essential to focus on the combination of prevention and treatment, emphasize early diagnosis and treatment of diseases, and promote the shift of medical models from "disease-centered" to "people-centered," from "treatment-oriented" to "prevention-oriented," and from "patient-centered" to "health-centered."

Ensuring basic services, strengthening primary care, and building mechanisms. The provision of basic public health and medical services should be ensured to meet the basic medical needs of the population. It is essential to strengthen the capacity of primary health services, promote the establishment of a tiered diagnosis and treatment system, and focus services and resources on primary care. It is also essential to establish and improve the development mechanisms of health undertakings, strengthen the formulation and implementation of health policies and regulations, and promote the scientific, standardized, and institutionalized development of health undertakings.

2.2.2 The Content and Evolution of the Healthy China Initiative

Since the founding of the People's Republic of China, the health policy guidelines formulated at different periods have collectively contributed to the formation of China's health development strategy. The Healthy China Initiative is the core content of China's health development strategy and is currently the main health development strategy in China. The Healthy China Initiative is an essential part of building a moderately prosperous society in all respects. Health is both the goal and the source of development; it is a necessary requirement for promoting comprehensive human development, an essential condition for economic and social development, a crucial indicator of national prosperity and strength, and a common pursuit of the broad masses.

2.2.2.1 The Development Process of the Healthy China Initiative

In the 1970s, the World Health Organization proposed the strategic goal of "Health for All by the Year 2000," which the Chinese government subsequently committed to achieving. In 1988, this goal was incorporated into China's overall economic and social development objectives for the year 2000. The "Decision of the Central Committee of the Communist Party of China and the State Council on Health Reform and Development" issued in 1997 identified rural health, preventive care, and the equal importance of TCM and Western medicine as strategic priorities for the development of the health work. The Fifth Plenary Session of the 18th Central Committee of the Communist Party of China and the report of the 19th National Congress of the Communist Party of China further established the crucial status of public health.

2.2.2.2 Main Characteristics of the Healthy China Initiative

The Healthy China Initiative adheres to both goal-oriented and problem-oriented approaches, highlighting its strategic, systemic, guiding, and operational nature. It has the following distinctive characteristics:

Emphasizing the comprehensive health development concept. Currently, the main health indicators of Chinese residents are generally better than the average levels in middle-and high-income countries. However, with the advancement of industrialization, urbanization, population aging, and changes in ecological environment and lifestyles, maintaining public health faces a series of new challenges. According to the World Health Organization's research, behavioral and environmental factors have an increasingly prominent impact on health. The treatment-centered approach is inadequate and unsustainable for addressing health issues. Therefore, the Healthy China Initiative establishes the concept of "comprehensive health" and "comprehensive hygiene" with "health promotion as the center." It emphasizes integrating this concept into the entire process of public policy formulation and implementation, coordinating responses to a wide range of health impact factors, and maintaining the health of the population throughout all aspects and across the entire life-cycle.

Combining long-term and current focus. The Healthy China Initiative is aligned with the national strategies of building a moderately prosperous society in all respects and achieving the "Two Centennial Goals." It fully considers the alignment with the objectives at various stages of economic and social development and the requirements of the United Nations' 2030 Agenda for Sustainable Development. At the same time, it addresses current prominent issues by innovating systems and mechanisms, and coordinating policies and measures across health and family planning, sports and fitness, environmental protection, food and drug safety, public safety, and health education from a holistic perspective to form a concerted effort to promote health.

Having clear and operational goals. The Healthy China Initiative sets several key quantitative indicators across various aspects such as overall health levels, health impact factors, health services and guarantees, the health industry, and the health promotion system. This concretizes the goals and tasks, making the work process operational, measurable, and assessable. Accordingly, the Healthy China Initiative proposes a "three-step" goal, which includes "by 2020, main health indicators will rank among the top in middle- and high-income countries," "by 2030, main health indicators will enter the ranks of high-income countries," and "by 2050, a health nation compatible with a modern socialist country will be built."

2.2.2.3 Goals of the Healthy China Initiative

First, by 2020, a system of basic medical and health services with Chinese characteristics covering urban and rural residents will be established, the health literacy level has continued to improve, the health service system will be complete and efficient, everyone will have access to basic medical and health services and basic physical fitness services, and a health industry system with rich connotations and a reasonable structure will be basically formed, with main health indicators ranking among the top in middle- and high-income countries.

Second, by 2030, the following specific goals should be achieved:

The health level of the population has continued to improve. The physical fitness of the population has improved significantly, with the average life expectancy reaching 79 years and a marked increase in average healthy life expectancy.

Major health risk factors have been effectively controlled. The health literacy of the population has been greatly improved, a healthy lifestyle has been popularized, a healthy working and living environment has basically taken shape, food and drug safety has been effectively guaranteed, and a number of major diseases have been eliminated.

The capacity of health services has been greatly improved. A high-quality and efficient integrated medical and health service system and a well-functioning public service system for physical fitness have been fully established, the health security system has been further improved, the overall strength of health science and technology innovation ranks among the top in the world, and the quality and level of health services have been significantly improved.

The scale of the health industry has expanded significantly. A comprehensive and well-structured health industry system has been established, and a number of large enterprises with strong innovation ability and international competitiveness have been formed, becoming pillar industries of the national economy.

The institutional system for promoting health has been further improved. The system of policies, laws and regulations conducive to health has been further improved, and the system and capacity for health governance have been basically modernized.

Third, by 2050, a health nation compatible with a socialist modern country will be built.

2.2.2.4 The Content of the Healthy China Initiative

The overarching strategy of the Healthy China Initiative is to center on human health, addressing health influencing factors such as individuals' lifestyles and behaviors, medical and health services and security, and production and living environment in a sequence from internal to external, and from individual behavior to environmental conditions. The strategy encompasses five main tasks: promoting healthy lifestyles, optimizing health services, enhancing health protection, building a healthy environment, and developing the health industry.

Promoting healthy lifestyles. Starting from the source of health promotion, it emphasizes individual health responsibility. This includes strengthening health education, improving the health literacy of the entire population, extensively conducting national fitness activities, fostering self-disciplined health behaviors, and guiding the public to adopt healthy lifestyles characterized by balanced diets, adequate exercise, smoking cessation, alcohol moderation, and mental well-being.

Optimizing health services. Focusing on women and children, the elderly, impoverished populations, and people with disabilities, it implements measures from both prevention and treatment perspectives. This includes strengthening public health services that cover the entire population, increasing efforts to prevent and control chronic and major infectious diseases, implementing health poverty alleviation projects, innovating the model for medical and health service delivery, leveraging the unique advantages of TCM in preventive care, and providing higher quality health services to the public.

Enhancing health protection. By improving the universal medical insurance system, and deepening reforms in the public hospital, pharmaceutical, and medical device distribution systems to reduce inflated prices, it aims to significantly ease the financial burden of medical expenses for the public, and improve patients' medical experience. This involves strengthening the integration and alignment of various medical insurance systems, refining insurance management service systems, and ensuring the long-term sustainability of the health protection capacity.

Building a healthy environment. Addressing environmental issues that impact health, it involves initiatives such as carrying out air, water, and soil pollution prevention and treatment, strengthening food and drug safety supervision, enhancing work safety and occupational disease prevention and treatment, promoting road traffic safety, deeply engaging in patriotic health campaigns, building healthy cities and villages, and improving emergency response capabilities to minimize the impact of external factors on health.

Developing the health industry. Differentiating between basic and non-basic health industries, it aims to optimize a diversified health service delivery structure, and promote the development of non-public medical institutions toward higher standards and larger scale. This involves advancing supply-side structural reforms, supporting the development of new health service models such as health tourism, actively developing fitness and leisure industries, enhancing the development of the pharmaceutical industry, and continually meeting the increasing and diverse health needs of the population.

Case Study: The "Healthy China Initiative (2019–2030)"

To effectively advance the implementation of the "Outline of the Healthy China 2030 Plan" and the achievement of its goals, the National Health Commission formulated the "Healthy China Initiative (2019–2030)" in June 2019. In July 2019, the State Council established the Healthy China Initiative Promotion Committee, which is responsible for coordinating the implementation, monitoring, and evaluation of the "Healthy China Initiative (2019–2030)." Focusing on two core areas of disease prevention and health promotion, the "Health China Initiative (2019–2030)" proposes 15 major special actions to promote the transformation from a disease-centered approach to a health-centered approach, and strive to minimize illness and improve health outcomes among the population. These 15 special actions include: health knowledge dissemination, balanced diet promotion, national fitness campaigns, smoking control, mental health promotion, health environment promotion, maternal and child health promotion, primary and secondary school health promotion, occupational health protection, elderly health promotion, cardiovascular disease prevention and treatment, cancer prevention and treatment, chronic respiratory disease prevention and treatment, diabetes prevention and treatment, and infectious and endemic disease prevention and control.

Chapter 3
China's Medical Service System

China's medical and health institutions mainly include hospitals and primary medical and health institutions. Since the reform and opening-up, the number of hospitals in China has maintained a continuous growth trend. By the end of 2021, there were 36,570 hospitals in China, 3.9 times that of 1978, of which 67.7% were private. Correspondingly, the number of hospital beds in China has also experienced continuous growth. In 2021, the number of beds in medical and health institutions per 1000 population reached 6.7. Although large-scale medical equipment is mainly concentrated in second-level and above hospitals, the equipment allocation of primary medical and health institutions is also improving year by year. In terms of informatization construction, the hospital management information system, clinical information system and regional health information system have all achieved rapid development. Government investment in the health field is concentrated in primary medical and health institutions and basic medical security.

China's health human resources are growing rapidly, with the number of health professionals per 1000 population reaching 7.97 in 2021, but there is a relative shortage of nursing staff. Health professionals in China's public medical and health institutions have clear career development plans, and their career development prospects are relatively broad. However, there is a certain gap between urban and rural areas in the allocation of health professionals. In 2021, the number of health professionals per 1000 population in urban areas was 9.87, while in rural areas it was 6.27. Other challenges to the development of China's health human resources include the lack of adequate health personnel at the grassroots level and the low level of education of health professionals. Although China has initially established a continuous and unified medical education system including medical school education, post-graduation medical education and continuing medical education, this system still needs to be improved and the quality of medical education still needs to be strengthened.

Z. Feng et al. (eds.), *China's Health System*, Introduction to China's S&T Innovation,
https://doi.org/10.1007/978-981-95-1205-8_3

3.1 Overview of China's Medical Service System

3.1.1 Medical and Health Institutions and Their Types

China's medical and health institutions can be divided into four categories: hospitals, primary medical and health institutions, professional public health institutions, and other medical and health institutions. Here is an overview of the hospitals.

Hospitals in China offer both inpatient and outpatient services. According to the objects or types of diseases they serve, hospitals can be divided into general hospitals, specialized hospitals, and others. General hospitals provide comprehensive medical services for various groups of people and diseases, while specialized hospitals such as children's hospitals, ear, nose and throat hospitals, obstetrics and gynecology hospitals, and dental hospitals provide specialized medical services. Hospitals in China include Western medicine hospitals and TCM hospitals. Most hospitals can offer Western medicine services. In China, almost every county has a traditional chinese medicine (TCM) hospital, which provides TCM services. In some ethnic minority areas, there are also ethnic hospitals, such as Tibetan medicine hospitals and Mongolian medicine hospitals. According to different ownership systems, hospitals in China can be divided into public hospitals and private hospitals. At present, public hospitals are the main body of China's medical service system. Private hospitals have also made some progress in recent years. Most private hospitals are for-profit hospitals, while some are non-profit hospitals.

In 1989, China began to implement a hierarchical hospital management system. According to the comprehensive level of the hospitals, such as their size and function, hospitals in China are divided into three levels.

A first-level hospital is a primary hospital that directly provides prevention, medical treatment, health care and rehabilitation services to a community with a certain population. Its responsibilities mainly include providing preventive health care (such as community health and epidemic prevention, maternal and child health care, family planning surgery and technical guidance, and health education), medical services (such as outpatient and inpatient diagnosis and treatment of common and frequent diseases in the community, and community rehabilitation medicine) and other services.

A second-level hospital is a regional hospital that provides comprehensive medical services to multiple communities and undertakes certain teaching and scientific research tasks. Its responsibilities mainly include providing medical services (providing comprehensive and continuous medical care, nursing, preventive health care and rehabilitation services to the community), carrying out teaching and scientific research in combination with medical care, and guiding the primary medical and health institutions in the region to do a good job in community treatment, preventive health care, rehabilitation and mental health.

A third-level hospital is a hospital above the regional level that provides high-level specialized medical services to several regions and undertakes higher teaching and scientific research tasks. Its responsibilities mainly include providing specialized medical services, solving critical and difficult diseases, accepting second-level referrals, providing professional and technical guidance and personnel training to lower-level hospitals, completing the teaching tasks of cultivating various senior medical professionals, undertaking scientific research projects at or above the provincial level, and participating in and guiding the primary and secondary prevention work.

Since the reform and opening-up, the number of hospitals in China has maintained a continuous growth trend. In 1978, there were only 9293 hospitals in China. By 2021, the total number of hospitals reached 36,570, 3.9 times that of 1978. Among them, the number of general hospitals, TCM hospitals and specialized hospitals has increased significantly. In 2021, 32.3% of all hospitals in China were public hospitals and 67.7% were private.

3.1.2 Capital Investment in Medical and Health Institutions

Most of China's medical and health institutions are public, and the government should be responsible for the construction and purchase of equipment for these public medical and health institutions. But from the 1980s to the 1990s, China's medical and health institutions gradually began to try to introduce market-oriented operation mechanisms, the government's fiscal investment in public medical and health institutions gradually decreased, and the fiscal autonomy of public medical and health institutions gradually expanded. Many hospitals and primary medical and health institutions can use their business income to build infrastructure or purchase medical equipment. Some medical and health institutions have even borrowed money to build houses and buy equipment.

Since the implementation of the new medical reform in 2009, the Chinese government has increased investment in basic medical security and primary medical and health institutions. From 2016 to 2021, China's fiscal expenditure on health care increased from 1315.9 billion yuan to 1914.27 billion yuan, including 22.35 billion yuan from the central government. From 2016 to 2020, the central government issued a total of 1448.4 billion yuan in medical insurance subsidies for urban and rural residents, and the fiscal subsidy standard for urban and rural residents basic medical insurance was raised from 420 yuan per person per year in 2016 to 550 yuan per person per year in 2020. From 2016 to 2020, the central government allocated a total of 50.8 billion yuan in subsidies for the comprehensive reform of public hospitals to support local governments in consolidating the achievements of eliminating the practice of "using drug sales to supplement medical income." In 2018 and 2019, half of the annual increase in per capita government subsidies for urban and rural residents basic medical insurance was used to improve the protection capacity of serious illness insurance in China. In 2017, China comprehensively implemented a comprehensive reform of public hospitals, and all public hospitals in the country abolished drug markups. In 2019, the markup for medical consumables in public hospitals was cancelled. Government investment at all levels plays different roles in the construction of infrastructure of medical and health institutions. The central government and provincial governments play a major role in the construction of infrastructure such as houses and equipment in primary medical and health institutions. Due to their weak fiscal capacity, county-level governments have invested less in the construction of infrastructure apart from being responsible for paying the salaries of health professionals, especially in the underdeveloped areas of the western regions.

In addition, although China's government has increased investment in second-level and above public hospitals, the investment is not as strong as that of primary medical and health institutions. Therefore, second-level and above public hospitals still need to use business income or other financing channels to strengthen the construction of infrastructure. China encourages private capital to run medical and health institutions, and the private medical and health institutions, whose number has been gradually increasing, mainly rely on private capital to invest in the construction of infrastructure such as houses and equipment.

3.1.3 Status Quo of the Scale of Medical and Health Institutions

The number of beds reflects the scale of a hospital's operations. According to the official data of China health statistics, the number of hospital beds is usually counted according to the following categories: 0–49, 50–99, 100–199, 200–299, 300–399, 400–499, 500–799, and 800 and above. At the end of 2021, there were 9.45 million beds in medical and health institutions nationwide, including 7.41 million (78.5%) in hospitals, 1.71 million (18.1%) in primary medical and health institutions, and 0.30 million (3.2%) in professional public health institutions. The number of beds in urban and rural medical and health institutions remained almost the same, accounting for 52.6% and 47.4% respectively. Among hospitals, 70.2% were in public hospitals and 29.8% were in private hospitals.

In line with the trend in the number of hospitals, the number of hospital beds in China has also experienced continuous growth, and the growth rate has outpaced that of the number of hospitals. In 1978, there were only 1.10 million hospital beds in China, but by 2021, this number had increased to 7.41 million, 6.7 times that of 1978. There has also been a significant increase in the number of beds in primary medical and health institutions, but at a slower rate than in hospitals. Taking into account the growth of the population, we look at the trend of the number of beds in medical and health institutions by examining the number of beds per 1000 population. In 2007, the number of hospital beds per 1000 population was 2.83, and by 2021, it had reached 6.70, representing an increase of 136.7% in 14 years.

There is little difference in the number of beds between urban and rural medical and health institutions in China. In recent years, the difference in bed allocation between urban and rural medical and health institutions has gradually narrowed. In 2010, the number of beds in medical and health institutions per 1000 population in urban areas was about 5.94, 2.28 times that of rural areas, and in 2020 this number was 1.78 times. In 2021, the number of beds in medical and health institutions per 1000 population in urban and rural areas was 7.47 and 6.01, respectively. In addition, there are certain differences in bed allocation and services provided between different medical and health institutions due to different regions and levels.

The bed occupancy rate and average length of stay for discharged patients reflect the use of hospital beds. The bed occupancy rate is the ratio of the total number of bed days actually occupied to the total number of bed days actually opened. The average length of stay for discharged patients is the ratio of the total number of bed days occupied by discharged patients to the number of discharged patients. In 2021, the occupancy rate of hospital beds in China was 74.6%, and the average length of stay for hospital dischargers was 9.2 days.

There are significant differences in bed occupancy rates among different levels of hospitals in China. Data for 2021 shows that the bed occupancy rate in third-level hospitals in China was 85.3%, compared with 71.1% in second-level hospitals and 52.1% in first-level hospitals, respectively. The average length of stay for hospital dischargers in China peaked at 16.2 days around 1992 and has been on a downward trend since then, falling to 9.2 days in 2021.

3.1.4 Current Status of Health Human Resources

By the end of 2021, the total number of health personnel in China was 13.98 million, of which 11.24 million were health professionals. In the same year, there were 3.04 practitioners and assistant practitioners and 3.56 registered nurses per 1000 population, and 3.08 general practitioners and 6.79 professional public health institution personnel per 10,000 population, respectively.

Since 1949, the total number of health personnel in China has generally maintained an upward trend. In the 1950s, the number of health personnel increased rapidly, by about 0.11 million per year. In the 1960s, the number of health personnel stagnated, fluctuating around 1.80 million. In the 1970s and 1980s, the number of health personnel increased rapidly again, by about 0.15 million per year, and the rate of increase slowed down after the 1990s. From 2001 to 2003, there was a negative growth in the number of health personnel. Since 2005, the number of health personnel has grown rapidly again, by more than 0.20 million per year. The number of health personnel in 2021 was 0.51 million more in 2021 (an increase of 3.8%) than in 2020.

3.1.4.1 The Structure and Distribution of Health Human Resources

In the early days of the People's Republic of China, the doctor-to-nurse ratio was about 10:1. But the number of nurses was growing significantly faster than that of doctors. By 2021, the doctor-to-nurse ratio in China reached 1:1.17. Health professionals in China are usually predominantly female. In 2018, 71.8% of China's health professionals were women, with the proportion of registered nurses being as high as 97.7%. In recent years, the age structure of China's health professionals has been dominated by young and middle-aged people. In 2018, 83.3% of China's health professionals were aged 25–54; 11% were aged 55 and over, up from 9.2% in 2017. The educational qualifications of health professionals in China are usually divided into graduate, undergraduate, junior college, technical secondary school, and others. In recent years, the educational qualifications of health professionals in China have been improving, with 42% of health professionals having a bachelor's degree or above in 2020, compared with 17.1% in 2005.

3.1.4.2 Education of Health Personnel

Since 1949, China has gradually established a continuous and unified medical education system, including medical school education, post-graduation medical education and continuing medical education. Since the 1990s, medical education in China has developed rapidly. In particular, with the encouragement of the policy of expanding the enrollment of higher education introduced in 1999, the scale of medical colleges in China has expanded rapidly. The number of students enrolled in higher medical education in 2019 was 6.7 times that of 2000. The number of medical colleges and universities had grown from 44 in the early days of the founding of the People's Republic of China to 192 in 2020. From the early days of the founding of the People's Republic of China to 2019, the number of students enrolled in medical colleges and universities increased from 15,200 to 3.32 million. In addition, 1.16 million students were enrolled in secondary medical education in 2019.

3.1.4.3 Careers of Health Personnel

There are three levels of health professional titles in China: junior, intermediate and senior. Taking doctors as an example, after graduating from technical secondary school and junior college, medical students can obtain medical assistant qualifications through examinations, and undergraduate graduates can obtain physician (or resident) qualifications. Medical assistant and physicians are both junior titles, and after working for a certain number of years (such as 5 years), they can be promoted to attending physicians (intermediate titles) through certain procedures. Senior titles include associate chief physician and chief physician. Other health personnel also have a corresponding career development system. Since the health personnel of the hospital affiliated to the medical school have the tasks of teaching, research and supervising graduate students, they also have the titles of associate professor and professor. If the medical institution has a corresponding promotion position (or title promotion quota), the health personnel who meet the promotion conditions can submit an application to the institution. After the medical institution has passed the review, it shall be reported to the health administrative department and the personnel department at the higher level for approval. Promotion to intermediate titles (such as attending physician) requires passing a provincial examination, which includes professional knowledge, foreign languages, and computer science. For promotion to senior titles (such as associate chief physician and chief physician), a defense is required. The provincial health administrative department and the personnel department invite experts in relevant fields to form a professional committee to review the applicant's qualifications and abilities. Based on the results of the defense, the provincial personnel department will make the final decision on whether to approve the applicant's promotion.

3.2 The Current Situation and Development Direction of China's Medical Services at all Levels

3.2.1 Residents' Healthcare-Seeking Pathways

In China, both urban and rural residents have their own choice to seek medical treatment in various medical and health institutions, as shown in Figs. 3.1 and 3.2. However, with the improvement of the level of medical and health institutions, the proportion of medical expenses and out-of-pocket medical expenses of residents has also increased. In addition, primary medical and health institutions are mostly located in residential areas and residents generally do not need to wait for treatment, so they often choose to seek treatment in primary medical and health institutions when they judge their condition is relatively mild.

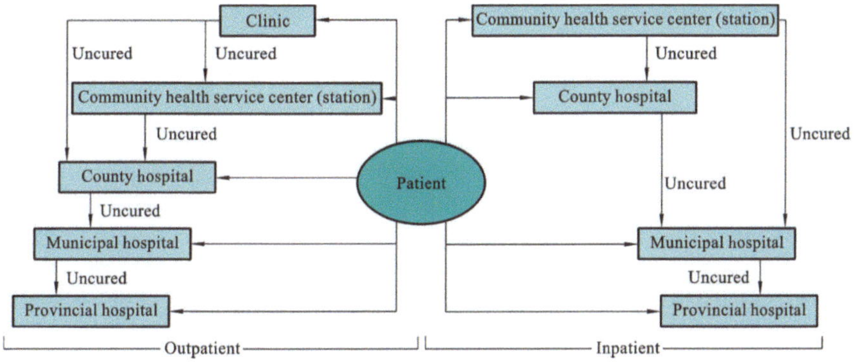

Fig. 3.1 Healthcare-seeking pathways for urban residents

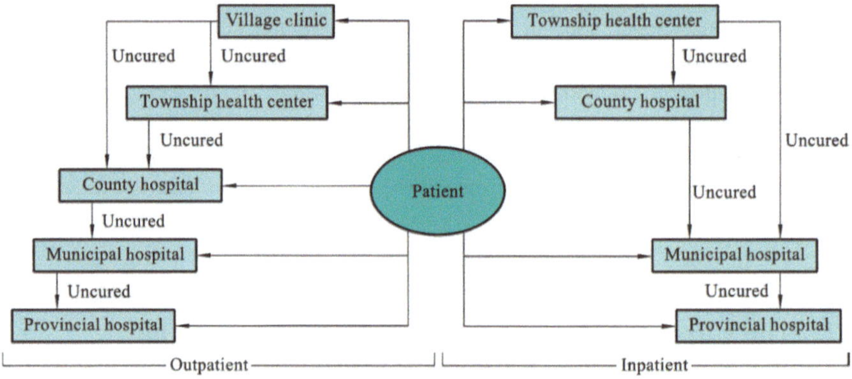

Fig. 3.2 Healthcare-seeking pathways for rural residents

3.2.2 Primary Medical Services

Primary medical services in China are mainly provided by community health service centers (stations), township health centers, village clinics and other primary medical and health institutions. Community health service centers implement integrated management of their subordinate community health service stations, and other community health service stations are subject to the operational management of community health service centers. The village clinics accept the operational management and technical guidance of the township health centers, and in some areas where the integration of rural health services has been realized, the township health centers shall implement unified management of the village clinics.

Community health service centers (stations) and township health centers are mainly responsible for providing local residents with health education, prevention, health care, rehabilitation services, as well as diagnosis and treatment services for common and frequently occurring diseases. Village clinics provide basic medical services to rural residents. The administrative departments of health are responsible for the daily supervision and management of primary medical and health institutions, and the centers for disease control and prevention, maternal and child health care hospitals (institutes, stations), specialized disease prevention and treatment centers (institutes) and other preventive health care institutions are responsible for conducting operational evaluation and guidance on the public health service work undertaken by primary medical and health institutions.

By the end of 2021, there were 36,160 community health service centers (stations), including 10,122 community health service centers and 26,038 community health service stations, 34,943 township health centers, 271,056 clinics and infirmaries, and 599,292 village clinics. Among the health personnel, there are 0.59 million health professionals in community health service centers (stations), 1.29 million health professionals in township health centers, and 1.36 million personnel in village clinics.

The number of diagnosis and treatment volume in primary medical and health institutions in China has generally shown an increasing trend. In 2021, it reached 4.25 billion (50.2% of the national total), an increase of 130 million compared with 2020, and the number of hospitalizations in primary medical and health institutions was 35.92 million (14.5% of the national total), a decrease of 1.15 million compared with 2020.

At present, China's primary medical services still have a long way to go in terms of talent team building, and the problems such as the insufficient number, low quality, and job instability of health professionals are still the bottleneck problems that restrict the further improvement of medical services and medical levels of primary medical and health institutions. In order to strengthen the capacity of primary medical services, various regions in China are actively promoting on-the-job training of rural health personnel, and implementing training programs for rural health personnel and free education programs for medical students with rural service commitments. In urban areas, China is vigorously carrying out on-the-job training for community health personnel, and implementing training programs for community health personnel and plans for the construction of primary medical and health teams focusing on general practitioners. In terms of system construction, China is improving the urban medical and health service system based on community health services, and gradually promoting the implementation of the community first diagnosis, hierarchical diagnosis and treatment, and two-way referral system.

3.2.3 Medical Services Provided by Second-Level and Third-Level Hospitals

China's second-level hospitals include general city and county hospitals, district-level hospitals in municipalities directly under the central government, as well as staff hospitals of industrial, mining, enterprises and institutions with a certain scale. Third-level hospitals include large municipal hospitals directly under the national, provincial and municipal governments, as well as affiliated hospitals of medical colleges and universities. As of the end of 2021, there were 3275 third-level hospitals and 10,848 second-level hospitals in China. China's second-level and third-level hospitals are divided into general hospitals, TCM hospitals, hospitals of integrated traditional Chinese and Western medicine, hospitals of traditional ethic medicine, specialized hospitals and nursing homes according to the different types of services provided. General hospitals generally have specialties such as internal medicine, surgery, obstetrics and gynecology, pediatrics, otolaryngology, ophthalmology, dermatology, and TCM, as well as medical and technical departments such as laboratory and imaging. TCM hospitals, hospitals of integrated traditional Chinese and Western medicine, and hospitals of traditional ethic medicine mainly provide medical services related to TCM and ethnic medicine. Specialized hospitals are hospitals set up for the diagnosis and treatment of various specialized diseases, such as obstetrics and gynecology hospitals, infectious disease hospitals, cancer hospitals, dental hospitals, occupational disease hospitals, etc. And nursing homes are medical institutions that provide long-term medical care, rehabilitation promotion, hospice care, and other services to patients.

In 2009, China launched a new medical reform, according to which the government encourages and guides private capital to run medical institutions, and encourages the free movement of medical and health professionals between public and private hospitals. In recent years, the number of private hospitals in China has been steadily increasing. In 2021, public hospitals accounted for 32.3% of the total number of hospitals in China, while private hospitals accounted for 67.7%.

In 2021, hospitals accounted for 3.88 billion (45.8%) of the total diagnosis and treatment volume in China, primary medical and health institutions accounted for 4.25 billion (50.2%), and other medical and health institutions accounted for 340 million (4%). In 2021, the occupancy rate of hospital beds in China was 74.6% (80.3% in public hospitals). In 2021, the average length of stay for hospital dischargers in China was 9.2 days (9.0 days in public hospitals), decreased by 0.3 days (0.3 days in public hospitals) compared with the previous year. Since 2005, a number of large general hospitals have started to open day wards to provide patients with emergency day surgery and day beds that do not require hospitalization. At present, day care services in China are still in the development stage.

For a period of time, issues such as high medical costs and inconsistent service quality were prominent in some second-level and third-level hospitals in China. To address this situation, China has launched a pilot project for the comprehensive reform of urban public hospitals since 2010, striving to achieve breakthroughs in improving the service system, innovating systems and mechanisms, strengthening internal management, and accelerating the formation of a diversified medical operation pattern. Since 2012, China has launched a pilot project for the comprehensive reform of county-level public hospitals, and has explored reform methods in aspects such as the compensation mechanisms of public hospitals.

3.2.4 The Relationship Between the Medical Services Provided by Second-Level and Third-Level Hospitals and Primary Medical Services

In order to guide general medical services at the primary level and promote the rational allocation of medical resources, China introduced a two-way referral system in 2016 to encourage patients to prefer primary medical and health institutions for treatment, and when necessary, primary medical and health institutions are responsible for transferring patients to second-level and third-level hospitals for treatment, and then these hospitals will transfer patients to primary medical and health institutions for rehabilitation and other follow-up treatment after the patient's condition is stable. Since the launch of the new medical reform in 2009, China has begun to explore the establishment of a division of labor and cooperation mechanism between second-level and third-level hospitals and urban and rural primary medical and health institutions, and these hospitals are responsible for driving the development of primary medical and health institutions in terms of technology, personnel and management. In order to achieve this goal, China has begun to explore the construction of medical consortia to promote the formation of a hierarchical diagnosis and treatment pattern.

3.2.5 TCM Services and Ethnic Medical Services

Most of China's comprehensive medical institutions and primary medical and health institutions have TCM departments, which provide TCM services mostly based on traditional therapies such as herbal medicine therapy, acupuncture therapy and massage therapy. To varying degrees, these services are included in the scope of compensation for the basic medical insurance for urban employees, the basic medical insurance for non-working urban residents, and the new rural cooperative medical care. As of 2021, the total number of TCM medical and health institutions in China was 77,336, including 5715 hospitals specialized in TCM, 71,583 outpatient departments and clinics specialized in TCM, and 38 institutions specialized in TCM research. In addition, there are a large number of private traditional medicine clinics and individual practitioners who provide TCM services. The total number of TCM health personnel reached 884,000, including 732,000 practitioners and assistant practitioners of TCM and 136,000 TCM pharmacists. The total number of consultations and treatments in TCM medical and health institutions nationwide was 1.2 billion, and the number of discharges from TCM medical and health institutions was 38 million.

The "Regulations of the People's Republic of China on Traditional Chinese Medicine" stipulates that the establishment of TCM medical institutions shall comply with the standards for the establishment of TCM medical institutions formulated by the health administrative department of the State Council and the local regional health plan, and go through the examination and approval procedures in accordance with the provisions of the "Regulations on the Administration of Medical Institutions" to obtain the practice license. TCM practitioners shall pass the qualification examination in accordance with the provisions of the laws, administrative regulations and departmental rules on health management, and obtain a practice certificate through registration before engaging in TCM service activities.

By the end of 2015, there were 3966 hospitals specialized in TCM in China, including 253 hospitals of traditional ethnic medicine and 446 hospitals of integrated traditional Chinese and Western medicine. There are 452,000 practitioners and assistant practitioners of TCM (including practitioners of ethnic medicine and integrated traditional Chinese and Western medicine). There are 42,528 outpatient departments and clinics of TCM, including 550 outpatient departments and clinics of ethnic medicine and 7706 outpatient departments and clinics of integrated traditional Chinese and Western medicine. In 2015, the total number of consultations and treatments in TCM medical and health institutions in China reached 910 million, and the number of discharges from TCM medical and health institutions nationwide reached 26.92 million.

According to the "14th Five-Year Plan for the Development of Traditional Chinese Medicine," China will build a high-quality and efficient TCM service system, improve the capacity of TCM health services, build a high-quality TCM talent team, establish a high-level TCM inheritance and protection, and scientific and technological innovation system, promote the high-quality development of the TCM industry, develop the TCM health service industry, promote the prosperity and development of TCM culture, accelerate the opening-up and development of TCM, deepen the reform of the field of TCM, and strengthen the support and guarantee for the development of TCM.

In addition to TCM therapies, there are also a large number of traditional therapies from ethnic minorities in China, and the discipline that studies this field is called "ethnic medicine." Some therapies in ethnic medicine are similar to those in TCM, such as herbal medicine therapy, cupping therapy, and acupuncture therapy. In addition, both ethnic medicine and TCM have their own unique therapies. There are dozens of categories of ethnic medicine in China, such as Tibetan medicine, Mongolian medicine, and Miao medicine. As of 2019, there were 699 integrated traditional Chinese and Western medicine hospitals and 312 hospitals of traditional ethic medicine in China. In addition to being carried out in hospitals of traditional ethic medicine, ethnic medical services are more often carried out in monasteries (for example, the educational and medical practice institutions set up in Tibetan Buddhist monasteries are called Manba Raseng), clinics and other places, or in the form of individual medical practice. Ethnic medicine is often taught in a more conservative way, such as oral transmission or even ancestral tradition, and retains more unique traditional healing methods and skills that are self-contained, but the extent of its application is not the same as that of TCM. In general, the management of ethnic physicians is carried out with reference to the management of TCM physicians.

3.3 High-Quality Development of China's Medical Service System

3.3.1 Medical Consortia

The construction of medical consortia is a major measure to promote the hierarchical diagnosis and treatment system in China. In 2017, the "Guiding Opinions of the General Office of the State Council on Promoting the Construction and Development of Medical Consortia" was issued, which clarified that medical communities should be established at the county level, strengthen the combination of medical and health and elderly care services, and provide patients with integrated and convenient disease diagnosis and treatment, rehabilitation and long-term care continuity services.

On the one hand, by adjusting and optimizing the layout of medical resources, the medical consortia can effectively expand high-quality resources and technical services to the grassroots level step by step, and improve the ability of primary medical services through various forms and means such as expert deployment to lower-level medical institutions, counterpart assistance, and telemedicine. On the other hand, as an important channel for the integration of medical resources and two-way referral, the medical consortia can gradually break down the barriers and obstacles in administrative division, financial investment, medical insurance payment, personnel management, etc., and promote the integration of high-quality medical resources.

In terms of the organizational model of medical consortia, China has proposed four mature models. First, in urban areas, medical groups are mainly formed, with third-level hospitals as the core and various medical institutions such as community health service institutions, nursing homes, and rehabilitation centers providing various types of services to meet the health, medical and rehabilitation needs of patients at different stages. Second, in county areas, medical communities are primarily established, focusing on exploring the integrated management of counties and townships with county hospitals as the leader, township health centers as the hub, and village clinics as the basis. A high degree of overall management and close division of labor and cooperation on personnel, finance, materials, prevention, security, and health is carried out, and a three-level linkage county-level medical service system is built. Third, for various specialized diseases, medical institutions with superior specialized medical resources are encouraged to take the lead and carry out cross-regional medical alliances. At the same time, China proposes to give full play to the resource advantages in national specialized medical care, and use specialist cooperation as a link to improve the treatment level of specialized diseases at the grassroots level and smoothen the channel of two-way referral. Fourth, China proposes to develop a telemedicine cooperation network in remote and impoverished areas, make full use of modern high-tech means such as telemedicine, distance teaching, and distance training, extend the medical technology and service capabilities of higher-level medical institutions, expand the service radius, and meet the medical needs of some grassroots areas, especially remote and impoverished areas.

At present, the construction of China's medical consortia has been fully launched, all third-level public hospitals have participated in the construction of medical consortia, the results of the two-way referral have initially appeared, regional medical resources have been shared, and the medical service capacity has been significantly improved. As of 2019, 607 urban medical consortium grids have been planned and constructed in 118 cities across China, and the state has promoted the pilot construction of county-level medical communities in 567 counties (cities, districts). By the end of 2020, there had been 25.08 million two-way referral patients from medical and health institutions across China. During the 13th Five-Year Plan period, the number of down-referred patients increased year by year, with an average annual growth rate of 38.4%. In 2020, the number of up-referred patients decreased for the first time, and the problem of "easy to transfer up and difficult to transfer down" gradually eased. According to the data of the Sixth National Health Service Statistical Survey, 46.9% of the two-way referral patients were referred within medical consortia, which was higher than other referral methods.

3.3.2 Reform of Primary Medical and Health Institutions

The development of primary medical and health institutions in China faces many challenges. Over-reliance on drug revenues has hampered the provision of reasonable health services. The establishment of a reasonable compensation mechanism and the increase of government investment are the focus of the reform of primary medical and health institutions in China. In addition, primary medical and health institutions need to strengthen the construction of human resources and other conditions.

Construction of the primary medical and health system. From 2009 to 2011, the main goals of the reform was to improve the three-tiered medical and health service network at the county, township and village levels. It focused on supporting the construction of urban and rural primary medical and health institutions, including county and rural health institutions and urban community health institutions, and supported the construction of village clinics in remote areas and urban community health service centers in difficult areas. After 2012, China continued to strengthen the construction of township health centers and the capacity building of TCM services in primary medical and health institutions.

Construction of primary medical and health teams. From 2009 to 2011, China began a program to train health personnel for rural primary medical and health institutions free of charge. In 2011, the "Guiding Opinions of the State Council on the Establishment of a General Practitioner System" was promulgated, which clarified the policy measures such as gradually establishing a unified and standardized general practitioner training system and reforming the practice methods of general practitioners. In 2012, the medical reform proposed to strengthen the construction of grassroots talent teams focusing on general practitioners and continue to train medical students free of charge for township health centers and grassroots troops in the central and western regions. On-the-job training for personnel in primary medical and health institutions is an important part of improving the capacity of health personnel. Since the new medical reform, China's governments at all levels invested funds to organize various forms of on-the-job training. In addition, China has also implemented a policy of counterpart support for rural hospitals in urban hospitals, that is, each urban third-level hospital is required to establish a long-term technical assistance relationship with about three county-level hospitals to improve the service capacity of county-level hospitals.

Establishment of compensation mechanisms for primary medical and health institutions. China clarifies that government subsidies and service charges (including medical insurance fees and public health service compensation) are the main compensation methods for primary medical and health institutions. Most importantly, drug markups are no longer the main compensation channel for primary medical and health institutions. The capital construction, equipment purchase, personnel expenses, and the operating expenses for public health services approved by township health centers and urban community health service centers (stations) in accordance with state regulations shall be compensated through project subsidies or purchase of services. For the public health services provided by non-government-run primary medical and health institutions, compensation shall be made in the form of government or basic medical insurance purchasing services, and the fiscal compensation for the implementation of the basic drug system in the village clinic is clarified.

Establishment of operational mechanisms for primary medical and health institutions. The reform measures implemented include the establishment of a two-way referral system, a primary care first diagnosis system, a performance appraisal mechanism for primary medical and health institutions and personnel, and an income distribution mechanism for primary medical and health institutions. In 2012, it was clearly proposed that the income distribution of personnel in primary medical and health institutions should be based on the quantity and quality of services and be tilted in favor of the core and backbone health professionals in China.

3.3.3 Future Development

Since the implementation of the new medical reform in 2009, China has made remarkable progress in improving the service capacity of primary medical and health institutions and reforming public medical and health institutions. At the same time, due to the complexity and systemic nature of health reform, it also faces many challenges and requires long-term persistence. In view of the new problems that have arisen, it is necessary to continuously improve the content of reform and effectively promote the implementation of reform policies and measures.

The reform of China's public hospitals needs to be continuously deepened, with a focus on addressing issues within the medical service system and driving the reform from the perspective of system construction and development. At the same time, the development of the health industry and the realization of a diversified medical pattern are also important development directions in the future. In the face of ongoing challenges of health and demographic transitions, China needs a more effective medical service system to address the challenges of chronic diseases and meet growing health needs. The focus of China's medical service system reform mainly includes the following four aspects:

First, deepen the reform of the medical and health system, including deepening the comprehensive reform of primary medical and health institutions and improving the operation mechanism of networked urban and rural primary medical and health services, perfecting the reasonable hierarchical diagnosis and treatment model and establishing a contractual service relationship between community doctors and residents, making full use of information technology to promote the vertical flow of high-quality medical resources, and strengthening the integration of regional public health service resources, etc. The main task is to establish a medical and health service system with clear functions, accurate positioning, and mutual cooperation, and give full play to the role of medical and health institutions with varying functions and at different levels. This requires the integration of medical and health service systems, including the integration of medical and public health service institutions, as well as institutional cohesion and vertical integration of medical and health institutions within the region, to improve the capacity of the system as a whole and address major health challenges.

Second, accelerate the reform of public hospitals, including innovating systems and mechanisms, and mobilizing the enthusiasm of medical staff. Among them, rationalizing the price of medicine and establishing a scientific compensation mechanism are the key points. The reform of county-level public hospitals is the key work in the next few years, and the content of this reform mainly includes adhering to public welfare and fulfilling the responsibilities of the government, deepening the reform of the distribution system and fully mobilizing the enthusiasm of medical staff, establishing a modern hospital management system and strengthening internal management, promoting the reform of the payment system, optimizing the allocation of resources and strengthening industry supervision, etc.

Third, strengthen the construction of medical and health talent team and the construction of medical and health informatization. The quality, structure and distribution of the medical and health talent team has always been one of the most important factors restricting the improvement of medical and health service capacity in China. China has established a standardized training system for residents and a training system for general practitioners, and has promoted the policy of stabilizing the ranks of rural doctors. In terms of medical and health informatization, China is studying the establishment of a unified national information standard system for electronic health records, electronic medical records, drugs and devices, medical services, medical insurance and other areas, and promoting the standardization of medical and health information technology.

Fourth, encourage the community to run medical and health institutions, and give priority to supporting social forces to set up non-profit medical and health institutions, including leaving a reasonable space for the development of social medical institutions and establishing a social medical system with non-profit medical and health institutions as the main body and for-profit medical and health institutions as the supplement in the regional health planning and planning for the establishment of medical and health institutions, improving preferential policies and measures in areas such as taxation for social medical services, promoting the improvement of multi-site practice policies for physicians, and ensuring the quality of medical services provided by non-public medical and health institutions, etc.

Chapter 4
China's Public Health Management System and Public Health Service System

China has established a relatively comprehensive public health management system and public health service system. In terms of public health management, health commissions at all levels, the National Disease Control and Prevention Administration, and centers for disease control and prevention at all levels are responsible for formulating and implementing public health development plans and policies. In terms of public health services, the content of services is continuously enriched and improved, the public health service network is continuously strengthened, and institutions ranging from centers for disease control and prevention at all levels to community health service centers (stations), township health centers, and village clinics are responsible for providing public health services such as infectious disease control and prevention, chronic disease prevention and treatment, health education, food safety surveillance and supervision, occupational health surveillance, handling of public health emergencies, and maternal and child health care for urban and rural residents.

Since the outbreak of SARS in 2003, the Chinese government has increased fiscal support for public health institutions and public health service programs. In recent years, the government has further adjusted the public health management system and institutional functions, which has greatly promoted the improvement of China's public health service system.

4.1 China's Public Health Management System

China's public health management system is primarily composed of national health management institutions such as the National Health Commission, the National Disease Control and Prevention Administration, and the Chinese Center for Disease Control and Prevention (China CDC), as well as these institutions at the provincial,

Z. Feng et al. (eds.), *China's Health System*, Introduction to China's S&T Innovation,
https://doi.org/10.1007/978-981-95-1205-8_4

prefectural, and county levels, each undertaking different management responsibilities. Health commissions at all levels are overall responsible for public health administrative management, disease control and prevention administrations at all levels are responsible for implementing disease control and prevention policies and decisions, and centers for disease control and prevention at all levels are responsible for technical support and work execution. From the national level to the provincial, prefectural, and county levels, the functions of planning and policy-making institutions at all levels are gradually detailed, and various decision deployments are gradually operationalized. Local public health policies sometimes serve as strong supplements to national policies.

4.1.1 National Health Commission

The National Health Commission is mainly responsible for organizing the formulation of national health policies, drafting laws and regulations, policies, and plans for health undertakings, formulating departmental regulations and standards, and organizing their implementation. It is also responsible for coordinating and promoting the deepening of the medical and health system reform, and researching and proposing recommendations for major guidelines, policies, and measures to deepen the medical and health system reform. In 2022, the General Office of the Central Committee of the Communist Party of China and the General Office of the State Council transferred some of the responsibilities of the National Health Commission, such as formulating and organizing the implementation of infectious disease control and prevention plans, national immunization plans, and intervention measures for major public health issues, to the National Disease Control and Prevention Administration.

Currently, the Department of Medical Emergency Response, the Department of Primary Health, the Department of Food Safety Standards, Risk Surveillance and Assessment, the Department of Maternal and Child Health, and the Department of Occupational Health under the National Health Commission are mainly responsible for the administrative management of public health-related services. Specifically, the Department of Medical Emergency Response is responsible for organizing and coordinating the response to infectious disease outbreaks, undertaking the construction of the medical emergency response system, organizing and guiding medical rescue for various public emergencies, drafting and implementing industry management policies and standards for medical safety, medical supervision, blood collection and supply institutions management and improvement of ethical conduct, drafting and supervising the implementation of major disease and chronic disease control and prevention management policies and norms, and so on. The Basic Public Health Division under the Department of Primary Health is responsible for the corresponding administrative management of grassroots public health. The Department of Food Safety Standards, Risk Surveillance and Assessment is responsible for organizing the formulation of national food safety standards, carrying out food safety risk surveillance and assessment, etc. The Department of Maternal and Child Health is responsible for drafting policies, standards, and norms for maternal and child health, promoting the construction of the maternal and child health service system, etc. The Department of Occupational Health is responsible for drafting and implementing policies and standards related to occupational health and radiation health, among others.

4.1.2 National Disease Control and Prevention Administration

In January 2022, according to the adjustment plan for the functional configuration of the National Health Commission, China abolished the National Health Commission's Bureau of Disease Control and Prevention and established the National Disease Control and Prevention Administration. The newly established National Disease Control and Prevention Administration is managed by the National Health Commission and has the status of a vice-ministerial-level national bureau.

The main responsibilities of the National Disease Control and Prevention Administration include organizing the drafting of laws, regulations, policies, plans, and standards for infectious disease control and prevention and public health supervision, leading the business work of disease control and prevention institutions at various local levels, formulating and organizing the implementation of the national immunization plans and intervention measures for major public health issues that seriously endanger people's health, coordinating and supervising the disease control and prevention work of infectious disease medical institutions and other medical institutions, planning and guiding the construction of infectious disease epidemic surveillance and early warning systems, responding to infectious disease epidemics, jointly guiding the construction of the disease control and prevention scientific research system, implementing the supervision and management of infectious disease prevention and treatment, environmental health, school health, public place health, and drinking water hygiene, and so on. Currently, provinces of China are also actively establishing provincial disease control and prevention bureaus.

4.1.3 China CDC

In China, centers for disease control and prevention are divided into four levels: national, provincial, municipal, and county levels, with different work focuses at each level. The China CDC is at the national level and is a public institution directly under the National Disease Control and Prevention Administration. The main responsibilities of the China CDC include carrying out work related to disease control and prevention, public health emergency response, environmental and occupational health, nutrition and health, aging health, maternal and child health, radiation health, and school health; organizing the formulation of national public health technical schemes and guidelines, and undertaking the comprehensive management of health standards related to public health; conducting surveillance of infectious diseases, chronic diseases, occupational diseases, endemic diseases, public health emergencies, suspected adverse reactions to vaccinations, and surveillance and assessment of the health status of the population; conducting investigations and risk assessments of major public health issues; conducting key scientific research and technological development in disease control and prevention, public health emergency response, and public health; guiding local implementation of national disease control and prevention plans and projects, providing business guidance to local disease control and prevention institutions, and participating in professional technical assessments and evaluations, and so on.

4.1.4 Other Public Health Management and Business Guidance Institutions

4.1.4.1 Mental Health Center of the China CDC

The Mental Health Center of the China CDC is the national technical center for mental health. Under the business leadership of the China CDC and entrusted by the China CDC, it mainly undertakes responsibilities including providing scientific basis and decision-making consultation for the formulation of laws, regulations, rules, policies, standards, technical specifications, and plans related to the control and prevention of mental disorders; guiding the establishment of a national mental disorder surveillance system, conducting epidemiological surveillance of the occurrence, distribution, and development patterns of common mental disorders, establishing a database, and regularly analyzing surveillance results; organizing the formulation of prevention and treatment plans for common mental disorders, and conducting quality control and effectiveness evaluation of the implementation of these plans; reporting, managing, predicting, and forecasting the information of mental disorders control and prevention; providing business guidance and technical training for mental health workers, and undertaking technical guidance in health work related to the control and prevention of mental disorders; conducting applied scientific research related to mental health, introducing, developing, and promoting new technologies and methods, and so on.

4.1.4.2 National Center for Women and Children's Health of the China CDC

The National Center for Women and Children's Health of the China CDC is the national technical guidance center for maternal and child health services. Its main responsibilities include carrying out maternal and child health work, providing technical support and consultation for the formulation of laws, regulations, policies, plans, and projects related to maternal and child health; organizing the formulation of technical schemes, guidelines, and standards for maternal and child health; conducting scientific research in the field of maternal and child health, and monitoring, evaluating, and assessing the health status of women and children and their influencing factors; undertaking the construction of maternal and child health information systems, and taking charge of technical support for the collection, management, and application service of related data; providing business guidance for local maternal and child health work, organizing business training, promoting new technologies and methods, and participating in professional technical assessments and evaluations related to maternal and child health services; conducting maternal and child health education, health science popularization, and health promotion activities; conducting graduate education and continuing education in the field of maternal and child health; conducting international exchanges and cooperation in related fields, and so on.

4.1.4.3 China Health Education Center

The China Health Education Center is a directly affiliated institution under the National Health Commission, responsible for providing technical guidance on national health education and public health communication, conducting research on related theories and practices, organizing and implementing large-scale activities related to health education and public health communication nationwide, and undertaking information management, media relations, business training, and other technical and service-related tasks. Specifically, its responsibilities include organizing research on theories, methods, and strategies in the fields of health education, health promotion, and public health communication, and providing technical consultation and policy recommendations for the government to formulate relevant laws, regulations, departmental rules, and technical standards; assisting in the organization, implementation, business training, and technical guidance of health education, health promotion, public health communication, and population education activities; assisting in the organization and coordination of news releases and major publicity activities of the National Health Commission, and conducting related policy publicity; organizing and carrying out research and promotion of practical technologies for health education policy advocacy and health science popularization, developing health science popularization information, conducting health education activities and research on tobacco control policy compliance and related publicity work, and assisting in the work related to the construction and content maintenance of the national health science popularization resource library and expert database, and so on.

4.1.4.4 Blood Collection and Supply Institutions

China's blood collection and supply institutions are divided into blood stations and single-donor plasma stations. Blood stations include general blood stations and special blood stations. They are non-profit health institutions that collect and provide blood for clinical use. General blood stations are divided into blood centers, central blood stations, and central blood banks. Special blood stations include umbilical cord blood hematopoietic stem cell banks and other blood banks. The planning and establishment of blood collection and supply institutions should be adapted to the status of local economic development, population, medical resources, and the planning and establishment of regional medical institutions. According to the *China Health Statistical Yearbook (2022)*, there were a total of 628 blood collection and supply institutions in China in 2021, including 365 in urban areas and 263 in rural areas. Blood centers, central blood stations, and central blood banks are established by local people's governments, and special blood stations are set up within the administrative regions of provinces according to national planning.

Blood centers are planned and established in cities and municipalities directly under the central government where provincial and autonomous regional people's governments are located. Central blood stations are planned and established in cities where municipal-level people's governments are located. Central blood banks are set up in county-level comprehensive hospitals where central blood stations do not cover. The main responsibilities of these three institutions include recruiting voluntary blood donors, collecting and preparing blood, supplying blood for clinical use, and providing guidance on medical blood use within the designated scope in accordance with the requirements of the health administrative departments of the provincial people's governments.

4.1.4.5 Specialized Disease Prevention and Treatment Institutions

Specialized diseases include various infectious diseases, occupational diseases, mental illnesses, dermatological diseases, and sexually transmitted diseases, among others. From the perspective of institutional level, specialized disease prevention and treatment institutions in China include specialized disease prevention and treatment institutes, specialized disease prevention and treatment centers, and specialized disease prevention and treatment stations. From the perspective of disease prevention and treatment types, specialized disease prevention and treatment institutions in China include institutions for the prevention and treatment of infectious diseases, tuberculosis, occupational diseases, oral diseases, mental illnesses, dermatological diseases and sexually transmitted diseases, as well as institutions for the prevention and treatment of endemic diseases and drug rehabilitation centers.

4.2 China's Public Health Service System

China's public health service system consists of specialized public health service network and public health services provided by medical and health institutions (Fig. 4.1). The specialized public health service network includes professional public health services such as disease control and prevention, health education, maternal and child health care, mental health, emergency treatment, blood collection and supply, health supervision, and specialized prevention and treatment. Specific content of specialized prevention and treatment services include the infectious disease prevention and treatment, oral disease prevention and treatment, dermatological disease and sexually transmitted disease prevention and treatment, tuberculosis prevention and treatment, occupational disease prevention and treatment, endemic disease prevention and treatment, and schistosomiasis prevention and treatment, among others. Within the medical service system, primary medical and health institutions with integrated medical and preventive functions (such as community health service institutions in urban areas and township health centers or village clinics in rural areas) not only provide basic medical services to residents in their jurisdiction but also offer basic public health services. Additionally, hospitals also provide public health services, such as specialized hospitals for infectious diseases and mental health, and public health-related departments in general hospitals (such as infectious disease departments and fever clinics).

In China, the specific content of public health services includes the infectious disease prevention and treatment, epidemic surveillance and the construction of the health emergency response network, maternal and child health surveillance and intervention, chronic disease prevention and treatment, endemic disease prevention and treatment, occupational disease prevention and treatment, environmental and health surveillance, as well as health education and health promotion. Below is an introduction to the specific content of public health services.

4.2.1 Basic Public Health Services

Since the initiation of the basic public health service equalization reform in 2009, China has been providing free basic public health services to all residents and continuously promoting the coverage of basic public health services for all residents. Basic public health services are defined as a shared fiscal responsibility between the central and local governments, with the central and local governments jointly bearing the expenditure. In 2022, the per capita fiscal subsidy standard for basic public health services in China reached 84 yuan. China's basic public health services are community-oriented, with specific public health service projects provided by a community service network covering both urban and rural areas. In 2021, a total of 119.41 million elderly people aged 65 and above, 109.38 million hypertension patients, and 35.71 million type 2 diabetes patients received health management

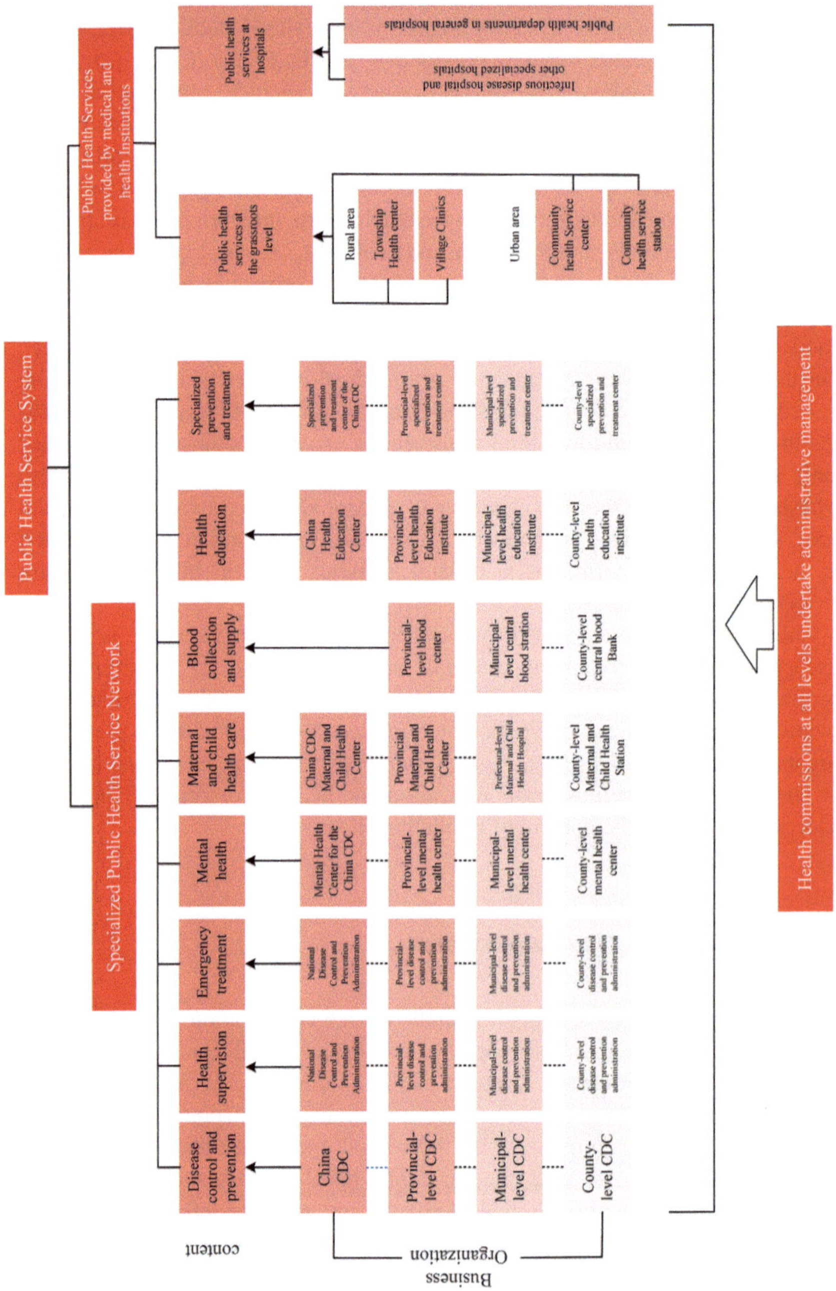

Fig. 4.1 China's public health service system. *Note* CDC stands for Center for Disease Control and Prevention. *Source* Refer to health systems in transition (Meng et al., 2015), with updates on institutional changes after 2015

services in primary medical and health institutions. As of the end of 2021, the vaccination coverage rate at the township and street level has been kept above 95%, and basic public health service programs have achieved full population coverage.

Currently, China's national basic public health service programs include 28 items, with some changes in recent years as shown in Table 4.1. Basic public health services are mainly provided free of charge to all residents through community health service centers (stations), township health centers, village clinics and other urban and rural primary medical and health institutions. The content of China's national basic public health service programs is adjusted annually by the National Health Commission, in collaboration with the National Administration of Traditional Chinese Medicine, the National Disease Control and Prevention Administration, the Ministry of Finance and other departments, based on the economic and social development situation, public health service needs, and fiscal capacity.

4.2.2 Infectious Disease Prevention and Treatment

The Law of the People's Republic of China on the Prevention and Treatment of Infectious Diseases stipulates a classified management system for infectious diseases. Legally defined infectious diseases are categorized into three classes (A, B, and C), totaling 40 diseases: 2 in Class A (plague and cholera), 27 in Class B, and 11 in Class C. China adheres to a prevention-first policy under unified government leadership for the prevention and treatment of infectious diseases. Disease control and prevention institutions at various levels are responsible for specific tasks such as epidemic surveillance, epidemiological investigation, and epidemic reporting. Public and private medical and health institutions are responsible for reporting and clinical treatment of infectious diseases within their scope.

Currently, the major infectious diseases threatening the health of Chinese residents include tuberculosis, AIDS, and viral hepatitis. In 2021, there were 6.23 million reported cases of legally defined infectious diseases nationwide, with 22,198 deaths. The reported incidence rate was 442.16 per 100,000, and the reported mortality rate was 1.57 per 100,000. The top five diseases by death toll were AIDS, tuberculosis, viral hepatitis, rabies, and epidemic hemorrhagic fever, accounting for 99.7% of deaths from Class A and B infectious diseases. Since China expanded its national immunization program in 2007, the number of vaccines has increased from 6 to 14, preventing 15 infectious diseases. China has eradicated smallpox, achieved the goal of being polio-free, and eliminated neonatal tetanus.

Table 4.1 Changes in China's national basic public health service programs from 2009 to 2022

Year	Item number or changes	Item name
2009	1	Management of urban and rural residents' health records
	2	Health education
	3	Health management for children aged 0 to 36 months
	4	Maternal health management
	5	Elderly health management
	6	Vaccination
	7	Infectious disease reporting and management
	8	Health management for hypertension patients
	9	Health management for type 2 diabetes patients
	10	Management of severe mental illness patients
2011	New item	Health supervision and co-management
	Item renaming	Renaming of "infectious disease reporting and management" to "reporting and management of infectious diseases and public health emergencies"
	Item renaming	Renaming of "health management for children aged 0 to 36 months" to "health management for children aged 0 to 6 years"
2013	Item merging	Merging of item 8 and item 9 into "health management for chronic disease patients"
	New item	TCM health management
	Item renaming	Renaming of "management of urban and rural residents' health records" to "establishment of residents' health records"
	Item renaming	Renaming of "health management for children aged 0 to 6 years" to "child health management"
2015	New item	Health management for tuberculosis patients
2017	New item	Free provision of contraceptive devices
	New item	Healthy manners promotion campaign
2018	Item cancellation	Free provision of contraceptive devices
	Item cancellation	Healthy manners promotion campaign

(continued)

Table 4.1 (continued)

Year	Item number or changes	Item name
2019	In addition to the above-mentioned 12 items, there are 19 new items implemented not limited to primary medical and health institutions (originally part of major public health and family planning program)	Endemic disease prevention and treatment, occupational disease prevention and treatment, surveillance of major diseases and health hazard factors, human avian influenza and SARS control and prevention program, plague prevention and treatment program, maintenance and support of national health emergency response teams, "two cancers" screening program for rural women, basic contraceptive services program, nutrition improvement program for children in poor areas, newborn disease screening program in poor areas, folic acid supplementation program for neural tube defect prevention, free pre-pregnancy health checkup program, thalassemia control and prevention program, food safety standards tracking and evaluation program, healthy manners promotion campaign program, national random supervision and inspection program, elderly health and medical care integration services, population surveillance program, supervision and management of health program
2022	Cancellation of 3 out of the 19 newly added service items in 2019	According to the joint issuance of the Ministry of Finance of the People's Republic of China and four other ministries on the "Notice on the Revision of the Management Measures for Five Subsidies including Basic Public Health Services," surveillance of major diseases and health hazard factors, national random supervision and inspection program, and population surveillance program are no longer included in basic public health services

Source National Health Commission

4.2.3 *Epidemic Surveillance and the Construction of the Health Emergency Response Network*

Following the SARS outbreak in 2003, China gradually established the world's largest direct reporting system for infectious disease epidemics and public health emergencies. This system enables medical and health institutions of all levels, including township health centers, to report infectious disease epidemics and public health emergencies directly to the national level, and has reduced the average reporting time from five days to within four hours. It covers 168,000 medical and health institutions nationwide, with 350,000 users, and achieves a timely reporting rate of over 99% for legally defined infectious diseases. Over the years, the effective operation of this system has reduced underreporting of infectious diseases and significantly improved the timeliness of the reporting of infectious diseases. Currently, 100% of disease control and prevention institutions above the county level, 98% of medical and health institutions above the county level, and 94% of primary medical and health institutions in China have achieved real-time online reporting of legally defined infectious diseases. Recently, this system has further enhanced the efficiency of China's health statistics work, providing robust data support for close contact tracing of infected individuals, epidemiological investigation, epidemic assessment, and big data comparative analysis.

4.2.4 Maternal and Child Health Surveillance and Intervention

China has established a relatively comprehensive maternal and child health care network. By the end of 2021, there were 3032 maternal and child health care institutions in China, including 26 at the provincial level, 377 at the prefectural (municipal) level, and 2554 at the county (district, county-level city) level, with 454,000 health technicians in these institutions. In terms of maternal and child health informatization construction, China has successively established the Maternal and Child Health Annual Report Information System, the Maternal and Child Health Surveillance Information System, and the Maternal and Child Health Care Institutions Surveillance Information System. China actively promotes hospital deliveries to ensure maternal and infant safety. In 2021, the prenatal examination rate for pregnant women reached 97.6%, the postpartum visit rate reached 96%, and the hospital delivery rate was 99.9% (100% in cities and 99.9% in counties), basically achieving full hospital deliveries; the systematic management rate for children under three years old reached 92.8%. China conducts screening work to prevent and treat common diseases among women. By 2020, the "two cancers" screening work has covered nearly 2600 counties (cities, districts) nationwide, and nearly 200 million people have been screened for the "two cancers" free of charge, including 130 million for cervical cancer and 64 million for breast cancer. In 2023, China released the "Action Plan for Accelerating the Elimination of Cervical Cancer (2023–2030)" to actively respond to the "Global Strategy to Accelerate the Elimination of Cervical Cancer" proposed by the World Health Organization, accelerating the process of cervical cancer elimination in China to protect and promote women's health. The action plan proposes the following goals: by 2025, promote pilot human papilloma virus (HPV) vaccination services for girls of appropriate age, achieve a 50% cervical cancer screening rate for women of appropriate age, and reach a 90% treatment rate for cervical cancer and precancerous lesions; by 2030, continue to promote HPV vaccination pilot work for girls of appropriate age, achieve a 70% cervical cancer screening rate for women of appropriate age, and reach a 90% treatment rate for cervical cancer and precancerous lesions.

In recent years, China has further strengthened comprehensive prevention and treatment of reproductive health and birth defects. China actively promotes premarital health care services; in 2018, 10.2 million newlyweds received premarital medical examinations, with a premarital examination rate of 61.1%. China has carried out the national pre-pregnancy health checkup program; from 2010 to 2018, free checkups were provided for 83.49 million couples planning to conceive. China has implemented a program of folic acid supplementation to prevent neural tube defects, providing free folic acid supplements to nearly 102 million women of childbearing age from 2009 to 2018. Prenatal screening and prenatal diagnosis coverage has gradually expanded, with a 61.1% serum screening rate for Down syndrome in 2018. Efforts to control and prevent thalassemia have been strengthened, with free screening for 1.65 million couples in 10 southern provinces by 2018, effectively reducing the birth of children with severe thalassemia. The coverage of neonatal disease screening has steadily expanded, with a 97.5% screening rate for neonatal genetic metabolic diseases nationwide in 2017. In 2018, neonatal congenital heart disease screening was initiated.

4.2.5 Chronic Disease Prevention and Treatment

The most common chronic diseases in China include cardiovascular diseases, diabetes, malignant tumors, and chronic respiratory diseases. To effectively control and prevent chronic diseases and curb the rapid rise in premature mortality caused by them, China began formulating a national chronic disease prevention and treatment plan in 2012. The "China's Medium- to Long-Term Plan for Prevention and Treatment of Chronic Diseases (2017–2025)" formulated by the Chinese government proposed the goals that by 2020, the environment for chronic disease control and prevention should be significantly improved, and the premature mortality rate from chronic diseases should be reduced, aiming to lower the premature mortality rate from cardiovascular diseases, cancer, chronic respiratory diseases, and diabetes among people aged 30–70 by 10% compared with 2015; by 2025, the risk factors for chronic diseases should be effectively controlled, the health management for the entire population across the life span should be achieved, and the goal is to lower the premature mortality rate from cardiovascular diseases, cancer, chronic respiratory diseases, and diabetes among people aged 30–70 by 20% compared with 2015; gradually increase residents' health life expectancy and effectively control the burden of chronic diseases.

To achieve these goals, China proposes to establish a division of labor and hierarchical management mechanism among disease control and prevention institutions, hospitals, specialized disease prevention and treatment institutions, and primary medical and health institutions in chronic disease prevention and treatment, with clear responsibilities and tasks. Disease control and prevention institutions and specialized disease prevention and treatment institutions should assist health administrative departments in formulating and implementing chronic disease control and prevention plans and programs, and provide business guidance and technical management. Hospitals are responsible for chronic disease-related information registration and reporting, providing diagnosis, treatment, and rehabilitation services for patients with severe and critical chronic diseases, offering technical guidance for primary medical and health institutions in chronic disease diagnosis, treatment, and rehabilitation, and establishing a two-way referral mechanism between themselves and primary medical and health institutions. Primary medical and health institutions are responsible for implementing chronic disease control and prevention measures. Moreover, China has made it clear that health education institutions are responsible for researching chronic disease health education strategies and methods, disseminating core information on chronic disease prevention and treatment, and guiding other institutions in conducting chronic disease health education activities. Maternal and child health care institutions provide consultation and guidance on chronic disease prevention related to women and children.

Currently, an important task in China's chronic disease prevention and treatment is to ensure the successful construction and innovative development of chronic disease comprehensive control and prevention demonstration areas. Since 2010, China has been creating chronic disease comprehensive control and prevention demonstration areas. In these demonstration areas, community surveys and diagnoses are conducted to identify major local health problems and risk factors, and appropriate technologies are applied to develop suitable chronic disease control and prevention strategies, measures, and long-term management models. Regarding the promotion of innovative development of chronic disease comprehensive control and prevention demonstration areas, the following measures are proposed in the "China's Medium- to Long-Term Plan for Prevention and Treatment of Chronic Diseases (2017–2025)": using the construction of national chronic disease comprehensive control and prevention demonstration areas as a starting point to cultivate chronic disease comprehensive control and prevention models suitable for different regions; the construction of demonstration areas should closely align with the requirements of creating healthy cities and towns, integrate with hierarchical diagnosis and treatment and family doctor contract services, comprehensively enhance the construction quality of demonstration areas, as well as play a leading role in strengthening the main responsibilities of the government, implementing the responsibilities of various departments, and providing comprehensive chronic disease prevention and treatment management services for the entire population throughout the life cycle, so as to drive the overall improvement of regional chronic disease prevention and treatment management levels.

4.2.6 Endemic Disease Prevention and Treatment

Endemic diseases are caused by geochemical and biological factors, as well as production and lifestyle habits, leading to region-specific occurrences. These diseases often occur in impoverished and rural areas, contributing significantly to poverty due to illness and poverty returning due to illness. Endemic disease prevention and treatment is a complex social system project and a significant livelihood project. In China, disease control and prevention institutions at various levels and specialized institutions for endemic disease prevention and treatment are responsible for the surveillance and health education of endemic diseases. They are also responsible for formulating endemic disease control and prevention measures and evaluating their effectiveness, as well as coordinating with relevant departments to implement control and prevention measures such as universal iodized salt use and improvement of water quality. China was once severely affected by endemic diseases, with iodine deficiency disorders, water-borne high iodine goiter, endemic fluorosis, endemic arsenic poisoning, Kashin-Beck disease, and Keshan disease being the main concerns. However, after years of efforts, most regions have effectively controlled or eliminated these hazards. The "three-year campaign on the prevention and treatment of endemic diseases" launched in 2018 has achieved sustained elimination of iodine deficiency disorder, basically eliminated coal-burning type fluorosis and arsenic poisoning, Kashin-Beck disease, and Keshan disease, and effectively controlled drinking water type fluorosis and arsenic poisoning, tea-drinking type fluorosis, and water-borne high iodine hazards. The prevention and treatment goals were achieved alongside poverty alleviation tasks, marking historic achievements in endemic disease prevention and treatment. Nevertheless, as endemic diseases are biogeochemical in nature, long-term consolidation and maintenance of prevention measures are required to prevent recurrence. Therefore, in the future, China will, on the basis of the "three-year campaign on the prevention and treatment of endemic diseases," further enhance nationwide comprehensive endemic disease prevention and treatment capabilities, establish long-term prevention and treatment management mechanisms, address key and difficult issues in current endemic disease prevention and treatment, and continuously consolidate and improve prevention and treatment outcomes to protect the health of the population.

4.2.7 Occupational Disease Prevention and Treatment

Occupational health is a fundamental and integral part of building a Healthy China, concerning the health and well-being of the vast workforce as well as economic development and social stability. China currently faces new challenges and requirements in safeguarding workers' health: the intertwining of new and old occupational disease hazards, and increasing difficulty in controlling and preventing occupational diseases and work-related illnesses; expanding scope of occupational health management and services, and prominent contradictions between the growing demand for occupational health services and the unbalanced and inadequate development of occupational health work. Additionally, the capacity for supporting services and guarantees for occupational disease prevention and treatment needs urgent strengthening, with lagging occupational health information system development. The foundation of occupational health needs to be further consolidated, and the regulatory responsibilities of some local governments and the main responsibilities of employers are not fully implemented.

China implements an occupational health supervision system. The work safety supervision and administration departments, health administrative departments, and labor security administrative departments under the State Council are responsible for supervising and managing occupational disease prevention and treatment nationwide according to the law. The diagnosis of occupational diseases and occupational health examinations are conducted by medical and health institutions approved by the provincial health administrative departments. In the event of an acute occupational disease hazard accident, employers must immediately take emergency rescue and control measures and report to the local health administrative departments and related departments. The health administrative departments are responsible for organizing medical treatment. The diagnosis, treatment, and rehabilitation costs for occupational disease patients, as well as social security for those who are disabled or have lost labor capacity due to occupational diseases, are covered by the national work-related injury insurance in which employers participate. If an employer does not participate in the national work-related injury insurance, the medical care and living security of the patient shall be borne by the employer.

In 2021, China issued the "National Occupational Disease Prevention and Treatment Plan (2021–2025)," setting the following goals: by 2025, establish a more complete occupational health governance system, significantly improve conditions regarding occupational disease hazards, notably improve working conditions in the workplace, further standardize the management of labor employment and working hours, effectively control key occupational diseases such as pneumoconiosis, realize the continuous enhancement of occupational health service capacity and guarantee level, significantly increase awareness of occupational health across society, and further improve the health of workers.

4.2.8 *Environmental and Health Surveillance*

In 2007, China issued the "National Action Plan on Environment and Health (2007–2015)," the first programmatic document in the field of environment and health in China. In 2022, the "14th Five-Year Plan for Environmental Health Work" formulated by the Chinese government proposed the goals that by 2025, the distribution characteristics of high environmental health risk sources in key areas nationwide will be basically understood, the layout of environmental health risk surveillance will be initially formed, the environmental health standard system will be further improved, and a batch of environmental health risk assessment technical specifications and model calculation software will be developed. Additionally, pilot projects for environmental health management will be carried out in 10–15 regions, achieving multilevel, diversified, and characteristic development of environmental health management. A professional team will be built, with cumulative business training for 50,000 people. A good social atmosphere supporting and participating in environmental health work will be fostered, with the national residents' environmental health literacy level reaching more than 20%.

4.2.9 *Health Education and Health Promotion*

China has initially established a health education system led by professional health education institutions, based on primary medical and health institutions in urban and rural areas, and including other medical and health institutions and key places such as schools, enterprises, government agencies, and public institutions. Professional health education institutions include health education centers, health education institutes, and health education stations. The China Health Education Center is responsible for providing technical guidance on health education and health news publicity nationwide, conducting related theoretical and practical research, organizing and implementing large-scale health education and health news publicity activities, and undertaking information management, media contacts, business training, and other technical and service work. At the local level, health education institutes or health education stations are set up to handle specific health education work. To promote the health of urban and rural residents, the Chinese government departments, social groups, and enterprises have jointly or independently carried out various health education and health promotion activities, covering areas such as tobacco control, maternal and child health, children's nutrition, and hepatitis prevention and treatment.

China has established a combined approach to population health surveillance, integrating routine surveillance and health checkups. Routine surveillance refers to the regular health surveillance work carried out by primary medical and health institutions as part of basic public health services. These surveillance efforts are mainly organized and implemented by township health centers and community health service centers, with village clinics and community health service stations conducting specific health surveillance under the management of them respectively. In recent years, health checkups have developed rapidly in China, primarily provided by health checkup institutions affiliated with hospitals, with some independent professional health checkup institutions also offering services.

Moreover, China has conducted special health surveillance programs, such as the Chinese Residents' Nutrition and Health Status Surveillance, which started in 1959. In recent years, other programs, including cause of death surveillance, tumor follow-up registration, chronic disease and nutrition surveillance, have also been carried out, with the coverage of surveillance sites expanding annually. All work has become increasingly standardized, and a chronic disease surveillance and information management platform covering morbidity, prevalence, mortality, and risk factors is gradually taking shape.

Case Study I: Schistosomiasis Prevention and Treatment in China

According to the World Health Organization, as of 2021, schistosomiasis transmission has been reported from 78 countries. However, preventive chemotherapy for schistosomiasis, where people and communities are targeted for large-scale treatment, is only required in 51 endemic countries with moderate-to-high transmission. In 2021, at least 251.4 million people worldwide needed preventive treatment for schistosomiasis. Schistosomiasis is a chronic parasitic disease caused by schistosomes. The Schistosomiasis prevention and treatment program is one of China's major infectious disease prevention and treatment programs. Statistics indicate that in the early days of the People's Republic of China, there were 11.6 million schistosomiasis patients, and over 100 million people were at risk. After more than half a century of efforts, by the end of 2004, the number of schistosomiasis patients in China had dropped to 843,000 (including 28,000 with advanced schistosomiasis), and the area infested with the host Oncomelania snails had reduced to a quarter of its original size. The number of infections and people at risk had significantly decreased, showcasing the tremendous achievements in China's schistosomiasis prevention and treatment efforts. These achievements are inseparable from China's emphasis on adopting a science-based approach and the participation of the entire population. The key experience from China's efforts is summarized as follows:

Adhering to the party's centralized and unified leadership and form synergy. In the early days of the People's Republic of China, Chairman Mao Zedong called for "mobilizing the whole party and the entire population to eliminate schistosomiasis." Under the unified leadership of the Communist Party of China, a leadership group for schistosomiasis prevention and treatment was established, rather than just health departments working alone. This group fully integrated resources from various departments, including health, agriculture, water conservancy, chemical industry, commerce, education, and civil affairs, as well as organizations like the military, Communist Youth League, and Women's Federation. The entire population was widely mobilized, including not only the residents of schistosomiasis-endemic areas but also a large number of farmers, students, and the People's Liberation Army from non-endemic regions.

Adopting a science-based approach and integrating traditional Chinese and Western medicine. China adhered to adopting a science-based approach. The Central Committee of the Communist Party of China carefully listened to the opinions of scientists and professionals, such as adopting fire-burning instead of soil-burying methods for captured Oncomelania snails. Scientific research was supported and promoted, and a combination of traditional Chinese and Western medicine was used, with comprehensive surveillance targeting humans, livestock, and host Oncomelania snails.

Mobilizing the entire population, adapting to local conditions, and doing the right thing at the right time. Taking the elimination of schistosomiasis as a political task, China has closely relied on the masses and mobilized the entire population to participate in various aspects such as Oncomelania snail elimination, patient treatment, fecal management, safe water use, and personal protection. For example, during the winter when farmers were less busy and water levels were low, most Oncomelania snails were exposed on the ground. The prevention and treatment focus was on mass treatment for able-bodied labor force, combined with water conservancy projects to bury soil and reclaim land to eliminate Oncomelania snails, along with fecal management. During the summer and autumn, when farmers frequently engaged in activities like cutting grass, collecting fertilizer, transplanting rice seedlings, and fertilizing, the risk of schistosomiasis infection was high. The prevention and treatment focus was on fecal management and personal protection, combined with treating semi-able-bodied labor force and children patients.

China is currently conducting planned, continuous, and systematic schistosomiasis surveillance, which is crucial for continuing effective control and prevention efforts. This includes the following aspects:

Establishing a nationwide surveillance network. China has been establishing and improving the epidemic surveillance system at county, township, village, and urban community levels to closely monitor the epidemic situation, socioeconomic conditions, and changes in the human and natural environment. The patient surveillance and new case reporting mechanisms are being improved, and comprehensive surveillance sites are being established to monitor not only the human population but also livestock, Oncomelania snails, and suspicious environments.

Carrying out timely epidemic reporting and case investigation. Various medical institutions, disease control and prevention institutions (schistosomiasis control institutions), health quarantine institutions, and their medical staff are required to report schistosomiasis cases within 24 h of diagnosis using an infectious disease report card through the network direct reporting system after distinguishing between acute and chronic cases. County-level disease control and prevention institutions are responsible for individual case investigations of reported acute schistosomiasis cases within one week, filling out case investigation forms, and promptly entering the data into the database, and then reporting through the schistosomiasis information reporting system network.

Conducting Oncomelania snail inspections and environmental surveillance. The significant success of China's schistosomiasis prevention and treatment efforts lies in the nationwide mobilization and Oncomelania snail elimination campaigns, which cut off the host transmission route. Despite the achievements, the Chinese government continues to conduct annual spring Oncomelania snail inspections. The inspection scope includes existing Oncomelania snail environments (including susceptible environments and other Oncomelania snail habitats) and suspicious environments. Systematic sampling and environmental sampling methods are used to check Oncomelania snail infection status.

Case Study II: Malaria Prevention and Treatment in China

According to the World Health Organization, globally in 2022, there were an estimated 249 million malaria cases and 608,000 malaria deaths in 85 countries. Malaria is a life-threatening disease transmitted to humans through the bites of certain types of mosquitoes. However, malaria is preventable and treatable. On June 30, 2021, the World Health Organization announced that China had been certified malaria-free, recognizing China's remarkable achievement of eliminating malaria after reporting around 30 million malaria cases annually in the 1940s and eradicating the disease entirely after 70 years of relentless effort. This accomplishment marks another significant eradication of a major infectious disease in China, following smallpox, poliomyelitis, filariasis, and neonatal tetanus, and represents a crucial milestone in both China's public health history and the global campaign to eliminate malaria.

Malaria was once one of China's most historically pervasive, widespread, and deadly infectious diseases. Before the founding of the People's Republic of China, approximately 30 million people contracted malaria annually, of which 300,000 died, with a fatality rate as high as 1%. Following the founding of the People's Republic of China, the Central Committee of the Communist Party of China and the State Council led the Chinese people in combating malaria through five arduous phases: carrying out key investigations and prevention and treatment measures (1949–1959), controlling severe epidemics (1960–1979), reducing the incidence rate (1980–1999), consolidating prevention and treatment achievements (2000–2009), and eliminating malaria (2010–2020).

In 2010, the Chinese government actively responded to the United Nations' global malaria eradication initiative by setting the goal of eliminating malaria by 2020. Through persistent efforts, China reduced the annual number of indigenous malaria cases from 30 million to zero, safeguarding the health and lives of its people. China established scientifically precise malaria control and prevention strategies, along with a sensitive and efficient system for reporting, detecting, treating, monitoring, and emergency response, thereby gaining the capacity to prevent the reintroduction and spread of malaria. China also developed artemisinin and other effective antimalarial drugs and treatment regimens and innovated the "1-3-7" malaria elimination protocol, which includes completing malaria case report within 1 day, case review and epidemiological investigation within 3 days, and focus investigation and response within 7 days. Additionally, China implemented multi-departmental and regional joint control and prevention measures and cooperated on malaria control and prevention in border areas, contributing Chinese expertise to global malaria control and elimination efforts. China reported its last local primary case of malaria in April 2016, has not detected any local primary case for four consecutive years since 2017, and submitted an application for malaria elimination certification to the World Health Organization in November 2020. After an on-site assessment by the World Health Organization, China passed the national malaria elimination certification on June 30, 2021.

Chapter 5
China's Medical Security System

The medical security system is an essential component of the social security system, encompassing common medical issues in most areas of social security system, such as illness, injury, childbirth, and elderly care. The establishment of a medical security system is a social responsibility that plays an increasingly important role in national affairs and social development. Countries around the world are attempting to improve their entire social security system by establishing a relatively comprehensive medical security system, so as to promote social harmonious development, and progress. China has already established a basic medical security system that covers all urban and rural residents. China's medical security system plays a significant role in safeguarding citizens' health and survival rights, improving population health levels, promoting the development of health care services, improving social fairness, and maintaining social stability.

China's medical security system includes multiple layers such as basic medical insurance, medical assistance, supplementary medical insurance, and commercial medical insurance (Fig. 5.1). Basic medical insurance, medical assistance, and supplementary medical insurance fall within the scope of social medical security, with funding and benefit policies formulated by the government and security services mainly provided by government-affiliated institutions, while commercial medical insurance is offered by insurance companies through market-oriented mechanisms. Basic medical insurance includes basic medical insurance for urban employees and basic medical insurance for rural and non-working urban residents. Urban employees are required to participate in basic medical insurance for urban employees, while non-working urban residents and rural residents voluntarily participate in basic medical insurance for rural and non-working urban residents on a household basis. The urban and rural medical assistance serves as the foundation of China's multi-level medical security system, encompassing urban medical assistance and rural medical assistance. The urban and rural medical assistance system raises funds through multiple channels such as government allocations and social donations, primarily

Z. Feng et al. (eds.), *China's Health System*, Introduction to China's S&T Innovation,
https://doi.org/10.1007/978-981-95-1205-8_5

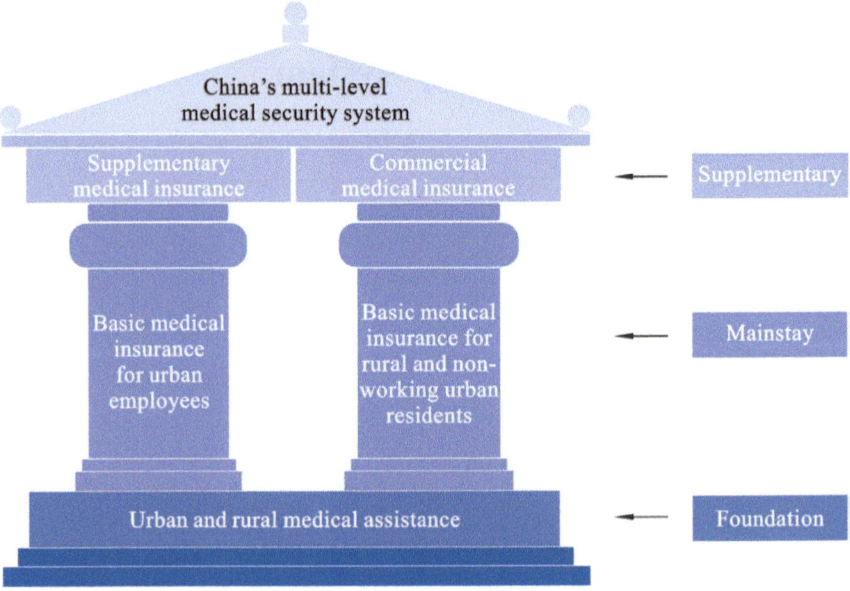

Fig. 5.1 China's multi-level medical security system

providing financial assistance to urban and rural low-income households, households enjoying five guarantees, and other economically disadvantaged families to ensure that impoverished populations enjoy basic medical services.

The following text will first provide a detailed introduction to basic medical insurance for urban employees and basic medical insurance for rural and non-working urban residents, and then introduce the urban and rural medical assistance, commercial medical insurance, and supplementary medical insurance.

5.1 Basic Medical Insurance for Urban Employees

5.1.1 Institutional Background

To safeguard the medical rights and interests of urban employees, China has successively established the socialized medicine and the labor insurance medical system (during the planned economy period), as well as the basic medical insurance for urban employees (which emerged under the socialist market economy environment). Starting from the comprehensive reform pilot of employee medical insurance conducted in Zhenjiang, Jiangsu Province, and Jiujiang, Jiangxi Province in 1994, to the promulgation of the "Decision of the State Council on Establishing the Basic Medical Insurance for Urban Employees" (hereinafter referred to as the "Decision") in December 1998, the framework of the basic medical insurance for urban employees was basically established in China. Currently, China's basic medical insurance for urban employees has been universally established nationwide.

The "Decision" proposes that the main task of the medical insurance system reform is to adapt to the socialist market economy system and establish a social medical insurance system that guarantees the basic medical needs of employees based on the fiscal, enterprise, and individual affordability. The "Decision" also proposes that the principles for establishing the basic medical insurance system for urban employees are as follows: the level of basic medical insurance should be commensurate with the level of productive forces in the primary stage of socialism;all urban employers and their employees must participate in basic medical insurance and this shall be subject to territorial administration; basic medical insurance premiums are jointly borne by both employers and employees; and the basic medical insurance funds implement a combination of social pooling funds with individual accounts.

5.1.2 Main Content

5.1.2.1 Coverage Range

According to the "Decision," the basic medical insurance system for urban employees should cover all urban employers, including enterprises (state-owned enterprises, collective enterprises, foreign-invested enterprises, private enterprises, etc.), government agencies, public institutions, social organizations, private non-enterprise units, and their employees. In other words, all formally employed individuals must participate in basic medical insurance to achieve "wide coverage."

With the further deepening of China's economic system reform and the adjustment of its industrial structure, the number of employees in flexible forms of employment such as part-time, temporary, and flexible work has gradually increased. To address the medical insurance issues of flexible employment personnel, in 2003, the Ministry of Labor and Social Security of the People's Republic of China issued the "Guiding Opinions on Urban Flexible Employment Personnel Participating in Basic Medical Insurance," which explicitly includes flexible employment personnel within the scope of the basic medical insurance system and encourages them to achieve overall participation through labor security agencies or community labor security service agencies.

Since entering the twenty-first century, the migration of rural labor to cities has accelerated, and the tide of migrant workers has further expanded in China. Although these individuals work and live in cities, they cannot enjoy the security and benefits of the cities they reside in. To improve the medical security for migrant workers, the Ministry of Labor and Social Security of the People's Republic of China launched a special campaign in 2006 to expand the coverage of medical insurance for migrant workers. As a result, all urban laborers are now covered by the basic medical insurance system for urban employees. By the end of 2022, the number of participants in China's basic medical insurance for urban employees reached 362 million.

5.1.2.2 Fund Collection

According to the "Decision," the basic medical insurance premiums for employees are jointly paid by employers and employees. The employers' contribution rate should be controlled at around 6% of the total wages of employees, while the employees' contribution rate is generally 2% of their personal income. With the development of the economy, the contribution rates of employers and employees can be adjusted accordingly. This funding level was formulated based on the actual situation of China's relatively low productivity level and limited fiscal and corporate affordability at that time. This document also stipulates that retirees participating in basic medical insurance do not pay basic medical insurance premiums personally. Currently, the average employer contribution rate in China is approximately 7.5%, and the average employee contribution rate is 2%. To address the medical insurance issues of retirees from closed and bankrupt state-owned enterprises, in May 2009, the Ministry of Human Resources and Social Security and three other ministries jointly issued the "Notice on Appropriately Addressing Issues Related to Medical Insurance for Retirees from Closed and Bankrupt State-Owned Enterprises." The notice clarifies that when an enterprise is closed or bankrupted, the required costs for retirees to participate in medical insurance should be paid through the enterprise's bankruptcy assets according to relevant provisions of the Enterprise Bankruptcy Law of the People's Republic of China. If the enterprise's bankruptcy assets are insufficient, they can be raised through various channels such as the proceeds from land sales that are not included in the bankruptcy assets, fiscal subsidies, and adjustments to the balance of medical insurance funds. Provincial governments should provide assistance and support to struggling cities and counties. For retirees from locally bankrupt state-owned enterprises participating in the basic medical insurance system for urban employees, the central government will provide a one-time subsidy based on the principle of "combining rewards and subsidies."

5.1.2.3 Fund Operation and Management

China's basic medical insurance funds consist of social pooling funds and individual accounts. According to the "Decision," all the basic medical insurance premiums paid by employees are credited to their individual accounts. The basic medical insurance premiums paid by employers are divided into two parts, one for establishing the social pooling funds and the other for crediting to individual accounts. The proportion credited to individual accounts is generally around 30% of the employers' contribution. The social pooling funds and individual accounts are accounted for separately according to their respective payment scopes and must not be misappropriated. In

2021, to further improve the basic medical insurance system for employees with mutual assistance and shared responsibility, the General Office of the State Council issued the "Guiding Opinions of the General Office of the State Council on Establishing and Improving the Outpatient Co-Insurance Mechanism for Employee Basic Medical Insurance," which modified the method of calculating individual accounts credits. In principle, the individual accounts credit standard is controlled at 2% of the individual's insured contribution base, and the basic medical insurance premiums paid by the employer are all credited to the social pooling funds. After adjusting the structure of the social pooling funds and individual accounts, the increased social pooling funds are mainly used for outpatient co-insurance and improving the outpatient benefits for insured individuals.

China's basic medical insurance funds are managed through special fiscal accounts. Fund collection is the responsibility of the medical insurance administrative institutions in the pooling area. The medical insurance funds first enter the fund income account of the administrative institutions, and then are handed over to the special fiscal account managed by the local financial department for unified management. Based on the payment plan of the medical insurance administrative institutions, the local financial department will allocate funds from the special fiscal account to the fund expenditure account of the medical insurance administrative institutions. Finally, the funds flow from the fund expenditure account of the medical insurance administrative institutions to medical institutions.

5.1.2.4 Scope of Coverage and Benefit Payment

China's basic medical insurance payment system implements a catalog management approach, primarily to ensure that insured individuals enjoy basic medical services legally, regulate reasonable prescriptions from medical institutions, and reasonably control medical expenses. The payment catalog includes the drug catalog, the diagnosis and treatment item catalog, and the medical service facility catalog. Among them, the drug catalog adopts an "admission method" for management, meaning that the listed drugs fall within the scope approved for payment by basic medical insurance; the diagnosis and treatment item catalog currently mainly adopts an "exclusion method" for management, but some regions adopt an "admission method" for management; the medical service facility catalog adopts an "exclusion method" for management.

The benefit payment of the basic medical insurance for urban employees covers three aspects: general outpatient services, outpatient services for major illnesses, and inpatient services. The basic medical insurance funds for urban employees implement a combination of social pooling funds and individual accounts (unified accounting). Specifically, the individual accounts cover outpatient services for minor illnesses, while the social pooling funds cover inpatient services and outpatient services for major illnesses. The basic medical insurance for urban employees sets a deductible threshold, coinsurance ratio, and ceiling limit. According to the requirements of the "Decision," the deductible threshold is controlled in principle at around 10%

of the local employees' annual average salary, and the maximum payment limit is controlled in principle at around four times the local employees' annual average salary. Medical expenses below the deductible threshold are paid from the individual accounts or borne by the individual. Medical expenses above the deductible threshold and below the maximum payment limit are primarily paid from the social pooling funds, with individuals also bearing a certain proportion.

5.1.2.5 Medical Service Management

The purpose of medical service management conducted by China's medical insurance institutions is to reasonably control medical expenses and ensure the quality of medical services. The content of medical service management can be summarized as "designated medical treatment and three catalogs." Designated medical treatment refers to the practice that the medical insurance administrative institutions and medical institutions sign the designated medical treatment agreements, the medical institutions accepts the assessment and supervision of the medical insurance administrative institutions, and only when insured individuals seek medical treatment at designated medical institutions can they obtain reimbursement from medical insurance. Designated medical institutions include general hospitals, specialized hospitals, and community health care facilities within the jurisdiction. With the expansion of medical insurance coverage, the number of designated medical institutions has also increased significantly. Generally, public medical institutions and private medical institutions with a certain scale within the jurisdiction are included in the scope of designated medical institutions.

The "three catalogs" refer to the drug catalog, the diagnosis and treatment item catalog, and the medical service facility catalog mentioned above. All three catalogs are formulated based on the principles of clinical necessity, safety, effectiveness, and appropriate pricing. Among them, the drug catalog is formulated by the Ministry of Human Resources and Social Security, while the diagnosis and treatment item catalog and the medical service facility catalog are formulated by the human resources and social security departments of various provinces. The drug catalog is divided into Class A and Class B. Class A is uniformly formulated by the state, and cannot be adjusted by local authorities. Class B is formulated by the state, but provinces, autonomous regions, and municipalities directly under the central government can make appropriate adjustments based on local conditions. The sum of the number of drugs added and reduced must not exceed 15% of the total number of drugs in the national Class B catalog. The human resources and social security departments of prefectural and county-level overall planning areas have no authority to adjust the drug catalog, but they can adjust the reimbursement ratio appropriately. Generally, about 20% of the self-paid expenses for drugs in Class B catalog are deducted, and the remaining amount can be reimbursed.

5.1.2.6 Medical Insurance Payment

Since 2011, China's medical and health system reform has taken the reform of medical insurance payment methods as an important task. An increasing number of regions have been transitioning from fee-for-service payment to mixed payment models.

Total budget control. It stipulates that the growth rate of medical institutions' business income must not exceed an agreed-upon value. For example, Shanghai and other places have adopted this approach.

Average cost per hospitalization. It stipulates that the average cost per hospitalization in medical institutions must not exceed an agreed-upon value. For instance, Nanjing, Zhenjiang, Guangzhou, Shenzhen, and other regions have implemented this method.

Diagnosis related groups (DRGs). For several specific diagnoses, fixed payment methods are implemented. For example, Beijing implemented DRGs in six pilot hospitals in 2011, covering 108 different diagnoses. Throughout the city, this payment method has been implemented for a small number of diseases such as appendicitis, goiter, cataract, benign ovarian tumor, uterine fibroid, hallux valgus, and gallstone. In Mudanjiang, Heilongjiang Province, however, single-diagnosis payment is implemented for the vast majority of diseases, with a total of 830 diagnoses in 2010.

Capitation. This method is primarily implemented in the management of chronic outpatient diseases (such as mental illnesses). Patients sign a contract with a designated medical institution, committing to seeking initial consultation at that institution for the entire year. The medical insurance institution then pays the designated medical institution a capitation fee for the outpatient services provided to chronic patients for one year. However, patients still need to pay a certain proportion of out-of-pocket expenses when seeking medical treatment.

Diagnosis-intervention packet (DIP). This is a payment method originally created in China. It relies on big data and groups cases based on the "diagnosis + operation" classification rule after collecting a large number of real-world cases. Medical insurance payments are then made according to certain settlement rules.

In China's practice, the prepaid system is combined with a risk-sharing mechanism. If the actual expenses of a medical institution exceed the pre-determined budget, the medical insurance institution will share a portion of the overrun expenses. The specific sharing method is negotiated between the medical insurance institution and the medical institution and is reflected in the designated medical treatment agreement.

5.1.2.7 Medical Service Regulation

In China, medical service regulation primarily includes aspects such as designated access, real-time monitoring, annual assessment, and reward and punishment mechanisms.

5.2 Basic Medical Insurance for Rural and Non-working Urban Residents

Case Study: China's Rural Cooperative Medical Care System Being Hailed as the "Chinese Model"

In the 1980s, the World Health Organization and the World Bank pointed out in their investigation report on China that the rural cooperative medical care system implemented in China was the only model for developing countries to solve health funding issues. Dr. Mahler, the then Director-General of the World Health Organization, actively recommended China's rural health work experience to developing countries.

China's rural cooperative medical care system has been praised by the World Health Organization and the World Bank as the "Chinese Model" that achieved the greatest health benefits with the least investment. It can be traced back to the earliest health pharmacies and health cooperatives in the 1930s, having undergone the embryonic stage in the 1930s to 1940s, the initial stage in the 1950s, the development and peak stage in the 1960s to 1970s, the disintegration stage in the 1980s, and the recovery and development stage since the 1990s (when the new rural cooperative medical care system was established). The development and improvement of China's rural cooperative medical care system laid the foundation for China to address the basic health issues of 800 million farmers with relatively low health expenditure in the 1960s to 1970s. In 1978, the coverage of China's rural cooperative medical care system reached over 90%. This system has improved the rural medical situation in China and enhanced the health level of the broad masses of the people. After implementing the rural cooperative medical care system, by 2003, China's infant mortality rate had dropped from 200‰ in the early days of the founding of the People's Republic of China to 25.5‰, the maternal mortality rate had decreased from 1500 per 100,000 to 51.3 per 100,000, the population mortality rate had declined from 17‰ to 6.4‰, and the average life expectancy had increased from 35 years to 72.4 years.

The early rural cooperative medical care system in China had the following characteristics: First, it was an important manifestation of promoting the development of the cooperative economy and improving its social service functions at that time. China's rural cooperative medical care system emerged in the form of health pharmacies and adhered to the principle of putting disease prevention first. Second, medical personnel played a significant role. These medical personnel did not receive salaries. They were busy with farm work most of the time, and served as doctors when needed, known as "barefoot doctors." They were trained by "mobile medical teams," which were a crucial pillar for consolidating and developing China's rural cooperative medical care system. Third, China's rural cooperative medical care system was primarily funded by farmers' voluntary contributions. Daily expenses of health pharmacies were secured through three sources: "health care fees" paid by farmers, 15% to

20% of the public welfare funds extracted from agricultural cooperatives, and medical income. Fourth, China's rural cooperative medical care system was a low-cost, widely covered rural health insurance system, enabling rural residents to enjoy basic primary health services nearby and ensuring fairness and accessibility of medical and health services for sick farmers.

Issues with the early rural cooperative medical care system in China include: First, there was a lack of relevant legal and organizational guarantees. Without formal legal documents, there was no legal basis, and management lacked scientific rigor. Second, during the "cultural revolution," there was an eagerness for quick success and immediate benefit. Under the influence of extreme left-wing ideologies, there was an overemphasis on catering to political needs, disregarding objective and subjective conditions as well as medical and health characteristics in health policy-making and management, which damaged the healthy development of the medical and health system and hindered the healthy development of rural medicine. Third, the technical level of health personnel was relatively low, resulting in an overall low performance of the rural cooperative medical care system. Fourth, the funding level was limited, and the ability to resist risks was poor. After the disintegration of the rural collective economy, the rural cooperative medical care system lost its primary source of funding, which was one of the fundamental reasons why it was difficult for the system to exist for a long time. Fifth, the rural cooperative medical care system adopted an approach that focused on outpatient clinics and minor illnesses. This increased the benefit coverage, but the level of protection was low, making it difficult to meet the multi-level needs of the rural population.

The basic medical insurance system for rural and non-working urban residents was established in 2016 by integrating the basic medical insurance system for non-working urban residents and the new rural cooperative medical care system. This section will first introduce the relevant content of basic medical insurance for non-working urban residents and new rural cooperative medical care separately, and then describe the integration of the basic medical insurance system for non-working urban residents and the new rural cooperative medical care system.

5.2.1 Basic Medical Insurance for Non-working Urban Residents

5.2.1.1 Institutional Background

In 2007, the pilot project for basic medical insurance for non-working urban residents was officially launched in China. 88 cities were selected across the country as pilot cities. In March 2008, the State Council issued the "Guiding Opinions of the State Council on Carrying Out the Pilot Project for Basic Medical Insurance for Non-Working Urban Residents" (hereinafter referred to as the "Guiding Opinions"). In 2010, the pilot project for basic medical insurance for non-working urban residents was fully implemented nationwide. The most distinctive feature of basic medical insurance for non-working urban residents is the government's universal subsidy for every insured resident.

Different from the main goal of basic medical insurance for urban employees, which is to guarantee the basic medical needs of the employed population in urban areas and establish a social insurance system combining individual accounts with social pooling funds, the goal of the basic medical insurance system for non-working urban residents is to establish a social security system that covers all non-working urban residents, with a reasonable funding mechanism, sound management system, and standardized operational mechanism, focusing primarily on comprehensive insurance for major illnesses.

The principles of the pilot project for basic medical insurance system for non-working urban residents are as follows: starting at a low level, determining the funding level and security standards reasonably based on the level of economic development and the affordability of all parties, focusing on guaranteeing the medical needs for major illnesses of non-working urban residents, and gradually improving the level of security; adhering to the principle of voluntariness and fully respecting the wishes of the people; clarifying the responsibilities of the central and local governments, with the central government determining the basic principles and major policies, and the local governments formulating specific measures to implement territorial management for insured residents; adhering to overall planning and coordination, ensuring the connection between the basic policies, standards, and management measures of various medical security systems.

5.2.1.2 Main Content

Similar to the basic medical insurance for urban employees, the basic medical insurance for non-working urban residents is also mostly formulated by the social security management departments of various localities, and managed by medical insurance administrative institutions. The basic medical insurance for non-working urban residents implements a catalog and management policy similar to that of the basic medical insurance for urban employees. Here, only the provisions that are inconsistent with the basic medical insurance for urban employees will be elaborated.

1. Coverage Range

According to the "Guiding Opinions," the coverage range of the basic medical insurance system for non-working urban residents includes "students in primary and secondary schools (including vocational high schools, technical secondary schools, and technical schools), children, and other non-working urban residents who are not covered by the basic medical insurance system for urban employees." Together with the basic medical insurance system for urban employees that covers all employed populations, it has achieved full coverage of urban residents' medical insurance.

2. Fund Collection

The basic medical insurance funds for non-working urban residents mainly come from two aspects: fiscal subsidies and individual contributions. When the pilot project was launched in 2007, the government provided subsidies at a standard of no less than 40 yuan per capita annually. For disadvantaged residents such as those receiving low-income assistance and severely disabled persons who have lost their ability to work, the government provided additional subsidies. The fiscal subsidy funds were included in the fiscal budgets of governments at all levels. With the introduction of the "Opinions of the Central Committee of the Communist Party of China and the State Council on Deepening the Reform of the Medical and Health System" in March 2009, the support of governments at all levels for the basic medical insurance system for non-working urban residents has gradually been strengthened, and the per capita fiscal subsidy standard for basic medical insurance for non-working urban residents has also been gradually increased, from 80 yuan per capita in 2009 to 450 yuan per capita in 2017, greatly improving the level of residents' medical and health security.

Regarding personal contributions, China currently does not have a unified standard. Local governments determine the appropriate level based on the local economic development level, basic medical consumption needs of different groups, and the affordability of local residents' families and the fiscal budget. In 2017, the per capita individual contribution standard for basic medical insurance for non-working urban residents reached 180 yuan.

3. Scope of Coverage and Benefit Payment

The basic medical insurance funds for non-working urban residents implement social pooling funds without setting up individual accounts. The funds are mainly used for the medical expenditures of inpatient services and outpatient services for major illnesses of insured residents. When the pilot project was launched in 2007, the basic medical insurance for non-working urban residents only covered inpatient services and outpatient services for major illnesses, and general outpatient services were not reimbursed. In 2009, the "Guiding Opinions of the Ministry of Human Resources and Social Security, the Ministry of Finance, and the Ministry of Health on Implementing the Risk Pooling of Outpatient Services for the Basic Medical Insurance for Non-working Urban Residents" was issued, requiring all localities to gradually include medical expenses for outpatient services for minor illnesses into the fund payment scope while focusing on ensuring the medical expenditures of inpatient services and outpatient services for major illnesses of insured residents.

When covering inpatient services and outpatient services for major illnesses, the basic medical insurance for non-working urban residents implements the same reimbursement catalog as the basic medical insurance for urban employees, but the level of benefits enjoyed by insured residents is generally lower than that of the basic medical insurance for urban employees. The specific thresholds for initiating medical insurance payments, payment ratios, and maximum limits for the basic medical insurance for non-working urban residents are determined by local authorities. During the 12th Five-Year Plan period, the reimbursement ratio for inpatient expenses covered by the basic medical insurance for non-working urban residents reached 75%. Currently, China has implemented the risk pooling of outpatient services for the basic medical insurance for non-working urban residents, which includes the outpatient expenses of insured residents into the reimbursement scope of the pooling funds, effectively addressing the burden of general outpatient medical expenses for non-working urban residents. The risk pooling of outpatient services generally requires insured residents to seek medical treatment at primary medical and health institutions, and the maximum limit is usually only a few hundred yuan.

5.2.2 New Rural Cooperative Medical Care System

5.2.2.1 Establishment of the New Rural Cooperative Medical Care System

To address the issue of farmers lacking medical security and the increasingly serious problem of poverty due to illness and poverty returning due to illness among rural residents, in October 2002, the Central Committee of the Communist Party of China and the State Council issued the "Decision of the Central Committee of the Communist Party of China and the State Council on Further Strengthening Rural Health Work," proposing the gradual establishment of the new rural cooperative medical care system. In 2003, the General Office of the State Council forwarded the "Opinions on Establishing a New Rural Cooperative Medical Care System" issued by the Ministry of Health and other departments, marking the official commencement of the establishment of the new rural cooperative medical care system. Since then, a new medical security system has gradually been implemented nationwide.

The new rural cooperative medical care system is a mutual medical assistance system for farmers that is organized, guided, and supported by the government. Farmers voluntarily participate in the system, with funding coming from individuals, collectives, and the government. The system focuses on providing comprehensive protection for major illnesses.

5.2.2.2 Objectives and Principles of the New Rural Cooperative Medical Care System

1. Objectives of the New Rural Cooperative Medical Care System

The new rural cooperative medical care system differs from any previous medical security system and has distinct Chinese characteristics. Its objectives are to establish a basic medical security system that meets the health service needs of the vast majority of farmers, address the issues of poverty due to illness and poverty returning due to illness among farmers, reduce farmers' economic burden of medical treatment, increase the utilization rate of health services, promote the construction of rural health service systems, and improve the health level of the population.

2. Principles of the New Rural Cooperative Medical Care System

The new rural cooperative medical care system follows unique principles that differ from previous cooperative medical care systems and align with China's rural development philosophy and the characteristics of farmers.

First, the principle of voluntary participation on a household basis. The most significant feature of the new rural cooperative medical care system is that it upholds the basic principle of "voluntary participation by farmers." The purpose is to allow farmers to recognize this beneficial system on their own and voluntarily participate in it, leveraging the situation to ultimately achieve full coverage of the new rural cooperative medical care system.

Second, the principle of government fiscal funding as the main source. In previous cooperative medical care systems, individual farmers or collective economies were the main funding sources. However, practice has shown that the amount of funding raised was relatively limited, the ability to resist risks was poor, and the systems were not sustainable. Since its inception, the new rural cooperative medical care system has clearly defined the principle of "government fiscal funding as the main source," specifying that central and local governments should provide certain subsidies to participating farmers.

Third, the principle of focusing on comprehensive protection for major illnesses while also considering outpatient services. The new rural cooperative medical care system primarily subsidizes hospitalization expenses while also compensating for outpatient expenses.

Fourth, the principle of using the county level as the unit of overall planning. In previous cooperative medical care systems, overall planning was conducted at the township level, which resulted in weaker management and lower risk resistance capabilities. Therefore, the new rural cooperative medical care system adopts the county level as the unit of overall planning and implementation, thus enhances the risk resistance capabilities and regulatory oversight.

Fifth, the principle of "operating through the health system with coordinated cooperation from various departments." China stipulates that people's governments at the county level and above are responsible for the unified coordination and guidance of the new rural cooperative medical care system within their respective administrative areas. The new rural cooperative medical care management committees shall be established, composed of relevant departments such as finance, health, and civil affairs, to clarify the responsibilities and tasks of the regulatory bodies and operating agencies.

5.2.2.3 Main Content

1. Fund Collection

The new rural cooperative medical care funds mainly come from fiscal subsidies and individual contributions. At the beginning of its launch in 2003, the per capita fund collection level for the new rural cooperative medical care system was only 30 yuan, with the central government and local governments each providing subsidy funds at a standard of 10 yuan per capita, and farmers paying 10 yuan out of their own pockets. In recent years, the per capita funding standard for the new rural cooperative medical care system has gradually increased, and the government finances have taken on the role of the main funding source for the new rural cooperative medical care system.

2. Compensation Mode

The new rural cooperative medical care funds primarily subsidize the inpatient medical expenses and outpatient expenses for major illnesses of participating farmers (some areas have already implemented risk pooling of outpatient services). Each region determines the scope, standards, and amount of fund payments based on the total funding amount, combined with local conditions. The competent departments of the new rural cooperative medical care system formulate a reimbursement drug catalog (generally at the provincial level) to constrain the scope of drug compensation. The reimbursement drug catalog is designed in a tiered manner, including the village level, township level, and county level and above. The higher the level of the designated medical institutions, the more types of drugs are allowed for use and reimbursement. The reimbursement drug catalog at the township level is primarily based on the National Essential Medicine List (primary level), with appropriate additions based on local outstanding health needs and the payment capacity of the new rural cooperative medical care funds. The reimbursement drug catalog at the county level adopts the National Essential Medicine List (primary level), and if there is a genuine need to add traditional ethnic medicines or drugs for special local diseases based on local conditions, appropriate additions can be made. The reimbursement rate for drugs within the National Essential Medicine List under the new rural cooperative medical care system is significantly higher than that for drugs outside the national essential medicine list.

3. Payment Method

The new rural cooperative medical care system implements total outpatient payment for designated medical institutions. Based on the handling method for the total outpatient budget surplus, it is divided into three types: outpatient total prepayment, outpatient total budget + flexible settlement, and outpatient total limit. The main inpatient payment methods under the new rural cooperative medical care system include single-diagnosis payment, per diem payment, total payment, and mixed payment.

5.2.3 *Integration of the Basic Medical Insurance System for Non-working Urban Residents and the New Rural Cooperative Medical Care System*

In January 2016, the State Council issued the "Opinions of the State Council on Integrating the Basic Medical Insurance System for Rural and Non-Working Urban Residents," merging the basic medical insurance system for non-working urban residents and the new rural cooperative medical care system into a unified basic medical insurance system for rural and non-working urban residents. This integration is a significant measure to promote the reform of the medical and health system, ensure that rural and non-working urban residents enjoy equal rights to basic medical insurance, promote social fairness and justice, and enhance people's well-being. It is of great significance for promoting the coordinated economic and social development of urban and rural areas and building a moderately prosperous society in all respects.

5.2.3.1 Integration of Basic Policies

The basic medical insurance for rural and non-working urban residents has achieved "six unifications." First, a unified coverage scope. The coverage scope of the basic medical insurance system for rural and non-working residents includes all individuals eligible for participation in the existing basic medical insurance system for non-working urban residents and the new rural cooperative medical care system, covering all urban and rural residents except those who should be covered by the basic medical insurance system for urban employees. Second, a unified fund collection policy. The basic medical insurance for rural and non-working urban residents continues to adopt a fund collection method that combines individual contributions with government subsidies, encouraging support or funding from collectives, units, or other social and economic organizations. Third, a unified benefit protection. Following the principles of moderate security and balanced revenue and expenditure, it ensures balanced urban and rural benefit protection, gradually unifying the scope of coverage and payment standards. The basic medical insurance funds for rural and non-working residents are mainly used to cover the inpatient and outpatient medical expenses of participants, with the inpatient reimbursement rate within the policy range maintained at around 75%. Fourth, a unified medical insurance catalog, including the drug catalog, diagnosis and treatment item catalog, and medical service facility catalog for basic medical insurance for rural and non-working urban residents. Fifth, a unified designated management. The management measures for designated medical institutions of basic medical insurance for rural and non-working urban residents have been unified, and a comprehensive evaluation and assessment mechanism as well as a dynamic entry and exit mechanism have been established and improved. Sixth, a unified fund management. The basic medical insurance for rural and non-working urban residents implements a unified national fund financial system, accounting system, and fund budget and final account management system. The basic medical insurance funds for rural and non-working urban residents are included in the special fiscal account and managed under the "two-line management" system of revenue and expenditure. The funds are independently accounted for and managed in a special account.

5.2.3.2 Integration of Management Systems

First, regions with suitable conditions are encouraged to streamline the management system of medical insurance and unify the administrative management functions of basic medical insurance. This includes integrating the medical insurance administrative institutions, personnel, and information systems of basic medical insurance for rural and non-working urban residents, standardizing operational procedures, and providing integrated service delivery. On the basis of integrating these institutions, it is further recommended to improve the management and operational mechanisms, and optimize the operational procedures. Second, regions with suitable conditions are encouraged to innovate in service delivery models, promote the separation of management from operations and introduce competitive mechanisms. Under the premise of ensuring the safety of the insurance funds and effective supervision, governments can purchase services and entrust qualified commercial insurance institutions and other social entities to participate in the operation of basic medical insurance, thereby invigorating the operational vitality.

5.3 Urban and Rural Medical Assistance, Commercial Medical Insurance, and Supplementary Medical Insurance

5.3.1 Urban and Rural Medical Assistance

The medical assistance system is able to provide medical security for the vast impoverished population, improve their health levels, and help them escape from the plight of poverty and illness as soon as possible. For China, the medical assistance system plays an important role and is of great significance in safeguarding people's rights and interests, fulfilling government responsibilities, embodying social fairness, and promoting higher-quality, more efficient, and fairer national economic development.

Therefore, building a medical assistance system for impoverished people plays a crucial role in the harmonious development of China's economy and society. The medical assistance system is an essential component of the medical security system, and its construction occupies an important position in the construction of the medical security system.

5.3.1.1 Collection and Management of Urban and Rural Medical Assistance Funds

Currently, the urban and rural medical assistance funds in China are raised through multiple channels, including fiscal allocations from the government, lottery welfare funds, social donations, and income from fund interest. Improving the health status of the impoverished population is an unshirkable responsibility of the government, and medical assistance for the impoverished requires a certain level of fiscal support from the government. In China, the central government allocates special funds to subsidize urban and rural medical assistance in disadvantaged areas, while local governments, especially provincial governments, effectively adjust the fiscal expenditure structure, increase investment, and further expand the scale of medical assistance funds. As China is still in the primary stage of socialism, with varying levels of economic development across regions, government fiscal allocations for medical assistance are heavily constrained by local economic development levels. In addition to government fiscal allocations, social donations are also an important component of the sources for urban and rural medical assistance funds.

Most of China's medical assistance funds are deposited in special fiscal accounts and managed in dedicated ledgers, ensuring that the funds are used specifically for their intended purposes (in this regard, China still lacks experience in maintaining and increasing the value of these funds through certain financial operations). For instance, establishing foundations to entrust specialized agencies with the operation of both fiscal funds and non-fiscal funds (funds obtained through social donations and other channels). These foundations are responsible for settling medical assistance expenses with medical institutions, strictly enforcing fund usage procedures, and assisting recipients in restoring their health.

To achieve legal and standardized management of medical assistance funds, the following points must be adhered to. First, implement specialized account storage and dedicated management. Civil affairs departments are the main entities responsible for managing medical assistance funds, while financial departments exercise oversight powers over the funds and assume corresponding responsibilities. It is necessary to establish a special fiscal account and implement budget-based management of medical assistance funds. Departments such as civil affairs, finance, and auditing at the county (city, district) level must conduct supervision and inspection of the use of medical assistance funds, promptly correct any issues found, and report them to the local people's government. Second, implement closed-loop operation. Closed-loop operation can be simply summarized as the separation of money and accounts, meaning that those in charge of money do not handle accounts, and those handling accounts do not manage money. Funds should always flow between the government's special fiscal accounts and the bank accounts of medical institutions. Third, the use of funds must be open and transparent. Information such as the collection, management, and use of medical assistance funds, as well as the recipients and the amount of assistance provided, should be regularly disclosed to the public through methods such as public notices. Fourth, continuously improve management efficiency and minimize management costs. All relevant departments involved in the management of medical assistance funds should coordinate with each other to continuously improve fund management efficiency and reduce management costs.

5.3.1.2 Target Recipients of Urban and Rural Medical Assistance

In China, urban and rural medical assistance serves as a supplementary form to the basic medical insurance for urban employees, basic medical insurance for rural and non-working urban residents, and commercial medical insurance. The target recipients of it are low-income groups.

Rural medical assistance is aimed at rural families receiving the "five guarantees," rural poverty-stricken household members, and other eligible rural poor farmers as stipulated by local governments. Urban medical assistance mainly targets those who are not enrolled in the basic medical insurance for urban employees among the recipients of the urban residents' minimum living security allowance, those who have participated in the basic medical insurance for urban employees but still face heavy personal financial burdens, and other specifically impoverished groups. In addition, China has also included members of low-income families with serious or critical illnesses, low-income elderly, severely disabled individuals, and other impoverished individuals who have difficulty paying for medical expenses due to serious or critical illnesses into the scope of urban and rural medical assistance.

Since the establishment of the urban and rural medical assistance system, the scope of recipients has been continuously expanded, including not only traditional disadvantaged groups but also other eligible recipients. The specific criteria for defining the recipients are formulated by local civil affairs departments, jointly with relevant departments such as finance, based on factors such as local economic conditions, the collection of medical assistance funds, the payment ability of impoverished populations, and their basic medical needs. These criteria are then submitted to the people's government of the same level for approval and implementation.

5.3.1.3 Methods and Services for Urban and Rural Medical Assistance

Medical assistance can be provided through various approaches. Different regions have adopted multiple medical assistance methods, taking into account factors such as local economic and social development levels, as well as fiscal revenue status. The primary methods are subsidizing insurance participation and reimbursing medical expenses. Subsidizing insurance participation involves assisting individuals who cannot afford to pay medical insurance premiums by funding part or all of their premiums, enabling them to obtain medical insurance coverage. Reimbursing medical expenses involves providing a certain percentage or amount of subsidy to recipients for their personal out-of-pocket medical expenses that exceed a certain threshold or for special diseases, after deducting the amounts covered by various medical insurance schemes, reimbursable portions from employers, and social assistance.

Currently, urban and rural medical assistance services primarily focus on inpatient assistance, while also taking into account outpatient assistance. Inpatient assistance is mainly used to cover the medical expenses borne by the recipients due to hospitalization for illness. Outpatient assistance is primarily used to cover the medical expenses for common illnesses, chronic diseases, long-term medication maintenance, as well as emergency and first-aid treatment, which are borne by the recipients themselves.

5.3.1.4 Management Departments for Urban and Rural Medical Assistance Work

Medical assistance involves multiple departments, and its management is jointly conducted by civil affairs departments, financial departments, human resources and social security departments, health departments, and other relevant departments.

The urban and rural medical assistance work in China is primarily managed by the civil affairs departments, which have set up specialized agencies from the central to local levels. These agencies are responsible for formulating the medical assistance system, coordinating the relationship between the various departments involved in its implementation, as well as the distribution and utilization of assistance funds. The financial departments are primarily responsible for compiling the annual budget for medical assistance funds, establishing special fiscal accounts for urban and rural medical assistance funds, managing the accounts, conducting accounting, and overseeing the use of funds. The human resources and social security departments are responsible for cooperating in the organization and implementation of medical assistance work, ensuring the integration of medical insurance and medical assistance policies. The health administrative departments are responsible for coordinating and overseeing the provision of medical services to ensure the specific implementation of medical assistance work. Other departments, such as audit departments, as well as organizations such as the Federation of Trade Unions and the Red Cross, also participate in the management of medical assistance work.

5.3.2 *Commercial Medical Insurance*

5.3.2.1 Market Position and Scale

With the further improvement of China's market economy system and the increase in residents' income, the demand for medical and health services among residents has been continuously increasing, and the role of commercial medical insurance in the medical security system has become increasingly significant. The new medical reform explicitly proposes to accelerate the establishment and improvement of a multi-level medical security system with basic medical security as the mainstay, supplemented by various forms of supplementary medical insurance and commercial health insurance, and covering both urban and rural residents. This clarifies the complementary role of commercial medical insurance in the medical security system. In the current commercial medical insurance market, student medical insurance, supplementary medical insurance, and comprehensive insurance that includes medical insurance, accident insurance, property insurance, and life insurance are relatively common. In 2012, the "Guiding Opinions on Carrying Out Critical Illness Insurance for Urban and Rural Residents" further clarified that commercial insurance institutions are supported to undertake critical illness insurance, leveraging market mechanisms to improve the operational efficiency, service level, and quality of critical illness insurance.

5.3.2.2 Market Structure

In China, collective participation in commercial medical insurance by enterprises or collectives is a relatively common form of group insurance. As enterprises provide benefits to their employees, they also enhance their employees' labor productivity. Such commercial medical insurance often serves as a supplement to basic medical insurance. For example, some commercial medical insurance can cover certain medications that are not included in the reimbursement catalog of basic medical insurance, and can also provide nutritional subsidies to insured individuals after illness. Collective participation by students is also common. Students can participate in the basic medical insurance for rural and non-working urban residents that covers hospitalization services, and those who have also participated in commercial medical insurance can obtain better coverage after falling ill. Participants in basic medical insurance can also obtain a higher reimbursement ratio or a wider reimbursement scope by participating in commercial medical insurance. Factors such as age, gender, economic status, education level, and geographical location have a certain influence on the choice of commercial medical insurance. At the same time, age, gender and other factors can also be limiting conditions for the purchase of commercial medical insurance.

In 2015, the "Opinions of the General Office of the State Council on the Full Implementation of Critical Illness Insurance for Urban and Rural Residents" was issued, further clarifying support for commercial insurance institutions to undertake critical illness insurance. The specific measures include the local government's departments of human resources and social security, health and family planning, finance, and insurance supervision jointly formulate basic policies for the financing, payment scope, minimum payment ratio, medical treatment, and settlement management of critical illness insurance, and solicit opinions through appropriate channels. In principle, commercial insurance institutions undertaking critical illness insurance are selected through government bidding. The bidding mainly includes specific payment ratios, profit and loss ratios, and the strengths of the undertaking and management team. Commercial insurance institutions that meet the basic entry conditions set by the insurance regulatory department voluntarily participate in the bidding. After winning the bid, they undertake critical illness insurance by signing insurance contracts, assuming operational risks, and being responsible for their own profits and losses.

5.3.2.3 Market Behavior

China encourages employers and individuals to participate in commercial medical insurance. The premiums of commercial medical insurance are generally calculated based on the positioning of the insurance, the payment capacity of the target population, combined with the operating costs of the insurance institutions. For individual insured persons, they are generally required to provide relevant health information before participating in the insurance to determine the premiums. If the participation is in the form of an enterprise or other groups, the personnel can enjoy group insurance rates.

Since the current market share of commercial medical insurance is relatively low, it is difficult to form negotiating power with medical institutions. Therefore, the coverage of commercial medical insurance is generally focused on reimbursement of medical expenses after treatment and subsidies for days off work such as hospitalization, and commercial medical insurance may have corresponding requirements for the medical institutions available for insured individuals to choose from.

The demand group for commercial medical insurance in China includes residents who already enjoy basic medical insurance. Such insured individuals have a greater demand for special examinations, treatments, and medications outside the scope specified by basic medical insurance. Commercial medical insurance can meet these non-basic medical service needs.

5.3.2.4 Public Policy

In China, commercial medical insurance is regulated by the National Financial Regulatory Administration. The "Measures on Administration of Health Insurance," which was first issued in 2006 and reissued in 2019 after revision, has unified the regulatory standards for the operation of health insurance businesses. To accelerate the development of the health service industry, the State Council has put forward the goal of "enriching commercial health insurance products, significantly increasing the number of insured individuals, significantly increasing the proportion of commercial health insurance expenditures in total health expenditures, and forming a relatively complete health insurance mechanism," laying a policy foundation for the development of commercial medical insurance. In addition, some regions have explored the operation of basic medical insurance models by commercial medical insurance institutions, which may provide more development opportunities for commercial medical insurance in the future.

5.3.3 Supplementary Medical Insurance

5.3.3.1 Overview of the Development of Supplementary Medical Insurance

China's supplementary medical insurance emerged along with the reform of the medical system. In 1993, the "Decision of the Central Committee of the Communist Party of China on Several Issues Concerning the Establishment of the Socialist Market Economic System" clearly stated that "a multi-level social security system should be established." In 1994, the "Pilot Opinions on the Reform of the Medical System for Employees" stipulated that employee medical mutual assistance funds and commercial medical insurance should be developed as a supplement to social medical insurance to meet medical needs beyond the basic medical security stipulated by the state, but the principle of individual voluntary participation and independent choice should be adhered to.

Under the guidance of the national macro policy, various regions have actively explored different forms of supplementary medical insurance. Many regions and cities have actively prepared and formulated various forms of supplementary medical insurance while establishing the basic medical insurance system for urban employees, and have formulated relevant policies and specific implementation measures.

5.3.3.2 Commercial Operation of Supplementary Medical Insurance

Currently, the management of supplementary medical insurance in China mainly falls into two categories: bundled operation and commercial operation. Bundled operation refers to the government's social security agencies operating supplementary medical insurance in the same way as basic medical insurance. Its characteristics include management difficulties, operational challenges, and heavy fiscal and corporate burdens. Commercial operation involves social security agencies utilizing commercial insurance institutions to manage and operate supplementary medical insurance. This approach can alleviate fiscal pressure, save human resources, optimize the allocation of medical resources, strengthen the management of medical institutions, and ultimately promote the standardization and scientization of basic medical insurance management. Supplementary medical insurance has received widespread attention. In China, commercial medical insurance is often operated as supplementary medical insurance, so the commercial operation of supplementary medical insurance will become an important aspect of improving the medical security system.

1. Development Potential for the Commercial Operation of Supplementary Medical Insurance

The unique advantages of commercial insurance institutions can increase their potential to occupy the medical insurance market. If they possess advanced management methods and flexible business strategies, they can also accept specific project management delegations from social security agencies and other supplementary medical insurance institutions. Overall, medical insurance demand in China has been growing rapidly in recent years. Due to the dual functions of commercial medical insurance as a health care and investment tool, individual commercial medical insurance products offered by various medical insurance institutions have been continuously increasing.

2. Issues to Consider in the Process of Commercial Operation of Supplementary Medical Insurance

First, it is important to reasonably define the nature of supplementary medical insurance. The government should only address basic medical issues, leaving the remaining medical issues to be resolved by the market. Additionally, the enthusiasm of medical insurance institutions should be fully mobilized.

Second, social security agencies and medical insurance institutions should strengthen the regulation of the behavior of both the supply and demand sides in medical services. It is necessary to establish a competition system among hospitals to improve the efficiency of medical services. At the same time, measures such as information management and irregular spot checks should be taken to prevent the waste of medical resources or collusion between doctors and patients for fraud.

Third, it is necessary to continuously strengthen the development of supplementary medical insurance products to meet the diverse needs of different levels of supplementary medical insurance.

Fourth, it is important to improve the professional level of institutions that offer supplementary medical insurance.

Chapter 6
China's Drug Supply Guarantee System

Drugs play an irreplaceable role in disease prevention and treatment, rehabilitation, health care, disaster relief, and epidemic prevention for the public. Their significance in economic development and national security has become increasingly prominent. As a special commodity, drugs face great challenges in research and development innovation, require strong professional technical expertise in production and use, can trigger adverse reactions even under normal use, and pose significant risks to patient health and social stability when of low quality or misused. The drug supply guarantee system stands alongside the public health service system, medical service system, and medical security system as one of the four beams of China's basic medical and health system. Moreover, the guarantee of drug supply is also one of the key tasks in the construction of Healthy China.

6.1 China's Drug Supply Guarantee Organization System

China's drug supply guarantee organization system can be divided into the following components: drug administrative supervision and management organization system, drug technical supervision and management organization system, pharmaceutical education, research organizations, and associations system, drug production and distribution organization system, and pharmaceutical organization system in medical institutions.

Z. Feng et al. (eds.), *China's Health System*, Introduction to China's S&T Innovation,
https://doi.org/10.1007/978-981-95-1205-8_6

6.1.1 The Drug Administrative Supervision and Management Organization System

China's drug supervision and management institutions are divided into four levels, namely, the National Medical Products Administration (NMPA), the medical products administrations at provincial (autonomous region, municipality directly under the central government) level, the market supervision and management institutions at municipal (prefecture, league) level, and the market supervision and management institutions at county (district) level. The basic framework is illustrated in Fig. 6.1.

6.1.1.1 The NMPA

The NMPA is a national agency under the supervision of the State Administration for Market Regulation. It holds vice-ministerial status and is primarily responsible for the safety supervision and management, standardization management, registration management, quality management, supervision inspections, and post-market risk management of drugs, medical devices, and cosmetics.

6.1.1.2 Provincial and Lower-Level Drug Supervision and Management Institutions

The provincial-level medical products administration in China functions as a working body under the provincial people's government and is responsible for statutory drug supervision and management within its jurisdiction. Its functional offices typically include Comprehensive Affairs, Planning and Finance Affairs Office, Policies and Regulations Office, Administrative Approval Office, Drug Registration Management Office, Drug Production Supervision and Management Office, Drug Circulation Supervision and Management Office, Medical Device Supervision and Management Office, and Cosmetics Supervision and Management Office. Drug supervision and management institutions below the provincial level are managed in a hierarchical manner by local governments, with their operations guided and supervised by higher-level authorities.

6.1.1.3 Other Institutions Related to Drug Supervision and Management

1. Market Supervision and Management Institutions

The market supervision and management institutions are responsible for registering and issuing business licenses to relevant market entities, investigating and

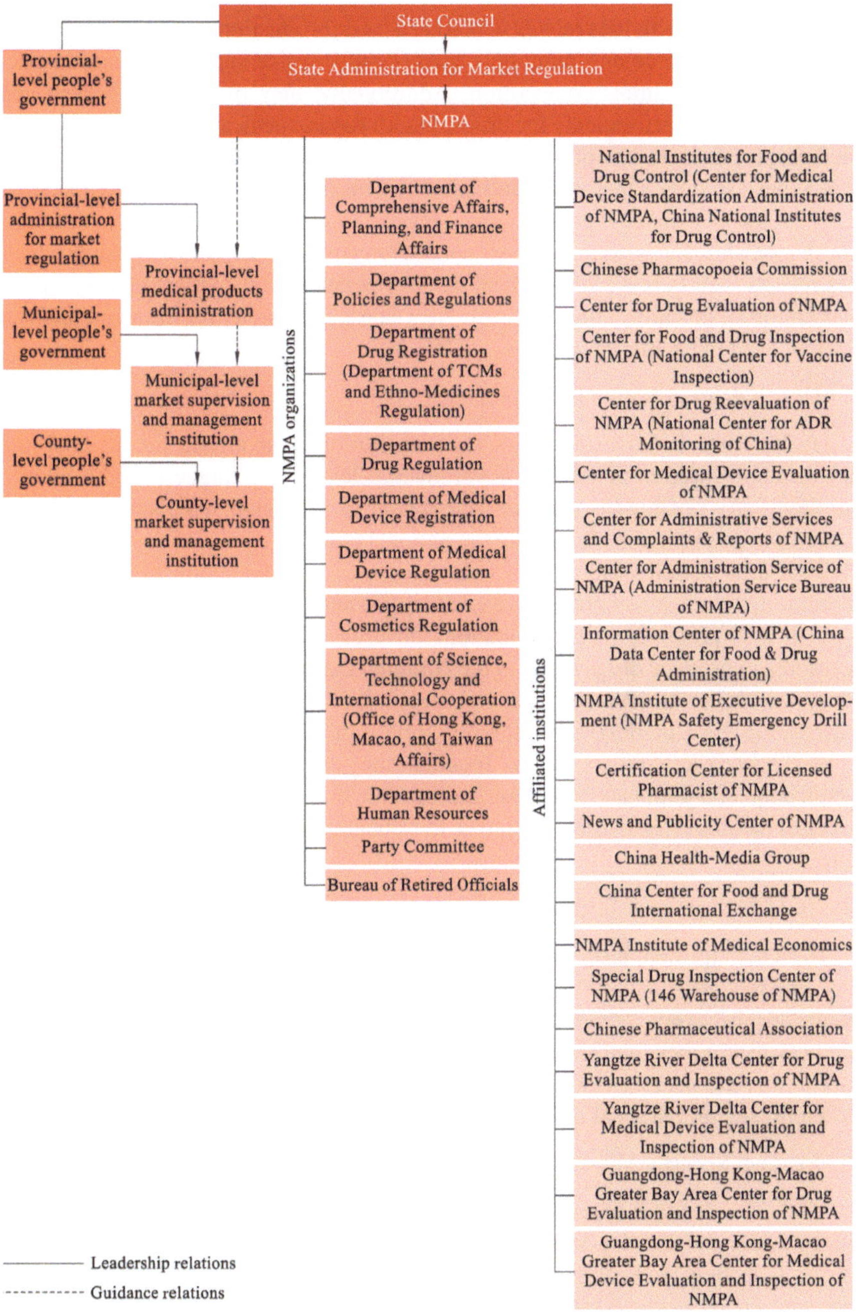

Fig. 6.1 The basic framework of China's drug supervision and management institutions

penalizing illegal activities related to market access, production, operation, and transactions. They enforce anti-monopoly laws, conduct price supervision and inspection, and address unfair competition. Additionally, they oversee the review and monitoring of advertisements for drugs, health foods, medical devices, and special medical purpose formula foods. The market supervision and management institutions also supervise drug supervision and management institutions at the corresponding level. At the city and county levels, market supervision and management institutions are responsible for issuing permits, conducting inspections, and imposing penalties related to drug retail and medical device operation, and conducting inspections and imposing penalties related to cosmetics sales, and quality for drug and medical devices used in healthcare settings.

2. Health Administrative Institutions

Health administrative institutions are institutions responsible for medical and health administration at various governmental levels. The highest health administration body in China is the National Health Commission. The National Health Commission is tasked with refining the national essential medicine system, drafting national drug policies and the essential medicines list, and conducting drug usage monitoring, clinical comprehensive evaluations, and early warnings for drug shortages. It also proposes recommendations on drug pricing policies and supportive measures to produce drugs listed in the National Essential Medicine List. In collaboration with the NMPA, the National Health Commission convenes the Chinese Pharmacopoeia Commission to compile, revise, and translate the *Pharmacopoeia of the People's Republic of China*. Together, they establish mechanisms for mutual notification and joint handling of serious adverse drug reactions and medical device events, ensuring a coordinated response to critical issues affecting public health and safety.

3. TCM Management Institutions

TCM management institutions are responsible for drafting strategies, plans, policies, and relevant standards for the development of TCM and ethnic medicine. They guide the discovery, organization, summarization, and enhancement of theories, medical techniques, and drugs of ethnic medicine. These institutions also organize comprehensive surveys of medicinal resources, and promote their protection, development, and rational utilization.

4. Medical Security Management Institutions

Medical security management institutions are responsible for drafting policies, plans, and standards for medical insurance, maternity insurance, medical assistance, and other medical security systems, and implementing them. They supervise the related medical security funds, improve medical expense settlement platforms, and organize the formulation and adjustment of prices and fee standards for drugs and medical services. These institutions also develop procurement policies for drugs and medical consumables and supervise their implementation, and oversee the service behaviors of medical institutions and medical expenses covered by medical insurance.

In addition, various departments in China such as the macroeconomic regulation and development department, the human resources and social security department, the industry and information technology management department, the Office of the Central Cyberspace Affairs Commission, the commerce management department, customs, as well as the public security department, undertake specific responsibilities within their respective scopes for drug supervision and management.

6.1.2 Drug Technical Supervision and Management Organization System

Drug supervision and management is highly technical, and technical support is necessary during the implementation of administrative supervision and management. Drug technical supervision and management institutions are integral to drug supervision and management, providing technical support and guarantees for administrative supervision. China's drug technical supervision and management institutions include drug testing institutions and other technical institutions directly under the NMPA.

6.1.2.1 Drug Testing Institutions

Drug testing institutions are statutory professional inspection institutions responsible for national drug quality supervision and inspection. They represent the state in supervising and inspecting drugs, and their results have legal effect. In China, drug testing institutions are divided into four levels: the National Institutes for Food and Drug Control, drug testing institutions at provincial (autonomous region, municipality directly under the central government), municipal (prefecture, league), and county levels.

According to the "Reply of the State Commission Office for Public Sector Reform on the Organization and Staffing of Institutions Directly Under the National Medical Products Administration," the National Institutes for Food and Drug Control is a public welfare institution of Category II under the NMPA, and it is the statutory institution and highest technical arbitration institution for national drug and biological product quality testing. The main responsibilities of the National Institutes for Food and Drug Control include testing and inspection of food, drugs, medical devices, cosmetics, and related drug excipients, packaging materials, and containers, conducting experimental research on the causes of serious adverse reactions and events of related products, organizing the planning, research, preparation, calibration, distribution, and management of national standard substances, conducting the verification of bacterial strains and cell lines for production, undertaking the collection, identification, preservation, distribution, and management of medical standard strains and cell lines, and so on.

6.1.2.2 Other Technical Institutions Directly Under the NMPA

1. Chinese Pharmacopoeia Commission

The Chinese Pharmacopoeia Commission is the earliest established standardization institution in China. It is responsible for organizing the compilation of the *Pharmacopoeia of the People's Republic of China* and formulating and revising national drug standards. The Chinese Pharmacopoeia Commission is the statutory professional management institution for national drug standards. The permanent office of the Chinese Pharmacopoeia Commission operates under the responsibility of the secretary general and includes the following departments: Business Management Department (Quality Management Department), Information Management Department (Editorial Office), TCM Department, Chemical Medicine Department, Biological Products Department, Office, Personnel and Party Affairs Department (Discipline Inspection Office), Finance Department, and General Provisions, Excipients, and Packaging Materials Department. It also has branches such as the "Drug Standards of China" magazine agency.

2. Center for Drug Evaluation of NMPA

The Center for Drug Evaluation of NMPA is the technical review institution for drug registration, providing technical support for drug registration. It includes the following departments: Business Management Department, Personnel Department (Services and Management Department for Retired Cadres), Quality Management Department, Compliance Department, Clinical Trial Management Department, Data Management Department, Office, Finance Department, Party Committee Office, Discipline Inspection Office, TCM and Ethnic Medicine Pharmacy Department, TCM and Ethnic Medicine Clinical Department, Chemical Medicine Pharmacy Department I, Chemical Medicine Pharmacy Department II, Pharmacology and Toxicology Department, Chemical Medicine Clinical Department I, Chemical Medicine Clinical Department II, Statistics and Clinical Pharmacology Department, Biological Products Pharmacy Department, and Biological Products Clinical Department.

3. Center for Drug Reevaluation of NMPA

The Center for Drug Reevaluation of NMPA includes the following departments: Office, Comprehensive Business Department, Chemical Medicine Monitoring and Evaluation Department, Biological Products Monitoring and Evaluation Department, TCM Monitoring and Evaluation Department, Medical Devices Monitoring and Evaluation Department, Cosmetics Monitoring and Evaluation Department, Scientific Research and Information Management Department, and Party Discipline Office (Personnel Department).

4. Center for Food and Drug Inspection of NMPA

The Center for Food and Drug Inspection of NMPA is a Category II public welfare institution directly under the NMPA (retaining bureau-level status). It includes the following departments: Office, Comprehensive Business Department (Quality Management Department), Information Management Department, Inspection Department I, Inspection Department II, Inspection Department III, Inspection Department IV, Inspection Department V, Inspection Department VI, Personnel Department (Party Committee Office), and Finance Department.

5. Certification Center for Licensed Pharmacist of NMPA

The Certification Center for Licensed Pharmacist of NMPA operates under the supervision and guidance of the Personnel Department of NMPA. It includes the following departments: Office (Personnel and Party Affairs Department), Examination Department, Registration Management Department, and Information Department.

6.1.3 Pharmaceutical Education, Research Organizations, and Associations System

Pharmaceutical education, research organizations, and associations are important components of China's pharmaceutical affairs organizations. Pharmaceutical associations include the Chinese Pharmaceutical Association and various pharmaceutical societies approved by Chinese government. Since the government institution reform, the industry management functions of pharmaceutical associations have been strengthened.

6.1.3.1 Pharmaceutical Education Organizations

Pharmaceutical education in China has developed over more than a century and consists mainly of higher pharmaceutical education, secondary pharmaceutical education, and continuing pharmaceutical education. This has resulted in a multi-type, multi-level, and multi-form educational system.

As of the end of 2016, China had 458 regular higher education institutions offering undergraduate programs related to pharmaceuticals, with 35 under the supervision of the Ministry of Education and 407 under the supervision of provincial, autonomous region, and municipal authorities. By 2021, China had 143 institutions authorized to award academic degrees in pharmacy, 46 institutions enrolling master's degree students in professional pharmacy programs, and a total of 498 higher education institutions offering pharmacy-related programs nationwide.

Continuing pharmaceutical education is primarily provided by higher education institutions and secondary schools with pharmacy programs, as well as pharmaceutical societies.

6.1.3.2 Pharmaceutical Research Organizations

Pharmaceutical research organizations in China mainly include independent drug research institutes and those attached to higher pharmaceutical education institutions, large pharmaceutical enterprises, and major hospitals. Independent drug research institutes are affiliated with national and local academy systems such as the Chinese Academy of Sciences, the Chinese Academy of Medical Sciences, the Academy of Military Medical Sciences, as well as relevant departments of central and local governments.

6.1.3.3 Pharmaceutical Associations

Pharmaceutical associations serve as a link between pharmaceutical affairs organizations, pharmacy personnel, and government institutions, assisting the government in management functions. Their roles include industry or professional social management, with tasks such as academic research and technical management of the industry and profession. Examples of these associations include the Chinese Pharmaceutical Association, the Chinese Pharmacists Association, and the China Pharmaceutical Enterprises Association.

6.1.4 Drug Production and Distribution Organization System

Drug production and distribution organizations are economic entities, mainly including drug production enterprises, drug wholesale enterprises, and drug retail enterprises. Drug production enterprises, commonly known as drug factories, are specialized or general enterprises legally established to engage in drug production activities and provide drugs to society, possessing corporate status. Drug distribution enterprises are also specialized or general enterprises that can be divided into drug wholesale enterprises and drug retail enterprises. Drug wholesale enterprises are typically referred to as drug companies or TCM companies, while drug retail enterprises are commonly known as retail pharmacies (drugstores).

6.1.5 Pharmaceutical Organization System in Medical Institutions

Pharmaceutical organizations in medical institutions are composed of departments that provide qualified drugs and engage in patient-centered, clinical pharmacy-based pharmaceutical technical services aimed at promoting the rational use of drugs and related drug management tasks. To achieve the transformation of pharmaceutical work functions under medical and health system reform, the "Regulations on Pharmaceutical Affairs Management in Medical Institutions" in China requires that medical institutions set up corresponding departments of pharmacy based on their functions, tasks, and scale and equip these departments with professional technical personnel, equipment, and facilities suitable for their tasks. The various departments within the departments of pharmacy are generally divided by function. Basic functional departments are those directly involved in drug supply and pharmaceutical services, such as outpatient and emergency pharmacies, inpatient pharmacies, TCM pharmacies, intravenous medication preparation center, and clinical pharmacy offices. Derivative functional departments are those that guarantee drug supply and support pharmaceutical services, such as drug logistics centers, formulation rooms, drug testing rooms, and pharmaceutical research offices.

The "Regulations on Pharmaceutical Affairs Management in Medical Institutions" in China clearly stipulates that second-level or above hospitals must establish a pharmaceutical affairs management and pharmacotherapeutics committee, while other medical institutions should form a pharmaceutical affairs management and pharmacotherapeutics group. These organizations are supervisory bodies for drug management in medical institutions and professional technical organizations that make specialized decisions on important pharmaceutical affairs. They develop policies for drug use in medical institutions based on national laws and policies, unify understanding, and collaboratively solve various drug-related issues. By supervising and guiding their affiliated medical institutions in scientific drug management and rational drug use, these organizations enhance drug management and improve medication practices in medical institutions.

Pharmaceutical organizations in medical institutions hold a significant position and proportion in pharmaceutical affairs organizations, and in China, they comprise the largest number of pharmacists. Fig. 6.2 depicts the possible organizational chart of the department of pharmacy in a third-level general hospital in China. Hospitals can refer to this and set up the necessary departments according to their specific circumstances.

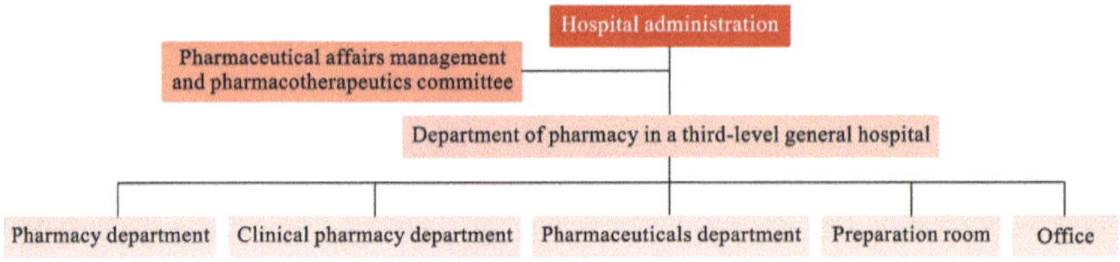

Fig. 6.2 The possible organizational chart of the department of pharmacy in a third-level general hospital in China

6.2 China's Drug Supply Guarantee Management System

The Drug Administration Law of the People's Republic of China clearly states that the purpose of this law is to "strengthen drug administration, ensure drug quality, protect drug safety and legitimate rights and interests of the public, and protect and promote public health." To achieve these objectives, China's drug supply guarantee management system focuses on several core areas.

6.2.1 Quality Management of New Drug Research and Drug Registration Management

From the perspective of drug registration management, new drugs refer to drugs that have not been marketed in China or abroad, categorized into innovative drugs and modified new drugs. New drug development research must verify the safety, efficacy, and quality stability of candidate drugs, involving a complex system engineering requiring multi-disciplinary and multi-departmental collaboration. The research process of new drugs mainly includes preclinical research, clinical research, and post-marketing surveillance, as shown in Fig. 6.3.

The safety evaluation of drug preclinical research must comply with the "Good Laboratory Practice for Non-Clinical Laboratory Studies." It is the guideline for conducting drug efficacy and toxicity animal studies, applicable to non-clinical studies conducted for drug registration applications. It is also a directive document guiding scientific research institutions to develop safe and effective drugs,

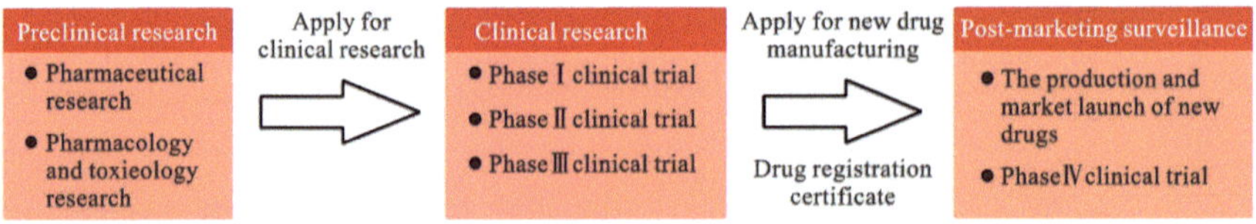

Fig. 6.3 The research process of new drugs. *Source* Drug Management (2nd Ed.) by Zhang and Liu, 2023

aiming to ensure the safety of preclinical researches and the reliability of data. The current "Good Laboratory Practice for Non-Clinical Laboratory Studies" in China was reviewed and approved by the State Food and Drug Administration on June 20, 2017, and has been in effect since September 1, 2017.

The "Good Clinical Practice" is the quality standard that regulates the entire process of drug clinical trials, including protocol design, implementation, monitoring, auditing, recording, analysis, summary, and reporting. Its purpose is to ensure the standardization of the clinical trial process and the scientific, true, and reliable nature of the data and results, as well as protect the rights, interests and safety of subjects and other parties involved in the research. With the rapid development of China's drug research and development and the deepening reform of the drug evaluation and approval system, the NMPA, together with the National Health Commission, issued the newly revised "Good Clinical Practice" on April 23, 2020, which took effect on July 1, 2020, to meet the needs of drug regulation.

Drug registration refers to the process where drug registration applicants submit applications for clinical trials, marketing authorization, and re-registration, as well as supplementary applications according to legal procedures and related requirements. The drug regulatory department reviews the safety, efficacy, and quality controllability based on laws, regulations, and current scientific knowledge, and decides whether to approve the application. The "Provisions for Drug Registration" in China classifies drug registration management into categories such as TCM, chemical drugs, and biological products, based on the nature of the drugs and the actual clinical use in China. Each major category is further subdivided based on the level of maturity of drug research and development, that is, people's understanding of the pharmaceutical properties, pharmacological and toxicological characteristics, and clinical characteristics of the drug developed, whether this type of drugs has already been marketed domestically or abroad, as well as whether there is an existing national drug standard.

6.2.2 Supervision and Management of Drug Production Quality

"Good Manufacturing Practice" (GMP) is a universally adopted statutory technical specification for supervising and managing the entire drug production process. In China, GMP is the fundamental guideline for drug production enterprises to manage production and quality. It applies to the entire process of drug formulation production and the critical processes in active pharmaceutical ingredient (API) production that affect the quality of the final product. The current GMP in China has been in effect since March 1, 2011. It has played a positive role in promoting the concentration of pharmaceutical industry resources in advantageous enterprises, eliminating outdated production capacity, adjusting the pharmaceutical economic structure, promoting industrial upgrading, fostering internationally competitive enterprises, and accelerating the entry of pharmaceutical products into the international market. Although the newly revised Drug Administration Law of the People's Republic of China in 2019 abolished the certification of the GMP, this does not mean the elimination of the GMP system. Instead, it is replaced by GMP compliance inspections conducted by provincial drug supervision and management institutions, changing the five-year certification inspection to random GMP compliance inspections, thereby imposing higher requirements on enterprises to continuously meet GMP standards.

6.2.3 *Supervision and Management of Drug Distribution Quality*

The newly revised Drug Administration Law of the People's Republic of China in 2019 stipulates that drug distribution enterprises must comply with the "Good Supply Practice" (GSP) for conducting drug distribution activities. The fundamental purpose of this regulation is to ensure that drug distribution enterprises focus on quality in all their operations, guaranteeing the quality of drugs.

In 2000, the China's NMPA revised the GSP based on the "Quality Management Standards for Pharmaceutical Commodities (Trial)." In the same year, the "Implementation Rules for Good Supply Practice" and the "Trial Measures for the Certification of Good Supply Practice (GSP)" were issued. This year marked a milestone for the implementation of drug distribution quality management in China. Subsequently, due to reforms in the governance mechanisms of China's pharmaceutical industry and changes in supporting laws and regulations, the GSP underwent two revisions and one amendment in 2012, 2015, and 2016, respectively. The GSP, along with its supporting documents such as the "Implementation Rules for Good Supply Practice" and the "Guiding Principles for On-Site Inspection of Good Supply Practice," collectively forms the normative system for drug distribution quality management in China.

6.2.4 *Pharmaceutical Affairs Management in Medical Institutions*

Pharmaceutical affairs management in medical institutions refers to the effective organization and management of the entire clinical medication process in medical institutions, with patients as the center and clinical pharmacy as the basis. It aims to facilitate pharmaceutical technical services supporting clinical scientific and rational use of drug, as well as related drug management. Specific responsibilities include drug supply management, management of institution-prepared medications, compounding and prescription management, clinical application management of medications, clinical pharmacy services, and pharmaceutical care, etc. This section primarily discusses management aspects such as drug procurement, prescription evaluation, and rational use of drug.

Drug procurement is a critical task to ensure the supply of drugs in medical institutions, essential for meeting medical service needs. The quality of drug procurement directly impacts the quality of medical services and economic efficiency of medical institutions. The main goals of drug procurement management include lawful and timely acquisition of high-quality drugs at appropriate prices. Methods for drug procurement include centralized bidding, invitation bidding, and inquiry-based procurement. China's implementation of centralized drug procurement involves specifying quantities during centralized drug procurement bids or negotiations, where companies bid and negotiate prices based on these specified quantities, with the lowest bid winning the contract. The core concept involves "quantity in exchange for price," akin to large-scale group purchasing or bulk buying. The "Opinions of the General Office of the State Council on Promoting the Normalization and Institutionalization of the Centralized Drug Procurement" issued in January 2021 marked the normalization, institutionalization and standardization of China's centralized drug procurement efforts, serving as a guideline for these activities.

Prescription evaluation involves assessing the compliance of prescriptions as well as the appropriateness of clinical drug use (including indications, drug selection, administration routes, dosage, drug interactions, and compatibility contraindications), identifying existing or potential issues, formulating and implementing interventions and improvement measures, and promoting rational clinical drug use according to relevant regulations and technical specifications. Prescription evaluation within hospitals is conducted under the leadership of the pharmaceutical affairs management and pharmacotherapeutics committee (group) and the medical quality management committee, organized jointly by the hospital's medical management and department of pharmacy.

Rational use of drug refers to the appropriate use of drugs in terms of their proper selection, dosage, timing, route of administration, and duration for the right patients to achieve appropriate treatment outcomes. Clinical rational drug use management involves overseeing the entire process of drug use in clinical diagnosis, prevention, and treatment within medical institutions. Medical institutions are required to formulate basic drug clinical application management methods in accordance with national macro-management regulations, establish and implement a graded management system for antibiotic clinical use, and establish systems for monitoring, evaluating, and early warning of clinical drug use safety, effectiveness, and economy, conducting reviews and interventions for prescriptions and medication orders, as well as monitoring and reporting adverse drug reactions, medication errors, and drug-related incidents. Upon discovery of such incidents, clinical departments must promptly treat patients, report to the department of pharmacy, and maintain observation and records. According to relevant national regulations, medical institutions are also mandated to report adverse drug reactions to relevant departments. And medication errors and drug-related incidents should be promptly reported to county-level health administrative departments.

6.3 China's National Essential Medicine System

The concept of essential medicines (EM) was introduced by the World Health Organization in 1977. In 2019, the Law of the People's Republic of China on Basic Medical and Health Care and the Promotion of Health defined essential medicines as those that satisfy basic medical needs of disease prevention and treatment, are adapted to the current basic national conditions and security capacities, and intended to be equitably available in appropriate dosage forms, at an appropriate price, and in adequate supply.

6.3.1 Objectives and Significance of China's National Essential Medicine System Construction

As a core policy in deepening reform of the medical and health system, China's national essential medicine system aims to ensure the accessibility, affordability, high quality, and rational use of essential medicines. This system encompasses the selection, production, distribution, use, pricing, reimbursement, monitoring, and evaluation of essential medicines, integrated with public health, medical service, and medical security systems. Since the new medical reform, the establishment and implementation of China's national essential medicine system have played a crucial role in improving the drug supply guarantee system, meeting basic medical and health needs, ensuring access to essential medicines for the population, and reducing the financial burden on patients.

6.3.2 Overview of China's National Essential Medicine System Construction

In April 1979, China actively responded to and participated in the World Health Organization's Essential Medicines Programme. Under the organization of the Ministry of Health and the State Administration of Medicine, the "National Essential Medicine Selection Group" was established to initiate the formulation of the national essential medicine list. In 1982, China officially issued the first edition of the "National Essential Medicine List," comprising 278 drugs, and the number of drugs in the list increased to 307 by 2009, covering major global diseases such as malaria, AIDS, tuberculosis, reproductive health diseases, as well as chronic diseases like cancer and diabetes.

The implementation of the new medical reform in 2009 marked a new phase for China's national essential medicine system. Policy documents such as the "Implementation Opinions on Establishing the National Essential Medicine System," "Management Measures for the National Essential Medicine List (Trial)," "National Essential Medicine List (Part of Primary Care)"(2009 Edition), "National Guidelines for Clinical Application of Essential Medicines (Part of Primary Care)," "National Formulary for Essential Medicines (Part of Primary Care)," and "Guidelines on Establishing and Standardizing a Mechanism for Purchasing Essential Medicines in Government-Run Primary Medical and Health Institutions" established an implementation system led by the government, supported by the market, and grounded in legal frameworks for the production, distribution, supply, use, and regulation of essential medicines.

From 2014 onwards, efforts have focused on consolidating and improving the national essential medicine system, addressing issues such as system coherence, shortages of some medicines, inadequate service capacity, ensuring supply of essential medicines, consistency in quality assessment, and promoting rational clinical use. On October 25, 2018, the "2018 National Essential Medicine List" was formally released by the National Health Commission, expanding the variety of drugs, optimizing the structure of the list, standardizing formulations and specifications, while maintaining the principle of emphasizing both TCM and Western medicine.

6.3.3 Overall Requirements of China's National Essential Medicine System

The fundamental goal of China's national essential medicine system is centered around promoting people's health, reinforcing the functional positioning of essential medicines to emphasize their basic nature, necessity for prevention and treatment, supply assurance, priority usage, quality assurance, and financial burden reduction. This comprehensive approach spans policies from the selection, production, distribution, use, payment, and monitoring of essential medicines, aiming to enhance the drug supply guarantee system, ensure that drugs are safe and effective, reasonably priced, and adequately supplied, alleviate the issue of high medical costs, facilitate the coordination of drug use between different levels of medical institutions, and support the development of a tiered diagnosis and treatment system. It also contributes to the transformation and upgrading of the pharmaceutical industry and supply-side structural reform.

6.3.4 Main Content of China's National Essential Medicine System

China's national essential medicine system effectively manages various aspects of essential medicines, including selection, production, distribution, use, payment, and monitoring.

6.3.4.1 Selection of Essential Medicines

The principles for selecting essential medicines include necessity for prevention and treatment, safety, effectiveness, reasonably pricing, ease of use, emphasizing both TCM and Western medicine, basic guarantee, clinical preference, and suitability for primary healthcare facilities. The selection and adjustment of the National Essential Medicine List should adhere to scientific, fair, transparent, and open principles, establishing evidence-based medicine and pharmacoeconomic evaluation standards and mechanisms. Scientific and reasonable formulation of the list should involve extensive consultation with all sectors of society and accept social supervision.

6.3.4.2 Production and Supply of Essential Medicines

The system emphasizes centralized procurement and implements categorized purchasing of medicines. Efforts are made to align drug use between different levels of medical institutions, promote centralized drug procurement for public medical institutions in cities and counties to lower drug prices, and ensure supply through measures such as market-based price determination, designated production, unified distribution, or inclusion in reserves for shortage-prone essential medicines.

6.3.4.3 Procurement Management of Essential Medicines

In 2019, the General Office of the State Council issued the "Pilot Plan for National Centralized Drug Procurement and Use," outlining strategies such as national organization, alliance procurement, and platform operations, principles including volume-based procurement, price based on quantity, linking quantity and price, unified bidding and procurement, quality assurance, and payment guarantee, and organizational forms like the Pilot Office and the Joint Procurement Office. The Joint Procurement Office conducts centralized procurement on behalf of the alliance regions and is supported by a supervision group, an expert group, and a centralized procurement team.

6.3.4.4 Management of the Use of Essential Medicines

Maintaining the leading role of essential medicines, the system specifies the proportion of essential medicines used in public medical institutions. It implements clinical usage monitoring and comprehensive evaluation of drug clinical efficacy. Reforms in medical insurance payment methods are deepened, with standards set for drug insurance payments, guiding medical institutions and personnel towards rational diagnosis, treatment, and drug use.

6.3.4.5 Quality Supervision of Essential Medicines

Comprehensive random checks are conducted on all types of essential medicines, strengthening supervision over their production processes to ensure quality and safety. Consistency evaluations of the quality and efficacy of generic drugs are promoted, and those passing such evaluations are prioritized for inclusion in the essential medicine list. Gradually, the essential medicine varieties that have not passed the consistency evaluation will be transferred out of the essential medicine list.

6.3.4.6 Performance Evaluation of the National Essential Medicine System

The implementation of the national essential medicine system is integrated into the performance evaluation systems at all levels of government to enhance supervision and assessment. A robust system for supervisory evaluation of the implementation of the essential medicine system is established to leverage third-party assessments and effectively utilize evaluation results.

6.3.5 Adjustment and Optimization of China's National Essential Medicine System

The "Outline of the Healthy China 2030 Plan" explicitly calls for the consolidation and improvement of the national essential medicine system. In September 2018, the General Office of the State Council issued the "Opinions of the General Office of the State Council on Improving the National Essential Medicine System" (hereinafter referred to as the "Opinions"). The "Opinions" reinforces the functional positioning of essential medicines to emphasize their basic nature, necessity for prevention and treatment, supply assurance, priority usage, quality assurance, and financial burden reduction. The "Opinions" focuses on improving the policy from the selection, production, distribution, use, payment, and monitoring of essential medicines.

First, in terms of the selection of essential medicines, there is a stronger emphasis on highlighting the clinical value of medicines, maintaining dynamic adjustments, and balancing additions and removals. Newly approved medicines with definite efficacy, reasonable pricing, and better suitability for disease prevention and treatment may also be considered for inclusion. At the same time, considering that the national essential medicine system has achieved full coverage in government-run primary medical and health institutions, allowing local supplements to the list is a transitional measure in the early stages of the system construction. The "Opinions" stipulates that, in principle, local supplements should not be allowed. This will facilitate comparative analysis of the use of essential medicines across different medical institutions.

Second, in terms of supply assurance, there is an increased focus on optimizing the roles of both government and market forces. Drawing from effective practices in recent years such as centralized procurement and addressing drug shortages, systematic arrangements are made to encourage technological upgrades in enterprises, improve procurement and distribution mechanisms, and strengthen early warning and response to shortages. Special emphasis is placed on preemptively preventing drug shortages through monitoring, early warnings, and timely responses, ensuring continuous availability and supply stability of essential medicines through multiple channels and methods.

Third, in terms of distribution and usage, there is a heightened focus on aligning drug use between grassroots and second-level medical institutions and above to support the development of tiered diagnosis and treatment system. Emphasis is placed on comprehensive provision and prioritized usage of essential medicines at all levels of medical institutions, standardizing the variety, dosage forms, and specifications of drugs used between different levels of medical institutions to ensure seamless coordination. This provides medication assurance for primary care first diagnosis, two-way referrals, managing minor ailments at the grassroots level, and facilitating recovery back to communities. Additionally, incentives and constraints for rational diagnosis, treatment, and medication are established for medical institutions and personnel through reforms in medical insurance payment methods and fiscal subsidies.

Fourth, in terms of quality assurance, there is an increased emphasis on linkage with consistency evaluations of generic drug quality and efficacy. It is stressed that medicines passing consistency evaluations should be prioritized for inclusion in the essential medicine list according to procedures, gradually phasing out generic versions of essential medicines that fail these evaluations. This further reinforces the concept that essential medicines are safe and reliable.

Fifth, in terms of financial burden reduction, there is an increased focus on aligning with medical insurance reimbursement policies, considering needs in public health and disease prevention and treatment. The treatment medicines within the essential medicine list are clearly defined. When adjusting the medical insurance catalog, medicines meeting criteria are prioritized for inclusion or reclassification as Class A or B, gradually improving the level of actual protection and maximizing reductions in patient medication expenses to enhance public satisfaction.

Chapter 7
TCM Services and Management

TCM is a gem of Chinese civilization, with its philosophy of "preventative treatment of disease" being integrated into the Healthy China Initiative. Currently, a preliminary TCM service system that encompasses both urban and rural areas, combining preventive care, disease treatment, and rehabilitation, has been established in China. The level and efficiency of TCM services are continually enhancing. Since the twenty-first century, China has undergone two large-scale public health campaigns against epidemics, creating a miracle in human history as a populous nation successfully emerging from major disease outbreaks. The combination of TCM and Western medicine, as well as the use of both TCM and Western medicine, has played a pivotal role in these campaigns, becoming distinctive features and highlights of China's epidemic control and prevention efforts. TCM, with its millennia-old heritage, has withstood numerous practical tests, safeguarding the health of the Chinese people, demonstrating the contemporary value of the Chinese treasure, and offering solutions to the world in combating infectious diseases and ensuring the health of all peoples.

7.1 TCM Services

7.1.1 TCM Service System

7.1.1.1 TCM Preventive Health Care Service System

The TCM preventive health care service system, primarily focusing on delivering TCM services, embodies the TCM principle of "preventative treatment of disease." Reinforcing the development of this system is a pivotal strategy in propelling medical reforms and advancing the growth of TCM undertakings in China. Presently, China has established a preliminary regional network for TCM preventive health care services, alongside a systematic and comprehensive content framework for such

Z. Feng et al. (eds.), *China's Health System*, Introduction to China's S&T Innovation,
https://doi.org/10.1007/978-981-95-1205-8_7

services that connects the entire care continuum. Distinct platforms showcasing TCM characteristics and capable of autonomously conducting preventive health care work have also been assembled. This system in China encompasses three integral parts: the provision system of TCM preventive health care services, the technology (and product) system of these services, and the support system backing them. Specifically, TCM preventive health care services are rendered by TCM preventive health care departments in various tiers of TCM hospitals, similar departments within general hospitals, as well as primary medical and health institutions like community health service centers and township health centers. The technology (and product) system encompasses methodologies and technologies for gathering, storing, integrating, and dynamically assessing and monitoring individual health status data. The construction of the support system includes establishing mechanisms for technological innovation and research and development institutions, cultivating specialized personnel, refining TCM-centric health assurance models, instituting pertinent management systems and standards, and promoting TCM health culture.

Currently, the TCM preventive health care service system in China is experiencing vigorous growth. A number of TCM medical institutions have set up preventive health care departments, effectively integrating existing resources to actively provide TCM preventive health care services, including therapies like massage and moxibustion. Privately-run TCM wellness and health preservation establishments are emerging in large numbers, akin to bamboo shoots after a spring rain, enriching the spectrum of services available and acting as a complement to the TCM preventive health care service system. Furthermore, the Ministry of Human Resources and Social Security has specifically designated occupations for those engaged in TCM preventive health care work, accompanied by the formulation of corresponding standards and regulations, which have significantly propelled the advancement of TCM preventive health care services.

7.1.1.2 TCM Medical Service System

The TCM medical service system constitutes a vital part of China's medical service system. In accordance with the "Several Opinions of the State Council on Supporting and Promoting the Development of Traditional Chinese Medicine," the TCM medical service system is jointly composed of TCM medical institutions and other medical institutions' TCM health resources, forming an interconnected system in the provision of TCM medical services. This includes both urban and rural TCM medical service networks. Currently, China has essentially established a comprehensive TCM medical service system covering both urban and rural areas. In urban settings, a TCM medical service network has taken shape, primarily consisting of TCM hospitals (hospitals of traditional ethnic medicine and integrated traditional Chinese and Western medicine), outpatient departments and clinics specialized in TCM, clinical department of TCM in general hospitals, and community health service institutions. In rural areas, another TCM medical service network is primarily built around county-level TCM hospitals, clinical department of TCM in general hospitals (specialized

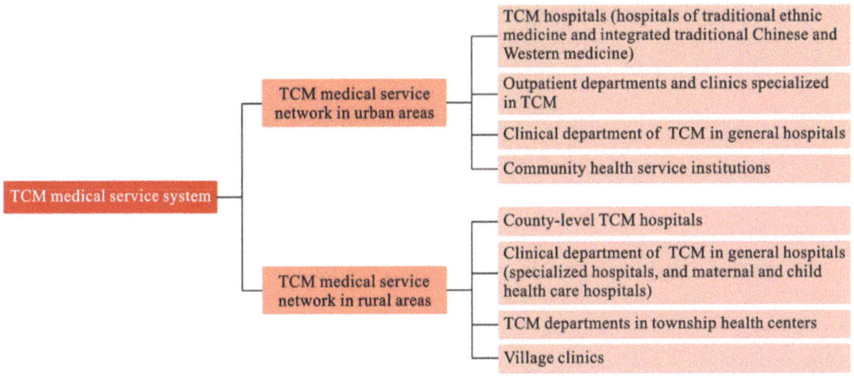

Fig. 7.1 China's TCM medical service system

hospitals, and maternal and child health care hospitals), TCM departments in township health centers, and village clinics, providing basic TCM medical, preventive, and healthcare services. For details, see Fig. 7.1.

Most comprehensive medical institutions and primary medical and health institutions in China have TCM departments, offering TCM services primarily based on traditional therapies such as herbal medicine, acupuncture, and massage. These services are, to varying degrees, included in the reimbursement scope of basic medical insurance for urban employees and basic medical insurance for rural and non-working urban residents.

By the end of 2020, China was home to 5482 hospitals specialized in TCM, comprising 2332 public TCM hospitals and 2094 private TCM hospitals. Among these, there were 535 third-level, 1926 second-level, and 1155 first-level TCM hospitals. In the effort to elevate TCM service standards, 6 hospitals specialized in TCM were included in the nurturing category for national medical centers, 20 TCM hospitals were incorporated into the scope of national regional medical centers as exporting hospitals, and 8 TCM projects were identified as national regional medical center construction projects.

7.1.1.3 Primary-Level TCM Service System

The primary-level TCM service network in China, featuring county-level TCM hospitals as leaders, community health service centers, community health service stations, township health centers, and village clinics as the main bodies, TCM departments in non-TCM medical institutions such as county-level general hospitals, maternal and child health care institutions as key supports, and privately-owned TCM hospitals, TCM outpatient departments and clinics as supplements, has gradually become more refined. By the end of 2020, 99.0% of community health service centers, 90.6% of community health service stations, 98.0% of township health centers, and 74.5% of village clinics were capable of providing TCM services. The enhancement of primary-level TCM service capabilities has yielded significant results, markedly improving the fairness, accessibility, and convenience for the public in seeking TCM services.

7.1.2 *Types of TCM Services*

7.1.2.1 TCM's "Preventive Treatment of Disease" Services

The concept of "preventive treatment of disease" in TCM originates from the *Yellow Emperor's Inner Canon*, which states that "the superior physician treats disease before it manifests, not after—it is this principle that is meant." The idea of "preventive treatment of disease," traceable to the *Yellow Emperor's Inner Canon*, emphasizes prevention over treatment, encapsulated in the principles of prevention before a disease arises, guarding against pathological changes when falling sick, and protecting recovering patients from relapse. This is also the basic idea that China's health sector has generally adhered to so far. "Preventive treatment of disease" in TCM necessitates not only treating diseases but also preventing their onset; it involves not just disease prevention but also forecasting disease trends, seeking remedies before pathology emerges, and seizing initiative during treatment.

In numerous Chinese policy documents, "preventive treatment of disease" in TCM is equated with TCM preventive health care. Promoting TCM health initiative of "preventive treatment of disease" and the construction of a TCM preventive health care service system constitute key directions for China's medical reforms and the development of TCM. Centered on individual wellness, TCM's "preventive treatment of disease" services employ unique preventive techniques to avert diseases. Over a decade has seen the development of China's TCM health initiative of "preventive treatment of disease." As China's new medical reform deepens, "preventive treatment of disease" in TCM is increasingly applied in safeguarding the health of urban and rural residents and preventing diseases. According to the *National Compilation of Traditional Chinese Medicine Statistics by National Administration of Traditional Chinese Medicine*, from 2019 to 2021, the number of health check-ups and "preventive treatment of disease" services completed in hospitals specialized in TCM in China notably increased, with an annual growth rate of 8.8%, marking a phased achievement in establishing the TCM preventive health care service system of "preventive treatment of disease."

7.1.2.2 TCM Outpatient Services

TCM outpatient services refer to the comprehensive application of fundamental TCM theories and clinical experience in diagnosing and treating patients, so as to offer them a holistic and systematic TCM health care experience. The scope of practice for TCM outpatient services in China is extensive, encompassing several key areas.

First, TCM diagnosis. This involves using traditional diagnostic methods such as inspection, auscultation and olfaction, inquiry, and palpation to ascertain patients' conditions. Second, TCM treatment. Patients are treated using various TCM modalities, including herbal medicine, acupuncture, massage and cupping therapy, and others. Third, TCM preventive health care. Based on theories and methods of TCM wellness and health preservation, patients receive guidance on maintaining good health and preventing diseases. Four, integrated treatment of traditional Chinese and Western medicine. In TCM comprehensive clinics, integration of Western medical examinations and therapies with TCM practices is employed for a combined therapeutic approach. Five, TCM health counseling. Through TCM theories and methods related to health, patients can receive guidance aimed at promoting and maintaining their overall well-being.

According to the "Guidelines for Medical Institution Setup and Planning (2016–2020)," China's provinces have essentially established clear functional roles for provincial, municipal, and county-level TCM hospitals, as well as township health centers and village clinics in TCM practices. This has led to the formation of a hierarchical, structurally sound, and functionally comprehensive TCM service system. Alongside China's sustained and rapid economic and social development, improvements in living standards and a rising demand for medical services have fueled the continuous advancement of China's medical services. As a vital component of these services, TCM outpatient services have also experienced substantial growth. In 2020, hospitals specialized in TCM in China provided approximately 596.99 million patient visits, among which outpatient departments specialized in TCM accounted for about 31.14 million visits, and clinics specialized in TCM saw around 157.38 million visits. Since 2013, the proportion of patient visits to TCM medical institutions out of the total patient visits nationwide has been on a consistent rise. By 2020, patient visits to TCM medical institutions accounted for 16.8% of all patient visits in China.

7.1.2.3 TCM Inpatient Services

TCM inpatient services refer to the comprehensive medical services provided within TCM medical institutions, where TCM practitioners, adhering to the core concepts of Yin Yang and the Five Phases, Zang-Fu organs, meridians and collaterals, holism, and treatment based on syndrome differentiation, comprehensively utilize the four diagnostic methods (inspection, auscultation and olfaction, inquiry, and palpation) along with auxiliary instruments. Primarily employing herbal formulations as the main therapeutic modality, these services also incorporate distinctive TCM treatments such as acupuncture, massage, cupping, and seasonal therapies (like treating winter ailments in summer) to offer inpatients a holistic approach to medical care.

In April 2019, the National Administration of Traditional Chinese Medicine in China issued the "Performance Appraisal Indicators for Third-Level Public Traditional Chinese Medicine Hospitals," aiming to conduct a comprehensive and unified data collection and evaluation of all third-level public TCM hospitals nationwide. This set clear standards and requirements specifically for TCM inpatient services. In

2020, approximately 29.07 million patients were discharged from hospitals specialized in TCM across China, accounting for 83% of the total discharges from TCM medical institutions nationally. The role of hospitals specialized in TCM in providing inpatient services has thus become increasingly prominent.

7.1.3 The Concept, Characteristics and Advantages of TCM Services

7.1.3.1 The Concept of TCM Services

The concept of TCM embodies the notion of "human beings are an inseparable part of nature," a perspective that emerged from a natural philosophical medical model over 2000 years ago. This concept underscores a human-centered approach, respects individuals' natural and social attributes, and pays close attention to the impact of psychological, emotional, environmental, and other subjective and objective factors on physical health. Through prolonged clinical practice, TCM has developed a unique theoretical framework and therapeutic approach centered on the "holism" and "treatment based on syndrome differentiation." With the transformation of disease spectrum, TCM's individualized "treatment based on syndrome differentiation" methodology and the notable efficacy of Chinese herbs in treating common and frequently-occurring diseases are gaining increasing global attention. Based on the patient's subjective experience, TCM offers distinctive perspectives and methods in addressing both physical and mental ailments, effectively tackling suboptimal health issues in populations.

7.1.3.2 The Characteristics of TCM Services

The concept of "harmony between form and spirit" in TCM aptly embodies the distinct characteristics of TCM services. TCM considers both the "spirit" (abstract thought) and the "form" (concrete expressions), recognizing that the well-being of both is essential for holistic health. In summary, the characteristics of TCM services are twofold. First, it resides in TCM's comprehensive and distinct theoretical framework, encompassing the theory of holism, treatment based on syndrome differentiation, and constant movement. Second, it is manifested in the TCM techniques employed in disease diagnosis and treatment, such as the four diagnostic methods of inspection, auscultation and olfaction, inquiry, and palpation, as well as therapies like acupuncture, massage, and cupping. In essence, TCM services are delivered under the guidance of TCM's characteristic theoretical system, utilizing TCM diagnostic and therapeutic techniques. TCM is often hailed as the "fifth great invention" alongside China's Four Great Inventions, and its resilience and continuing enhancement in service quality over 2000 years can be attributed to its unique diagnostic and therapeutic methods, efficacious treatments, and distinct theoretical system.

7.1.3.3 The Advantages of TCM Services

The TCM diagnostic and therapeutic equipment is simple and its techniques are straightforward, which helps alleviate the burden on medical institutions. TCM services boast the advantages of low investment and cost-effectiveness. The concept of "preventive treatment of disease" in TCM encompasses both prevention before a disease arises and guarding against pathological changes when falling sick, echoing the primary medical and health service's emphasis on an integrated approach that includes prevention, health protection, medical care, rehabilitation, health education, family planning, and technical guidance. Guided by this concept, shifting the focus of health upstream involves differential diagnosis and treatment tailored to different population groups, regulating body balance to prevent diseases, thereby fostering a healthy living environment and enhancing the quality of life. This approach presents a novel solution to break the vicious cycle of poverty due to illness and poverty returning due to illness.

TCM theories embody a health paradigm that starkly contrasts with the reductionism of Western medicine. Unlike modern Western medicine's focus on treating existing diseases, TCM advocates "preventive treatment of disease," aiming to achieve the goals of prevention before a disease arises, guarding against pathological changes when falling sick, and protecting recovering patients from relapse. One of China's earliest surviving medical classics, the *Yellow Emperor's Inner Canon*, clearly records this concept of "preventive treatment of disease," stating that "the superior physician treats disease before it manifests, not after—it is this principle that is meant." In recent years, a series of policy documents issued and implemented in China, such as the "13th Five-Year Plan for the Development of Traditional Chinese Medicine" and the "Guidelines for the Establishment and Management of 'Preventive Treatment of Disease' Departments in Traditional Chinese Medicine Hospitals (Revised Edition)," highlight a prominent orientation towards "preventive treatment of disease." This concept, characterized by promoting health, putting disease prevention first, and combining prevention with treatment, is gradually gaining recognition and importance among the people in China.

7.1.4 TCM Service Resources

7.1.4.1 TCM Medical and Health Institutions

According to the "Statistical Bulletin on Health Development in China," the structure of China's medical and health institutions consists of hospitals, primary medical and health institutions, professional public health institutions, and other institutions. Among these, TCM medical and health institutions encompass hospitals specialized in TCM, outpatient departments specialized in TCM, clinics specialized in TCM, institutions specialized in TCM research, as well as clinical departments of TCM within non-TCM medical institutions. These institutions serve as the main providers of TCM services. The total number of TCM medical and health institutions across China has grown from 46,541 in 2015 to 80,319 in 2022, demonstrating an average annual growth rate of 8.1%, and representing a 72.6% increase compared with 2015.

1. Hospitals Specialized in TCM

According to the "Statistical Bulletin on Health Development in China," hospitals specialized in TCM in China encompass TCM hospitals, hospitals of integrated traditional Chinese and Western medicine, and hospitals of traditional ethnic medicine. By the end of 2022, there were a total of 5,862 hospitals specialized in TCM in China, among which 4,779 were TCM hospitals, accounting for 81.5% of the total. Hospitals of integrated traditional Chinese and Western medicine and hospitals of traditional ethnic medicine represented 13% and 5.5% respectively.

2. Outpatient Departments and Clinics Specialized in TCM

According to the "Statistical Bulletin on Health Development in China," outpatient departments specialized in TCM in China consist of TCM outpatient departments, outpatient departments of integrated traditional Chinese and Western medicine, and outpatient departments of traditional ethnic medicine, while clinics specialized in TCM include TCM clinics, clinics of integrated traditional Chinese and Western medicine, and clinics of traditional ethnic medicine. These outpatient departments and clinics form part of the grassroots network for TCM services, with the majority being established by social entities. From 2015 to 2020, the number of outpatient departments specialized in TCM in China experienced an average annual growth rate of 16.6%, significantly higher than that of clinics specialized in TCM. By 2022, there were 3,786 outpatient departments specialized in TCM and 70,631 clinics specialized in TCM in operation.

3. Institutions Specialized in TCM Research

According to the "Statistical Bulletin on Health Development in China," institutions specialized in TCM research in China comprise TCM institutions, institutions of integrated traditional Chinese and Western medicine, and institutions of traditional ethnic medicine. By the end of 2020, China was home to a total of 43 institutions specialized in TCM research, including 34 TCM institutions, 2 institutions of integrated traditional Chinese and Western medicine, and 7 institutions of traditional ethnic medicine.

4. Clinical Departments of TCM within Non-TCM Medical Institutions

According to relevant Chinese standards, the clinical departments of TCM in general hospitals should be established as primary clinical departments within the hospital. The general hospitals should provide TCM beds, with the number not less than 5% of the hospitals' standard bed capacity. Larger hospitals, based on actual needs, may establish independent TCM wards. Furthermore, independent TCM outpatient services must be set up, with third-level general hospitals offering no fewer than three TCM specialties and second-level general hospitals offering no fewer than two. By the end of 2020, among China's general hospitals, 4,071 had clinical department of TCM, constituting the highest proportion (86.7%) among similar institutions. Among community health service centers and township health centers, 4,590 and 17,414 respectively had clinical department of TCM, accounting for 63.1% and 50.1% of their respective categories.

7.1.4.2 The Number of TCM Beds

TCM beds refer to those provided by TCM medical and health institutions including hospitals specialized in TCM, outpatient departments specialized in TCM, and clinical departments of TCM within non-TCM medical institutions, with hospitals specialized in TCM being the predominant provider. In 2020, China had approximately 9.10 million beds in medical and health institutions in total, among which around 1.43 million were in TCM medical and health institutions, accounting for 15.7%. Specifically, the beds in hospitals specialized in TCM numbered around 1.15 million (a 40.1% increase compared with 2015), representing 16.1% of all hospital beds nationwide, and indicating a steady growth trend. Among the beds in hospitals specialized in TCM, TCM hospitals provided about 0.98 million beds (accounting for 85.5%), hospitals of integrated traditional Chinese and Western medicine had roughly 0.13 million beds (accounting for 10.9%), and hospitals of traditional ethnic medicine had 42,379 beds (accounting for 3.7%).

7.1.4.3 TCM Resources

1. Definition and Classification of TCM Resources

TCM resources are integral components of natural ecological resources and constitute a crucial material foundation for the development of TCM. These resources encompass medicinally used animals, plants, and minerals scattered within specific regions or areas, which are utilized under the guidance of TCM's fundamental theories for traditional medicinal purposes. The term does not solely refer to the narrow definition of TCM resources; it also encompasses folk herbal medicines and ethnic medicinal resources such as Zhuang and Miao medicines. With the continuous exploitation and utilization of natural resources, some have become scarce, leading to the development of artificially cultivated, bred, or manufactured medicinal resources through biochemical technologies, known as artificial TCM resources. Natural TCM resources, in contrast to artificial ones, can be broadly classified into two categories: biological resources and non-biological resources. Approximately 99.4% of these resources fall under biological resources, including medicinal animals and plants, which are renewable. Conversely, medicinal mineral resources, classified as non-biological resources, are non-renewable and account for about 0.6% of the total.

2. The Status Quo of the Existing TCM Resources

Information regarding the types, distribution, and reserves of TCM resources is primarily obtained through conducting national surveys of them. China has carried out four such surveys since 1960. According to the data from the Fourth National Survey of TCM Resources, China boasts a total of 18,817 species of TCM resources. Among these, there are 826 species of medicinal fungi (approximately 4.39%), 15,227 species of medicinal plants (about 80.92%), 2,611 species of medicinal animals (around 13.88%), and 153 species of medicinal minerals (about 0.81%). Furthermore, to understand the regional variations in the distribution of TCM resources, China has conducted detailed classifications based on administrative regions. Specifically, Hainan province possesses nearly 2,500 species of TCM resources, while Yunnan province has 8,875, highlighting a significant difference in distribution across regions.

7.1.4.4 TCM Human Resources

TCM human resources encompass three main categories: practitioners and assistant practitioners of TCM (encompassing practitioners of TCM, integrating traditional Chinese and Western medicine, and ethnic medicine), TCM pharmacists, and intern practitioners of TCM. Personnel engaged in TCM management tasks are not included in this statistical count.

1. Total Human Resources of TCM

As China attaches greater importance to TCM and the demand from the public for TCM services rises, the total volume of TCM human resources in the country has seen a rapid increase. By 2021, the overall number of TCM human resources in medical and health institutions nationwide reached 884,815. From 2017 to 2022, both the total number of practitioners and assistant practitioners nationwide and those specializing in TCM categories experienced continuous growth, increasing from 3.39 million to 4.44 million and from 527,000 to 764,000 respectively, with average annual growth rates of 5.5% and 7.7%. During the same period, the number of TCM pharmacists grew from 120,000 in 2017 to 139,000 in 2022, with an average annual growth rate of 3%. Evidently, within TCM human resources, the number of practitioners and assistant practitioners of TCM was expanding at a faster pace, whereas the growth in the number of TCM pharmacists was slower.

2. The Allocation and Age Structure of TCM Human Resources

During the 13th Five-Year Plan period, the allocation of TCM human resources per 10,000 population in various regions of China steadily increased, with the maximum allocation rising from 4.43 to 5.87 personnel, and the minimum allocation of TCM pharmacists per 10,000 population growing from 0.84 to 0.93. In central regions, the overall allocation of TCM personnel, practitioners and assistant practitioners of TCM, and TCM pharmacists per 10,000 population was lower than the national average. However, the allocation of health technicians per 10,000 population in TCM hospitals in these regions, which was in the middle range during the 12th Five-Year Plan period, rose to lead the nation by the end of the 13th Five-Year Plan period. Regarding the allocation of practitioners and assistant practitioners of TCM per 10,000 population, western regions consistently held the lead. Given the relatively smaller population in these areas, the number of practitioners per 10,000 population tended to be higher. As for the allocation of TCM pharmacists per 10,000 population, eastern regions exceeded the national average. These regions enjoy relatively abundant TCM human resources, and despite having a larger population base, they maintain their leading position.

Compared with 2017, there were changes in the age structure of TCM human resources in China in 2021. Specifically, for practitioners and assistant practitioners of TCM in public TCM hospitals, the proportion of those aged below 25 increased by 0.5%, those aged 25 to 34 rose by 7%, those aged 35 to 54 decreased by 6.3%, those aged 55 to 59 saw an increase of 1.3%, while the percentage of those aged 60 and above declined by 2.5%.

7.2 TCM Management

7.2.1 TCM Management System

Since the founding of the People's Republic of China, to ensure and promote the development of TCM, the state has established specialized organizations for TCM management and built a hierarchical TCM management system extending from the central government to local levels. Through ongoing practical exploration, central-level TCM management bodies have undergone four major transitions, evolving from the Department of Traditional Chinese Medicine, to the Bureau of Traditional Chinese Medicine, then to the State Administration of Traditional Chinese Medicine, and finally to the current National Administration of Traditional Chinese Medicine. As the central-level TCM administrative institutions have continually upgraded, local governments have also successively established corresponding TCM management agencies. Currently, China's TCM management structure encompasses four tiers: central, provincial, municipal, and county levels, with management responsibilities covering areas such as medical services, education, scientific research, and cultural dissemination.

The National Administration of Traditional Chinese Medicine of China, serving as the national governing body, is responsible for planning and guiding the development of TCM management across the country. By 2018, all 31 provincial-level administrative regions had completed institutional reforms, with basically established

TCM administrations (bureaus, offices) at the provincial level. The municipal-level TCM management system was further refined, and the grassroots TCM management system witnessed a leap from nonexistence to establishment. Provinces including Hebei, Jilin, and Sichuan have set up relatively independent TCM administrations under the provincial health commission. Most provincial-level TCM administrations are at the deputy director-general level, with Jilin Province being a notable example. This province has formed a relatively complete TCM management system. The model of relatively independent TCM administrations, which grants these institutions independent staffing quotas, personnel authority, and dedicated financial budgets, facilitates autonomous operations of them. This, to a certain extent, promotes the implementation of TCM policies.

China's TCM undertakings operates under a divided departmental and hierarchical regulatory framework, involving multiple ministries and commissions, chiefly including the National Development and Reform Commission, the Ministry of Agriculture and Rural Affairs, the National Health Commission, and the National Administration of Traditional Chinese Medicine. At the national level, the National Administration of Traditional Chinese Medicine is established to oversee TCM affairs comprehensively. Both provincial and municipal levels have set up TCM administrations, while each county-level health administrative body houses a TCM management department. Relevant departments at all levels collaborate to ensure the effective implementation of policies and regulations pertaining to TCM. This multi-department cooperative management system provides a reliable organizational guarantee for the development of TCM in China.

7.2.2 The Legal System of TCM

The development of TCM is inseparable from legal safeguards. The issuance of the "Regulations of the People's Republic of China on Traditional Chinese Medicine" in 2003 played a vital role in promoting and regulating the development of TCM. However, with the rapid economic and social development, a series of issues emerged in the development of TCM in China, including insufficient service capabilities of TCM, a decline in the TCM service market, and difficulties for the current physicians, clinics, and drug management systems to adapt to the characteristics and development needs of TCM. To further ensure and facilitate the development of TCM, in 2008, the Standing Committee of the 11th National People's Congress included the TCM law in its legislative plan. The Law of the People's Republic of China on Traditional Chinese Medicine was officially adopted at the 25th Session of the Standing Committee of the 12th National People's Congress on December 25, 2016, and came into effect on July 1, 2017. This marked a milestone event in the history of TCM development. As the first comprehensive and systematic law that fully embodies the characteristics of TCM, the Law of the People's Republic of China on Traditional Chinese Medicine codifies China's policies and guidelines for managing the development of TCM, legally affirming the significant position of TCM and embodying the expectations and demands of the people for TCM in a legal form. Based on the Constitution of the People's Republic of China, the Law of the People's Republic of China on Traditional Chinese Medicine ensures the legal status of TCM and provides fundamental guidance for its development.

7.2.3 *TCM Quality Control*

7.2.3.1 Whole Process Quality Control

TCM encompasses a variety of forms, such as Chinese crude drugs (derived from plants, animals, and minerals), TCM decoction pieces, and Chinese patent medicines, which constitute the primary manifestations of medicines found in a Chinese pharmacy. TCM decoction pieces and Chinese patent medicines, among other TCM preparations, are processed and prepared from Chinese crude drugs through specific stages. High-quality medicines form the material basis for effective treatment, and superior TCM decoction pieces and Chinese patent medicines ensure optimal clinical outcomes in TCM practice. Thus, the quality assurance of TCM necessitates rigorous control starting from the sourcing of raw materials. Chinese crude drugs possess multiple attributes as pharmaceuticals, commodities, and agricultural and sideline products, and their circulation process spans cultivation, harvesting, processing, packaging, storage, transportation, and sales, with potential quality issues arising at any step along this chain. This complexity inherents in these steps consequently dictates the intricacy of quality control required.

Chapter III of the Law of the People's Republic of China on Traditional Chinese Medicine contains provisions specifically addressing the "Protection and Development of TCM." Article 21 stipulates the overarching requirements for the supervision of the entire process from the production to circulation of Chinese crude drugs, stating that "the state shall formulate technical norms and standards for the cultivation, breeding, collection, storage, and primary processing of Chinese crude drugs, and strengthen the quality supervision and management throughout the entire process of production and circulation of Chinese crude drugs to ensure their quality and safety." Article 24 sets regulations for the establishment of a quality monitoring system for Chinese crude drugs and the construction of a traceability system for their circulation. Furthermore, Article 31 provides regulations concerning the preparation of TCM preparation formulations by medical institutions.

From a legal standpoint, China's current TCM supervision system is centered around the Drug Administration Law of the People's Republic of China, complemented by administrative regulations and departmental rules including the "Regulations for the Implementation of the Drug Administration Law of the People's Republic of China," "Good Manufacturing Practice," "Good Supply Practice," and "Good Agricultural Practice for Chinese Crude Drugs." The "Regulations for the Implementation of the Drug Administration Law of the People's Republic of China" outlines the rules governing drug research and development, production, distribution, usage, and supervision, encompassing TCM. The "Good Manufacturing Practice," "Good Supply Practice," and "Good Agricultural Practice for Chinese Crude Drugs" establish detailed guidelines and operational standards for drug production and distribution practices. Additional normative documents also play a pivotal role. For instance, the national food and drug administration authorities have issued a series of notices, including "Notice on Strengthening Supervision over the Administration of TCM Decoction Pieces," "Notice of the China Food and Drug Administration on Further Strengthening the Supervision over the Production and Operation of TCM Decoction Pieces," and "Notice of the China Food and Drug Administration on Further Strengthening Quality Supervision over Special Chinese Crude Drug Markets," which lay down explicit regulations for the production and management supervision of TCM decoction pieces, Chinese crude drugs, and Chinese patent medicines. Overall, a preliminary legal and regulatory system for TCM has been established in China.

In terms of the organization and management of TCM, after the reform and opening-up, the State Council established the State Pharmaceutical Administration to oversee drug regulation. With the emergence of dispersed drug supervision, the authority for TCM regulation was transferred to the State Administration of Traditional Chinese Medicine. During the institutional reform in 1998, the State Council integrated the relevant functions of the Pharmaceutical Administration Bureau of the Ministry of Health, the State Pharmaceutical Administration, and the State Administration of Traditional Chinese Medicine, forming the National Medical Products Administration, which reported directly to the State Council and was responsible for comprehensive supervision of drugs from research and development to sales. In 2003, with the addition of food and cosmetic supervision responsibilities, the National Medical Products Administration was renamed the State Food and Drug Administration, assuming administrative and technical oversight of drugs (including Chinese crude drugs, TCM decoction pieces, and Chinese patent medicines) throughout their lifecycle from research and development, production, distribution to usage. The management below the provincial level was organized on a vertical basis. Under the context of the large-scale institutional reform in 2008, the State Food and Drug Administration changed from being a directly affiliated agency of the State Council to being under the jurisdiction of the Ministry of Health, and the drug regulatory bodies below the provincial level shifted from vertical management to local management. In 2013, the State Food and Drug Administration was renamed the China Food and Drug Administration, and in 2018, it was again renamed the National Medical Products Administration, which is managed by the State Administration for Market Regulation, overseeing the unified regulation of drugs across different stages such as production, distribution, and consumption.

7.2.3.2 Construction of the Quality Traceability System

The International Organization for Standardization defines traceability as the ability to track and identify the history, usage, or location of goods or actions through recorded identification codes. Establishing a traceability system is a critical measure to reinforce quality and safety supervision. The concept of a quality traceability system for Chinese crude drugs was first proposed at the 3rd International Conference on the Modernization of Traditional Chinese Medicine in 2010, aiming at enforcing quality control throughout the entire process of production and usage of these materials. The TCM quality traceability system employs modern Internet of Things (IoT) technology, block chain, cloud computing, big data, and other information technologies to manage key information throughout the entire process of TCM production, from planting, processing, manufacturing, distribution to usage. This enables the realization of a system where "the source is identifiable, the destination is traceable, the quality is verifiable, and the responsibility is accountable," essentially achieving "traceability from farm to patient" or "traceability regulation from patient back to farm." The development of such a traceability system for TCM quality is a public welfare project that ensures the safety, efficacy, and controllability of TCM quality, thereby safeguarding public health.

Case Study: Chinese Pharmaceutical Chemist Tu Youyou Discovered an Anti-Malaria Medicine—Artemisinin

Since ancient times, humans have been engaged in a protracted battle against malaria, with records dating back to China's *Yellow Emperor's Inner Canon: Basic Questions*, compiled before the Common Era. Even to this day, malaria continues to wreak havoc in numerous countries, posing a threat to people's health and lives.

On October 5, 2015, the Karolinska Institute in Sweden announced the awarding of the 2015 Nobel Prize in Physiology or Medicine to pharmaceutical chemist Tu Youyou and two other scientists, in recognition of their contributions to the research on treatments for parasitic diseases such as malaria. Tu Youyou thus became the first Chinese native scientist to win a Nobel Prize in a scientific discipline.

Before artemisinin was discovered, quinine and chloroquine were the primary medicines used to combat malaria. However, the effectiveness of these medicines against malaria did not persist for long. In the 1960s, many regions of the world began to witness the emergence of malaria parasites resistant to these medicines, particularly in Southeast Asia and Africa, reaching a point where no effective medicines were available. Consequently, the development of new anti-malaria medicines became imperative. By 1972, after screening over 2000 traditional Chinese herbal medicine recipes, Tu Youyou and her team found that an extract from the Artemisia annual plant, a member of the Compositae family, showed some inhibitory effects on mouse malaria parasites. Initially, the effectiveness was limited due to improper extraction methods resulting in low concentrations of the active ingredient. Inspired by Ge Hong, a medical scholar from China's Eastern Jin Dynasty, and adopting a low-temperature ether extraction method instead, the team successfully extracted the effective antimalarial compound, artemisinin, which achieved a 100% inhibition rate against the malaria parasites.

Compared with other anti-malaria medicines, artemisinin-based medicines exhibit high efficiency and rapid clearance of malaria parasites. However, due to the short half-life of artemisinin compounds in the human body, researchers recommend combining artemisinin and its derivatives with other anti-malaria medicines to achieve complete eradication of the parasites and mitigate the development of resistance. A 2004 publication in *The Lancet* demonstrated that when artesunate, a derivative of artemisinin, is used in combination with other medicines, the cure rate for Plasmodium falciparum (the most severe form of malaria) exceeds 80%, accompanied by a significant reduction in recurrence rates and gametocyte infection rates. By 2013, out of the 87 countries where Plasmodium falciparum malaria was prevalent, 79 had adopted artemisinin-based combination therapies (ACTs) as the first-line treatment for this deadly form of malaria.

Artemisinin has paved the way for the development of a new generation of anti-malaria medicines. It originates from TCM, and its discovery has saved millions of lives worldwide, particularly in developing countries. It is believed that through the sustained efforts of researchers and health care workers, global malaria control and ultimately its eradication will be attainable goals.

Chapter 8
China's Health Resource Planning

Formulating health resource planning is a pivotal instrument for materializing the Healthy China Initiative and significantly contributes to the construction of China's medical and health service system. China's health resource planning encompasses a diverse array of categories, spanning from talent cultivation, infrastructure, pharmaceutical resource allocation, to capital within the health domain. This chapter will first provide an overview of China's health resource planning. It encompasses the delineation of health resources, their categorization, allocation methodologies, as well as the fundamentals of health resource planning such as its concept, types, and formulation principles. Subsequently, the chapter delves into the indicators employed in China's health resource planning, utilizing these metrics as a foundation to elaborate on the planning formulation process. This intricate procedure encompasses defining strategic objectives, and formulating health resource development strategies and budget. Finally, a case study of China's health talent team construction planning is presented to help readers understand the specific forms of China's health resource planning.

8.1 Overview of China's Health Resource Planning

8.1.1 Concepts Related to Health Resource Planning

Health resources encompass the aggregate of various elements utilized or consumed in the provision of health services, comprising human resources, funds, infrastructures, equipment, medications, information, knowledge, and technological resources. Illustrative measures of a nation's or region's health vitality include the quantity of health institutions, hospital beds, health personnel, allocated health funds, and the

Z. Feng et al. (eds.), *China's Health System*, Introduction to China's S&T Innovation,
https://doi.org/10.1007/978-981-95-1205-8_8

ratio of health funds to Gross Domestic Product (GDP). Health resources are important indicators to measure the health status of a country or region and the material and technical foundations upon which health programs rest.

These resources can be further categorized into health human resources, health material resources, health financial resources, and health information and technology. Health human resources are individuals capable of delivering health services, encompassing both active practitioners and those undergoing training for future engagement. Health material resources include physical assets such as facilities, equipment, and medicines dedicated to health delivery. Health financial resources pertain to monetary inputs for health provision, stemming from governmental, societal, and personal sources, and are commonly referred to as "health expenditure." Health information and technology revolve around data, patents, norms, procedures, and other knowledge-based assets relevant to health.

In China, the allocation of health resources is executed through three principal modalities: first, planned allocation, wherein the government takes the responsibility of deciding resource distribution; second, market allocation, driven by market dynamics like pricing and competition, determining resource allocation patterns; third, a hybrid model combining planning and market mechanisms, enabling collaborative governance of resource allocation by both the government and market forces.

Health resource planning embodies a systematic approach aimed at defining the developmental objectives, scale, and pace of health resources, grounded in considerations such as the natural ecology, socioeconomic progression, population health challenges, and health demands. It endeavors to devise comprehensive plans for the rational allocation of these resources, with the overarching goal of augmenting the quality and availability of health services and optimizing the effectiveness and efficiency of resource usage. Enhancing resource allocation efficiency through meticulous planning constitutes a globally recognized practice and a cornerstone strategy for the Chinese government in ensuring equitable and efficient health resource allocation to address public health necessities. In devising such plans, the government meticulously considers three key dynamics: first, macro–micro relations, reflecting the interplay between national oversight of society-wide health resources and institutional-level health resource management; second, stock-increment balance, examining the interdependence between existing and forthcoming health resources; third, equity-efficiency nexus, striking a balance between the dual values of equity and efficiency in health resource allocation decisions.

8.1.2 *Types of Health Resource Planning in China*

China's health resource planning can be classified according to planning levels, planning subjects and planning periods (Fig. 8.1).

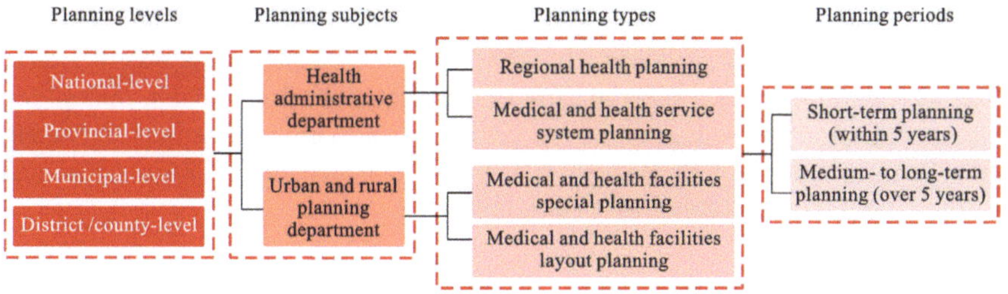

Fig. 8.1 Types of health resource planning in China

In terms of planning levels, China' health resource planning is divided into national and regional tiers. National planning sets the tone by outlining developmental objectives, guiding principles, and strategic frameworks for the nation's health undertakings, thereby serving as a guiding framework. Conversely, regional planning is more nuanced, tailoring health development directions, models, and objectives according to the specific socioeconomic context and health profile of each area. It involves the rational distribution of medical and health institutions across various tiers, functions, and sizes, culminating in a cohesive blueprint for regional health progress. In China, the state often initiates regional planning directives, establishing resource allocation guidelines for defined periods. Subsequently, provincial health administrative departments establish baseline standards, followed by prefectural and county-level health administrative departments defining localized goals, allocation benchmarks, key tasks, and implementation guarantees. Execution of the regional health planning underpins the macroeconomic regulation of the health undertakings by governments at all tiers and facilitates comprehensive industry management in health.

Regarding planning subjects, the demarcation in China's health resource planning splits into two branches. The first, spearheaded and led by health administrations across all levels, encapsulates regional health planning and medical and health service system planning. It revolves around intra-system resource allocation, service provision, and developmental management. The second, handled by urban and rural planning departments, focuses on the land allocation and spatial arrangement for medical and health facilities through specialized plans and layout strategies such as medical and health facilities special planning and medical and health facilities layout planning. This chapter primarily delves into the former category—planning spearheaded and led by health administrative departments across all levels for execution.

When viewed through the lens of planning periods, China's health resource planning is bifurcated into short-term planning and medium- to long-term planning. Short-term planning, exemplified by that aligned with the national five-year economic and social development plans such as the "14th Five-Year Plan for National Health," the "14th Five-Year Plan for National Medical Security," the "14th Five-Year Plan for Health Standardization," set forth during the 14th Five-Year Plan period, encapsulates the period from 2021 to 2025. Conversely, medium- to long-term planning, epitomized by the "Outline of the Healthy China 2030 Plan" issued by the Central Committee of the Communist Party of China and the State Council on October

25, 2016, covers a longer time frame. As the inaugural national-scale, medium- to long-term health strategy since the founding of the People's Republic of China, it outlines ambitious goals spanning from enhancing population health, optimizing demographic structure and health literacy, restructuring a modern medical and health systems, fostering comprehensive health service models, propelling medical and health reforms, and bolstering the health industry's growth.

8.1.3 Principles for the Formulation of China's Health Resource Planning

To ascertain the precision and viability of health resource planning, governments worldwide adhere to a set of principles that not only conform to the health sector's developmental trajectories but also align with their unique political landscapes in formulating health resource planning. Universally embraced principles guiding the formulation of health resource planning encompass five main tenets: the first is the target-oriented principle, which delineates, actionable, quantifiable, achievable and assessable objectives; the second is the process-oriented principle, adhering to a scientific planning methodology entailing situational analysis, goal formulation and adjustment, strategy development and execution, and performance monitoring; the third is the coordination principle, emphasizing harmonious integration among diverse health institutions and personnel, fostering judicious and productive resource allocation; the fourth is the systemic principle, necessitating a holistic and dynamic examination of the health system's multifaceted internal and external factors and their reciprocal impacts, and finally establishing a complete health planning system; and the fifth is the sustainability principle, ensuring alignment with socioeconomic progress and public health needs, supporting the health sector's enduring expansion while safeguarding environmental and resource integrity.

China, anchored in its distinct national context and cumulative experience, has distilled its health resource planning approach into five tailored principles.

First, the coordination principle. It underscores that China's health resource planning should be coordinated with the national economic and social development. The government must calibrate health development aspirations, scale, and pace according to regional disparities, factor in socioeconomic influences on the development of health undertakings and population health, leverage conducive conditions and seize development prospects, dynamically adjust to socioeconomic transformations to tackle health challenges posed by industrialization, urbanization and demographic aging, and determine the number, scale and distribution of medical and health institutions scientifically and reasonably on a health needs-oriented basis. It also necessitates stakeholder collaboration, ensuring diverse viewpoints are incorporated to forge consensus. The solution of many health problems requires the joint efforts of the government and society. Therefore, it is necessary to strengthen the interaction, communication and coordination among all parties.

Second, the systemic principle, also known as the integrity principle. It underscores that health planners should view the health system or its components as an interconnected whole, recognizing that health system functionality is intertwined with broader societal systems. Similarly, each part of the health system is interconnected with others. The formulation of health resource planning, therefore, goes beyond simple allocation, aiming to enhance the health system's operational effectiveness holistically. To ensure that health resources are used more effectively, cooperation both within the health system and with external systems must be strengthened. This requires coordinated efforts between the government and market forces, with the government assuming a pivotal role in systemic design, planning, financing, service provision, and oversight to uphold public health's welfare orientation and cater to varied health service demands.

Third, the sustainability principle. As important planning to guide the operation of the health system, the concept of sustainable development should be emphasized in the process of formulating health resource planning. One of the objectives of health resource planning is to address health issues. Health resource planning must contemplate both immediate and future health necessities, addressing prevailing issues while averting emerging ones. Sometimes, the government formulates a certain plan to address a specific existing health issue. Due to the high level of attention from the government, the function of the plan is effectively implemented, and the health issue is resolved. However, once the issue is resolved, the implementation of the plan often ceases, leading to the recurrence of the same health issue after some time.

Fourth, the differentiated guidance principle. China has a large population and a vast territory, with significant regional economic disparities. There are substantial differences in the quantity and distribution of health resources, the level of health services, and the health status of the population across different regions. When formulating health resource planning, it is necessary to consider the specific conditions of different regions, systems, institutions, and organizations, as well as the health needs of the population, the level of economic and social development, and the current status of health resources. The quantity and distribution of health resources across different regions, types, and levels should be rationally coordinated, and allocation standards should be developed accordingly. This principle is reflected in setting goals, choosing strategies, and allocating resources, which includes clearly defining and implementing the functions and tasks of medical and health institutions at various levels and types, implementing the strategy of "centralized control with peripheral development" based on factors such as population size, distribution, age structure, transportation conditions, and diagnosis and treatment needs, as well as rationally allocating the number of medical and health institutions in each region, and promoting the balanced distribution and homogeneous development of medical resources in each region.

Fifth, the principle of balancing equity and efficiency. Equity and efficiency are fundamental to the government's agenda, with efficiency enabling the sustainability of health initiatives and equity reflecting the purpose of the health undertakings development. Thus, the formulation of health resource planning requires achieving a balance between equity and efficiency, optimizing resource usage while upholding universal access to health resources and health services, particularly for marginalized communities. Specifically, this involves securing universal access to basic medical and health services to promote fairness and justice, coupled with the optimized, cost-effective allocation and usage of health resources to harmonize equity and efficiency.

8.2 Formulation of China's Health Resource Planning

8.2.1 Health Resource Planning Targets

Health resource planning targets serve as metrics, quantitatively or qualitatively reflecting the efficacy of planning execution. They play a pivotal role in guiding regional health advancements, optimizing health resource allocation and activities, assessing health resource planning outcomes, bolstering health strategies and policies, propelling enhancements in health service quality, and safeguarding public health.

In China, health resource planning targets are bifurcated into two types: obligatory targets and anticipated targets. Obligatory targets denote compulsory targets to be attained by the planning cycle's conclusion, embodying the government's accountability, commitments, and directives to subordinate levels. Governments are duty-bound to harness public resources and administrative authority to guarantee the fulfillment of obligatory targets. Conversely, anticipated targets represent the government's desired achievements by the planning horizon, expressing its policy intent. Here, the government employs policy levers to orient, regulate, and mediate societal resources to attain or remain proximal to these benchmarks. The targets can further be categorized based on the type of health resources, encompassing health workforce allocation targets, targets of bed allocation in medical and health institutions, health expenditure allocation targets, and others.

Within health workforce allocation targets, quantitative and structural targets coexist. Notable targets consist of the number of health technicians per 1000 population, reflecting the aggregate of locally active health professionals across various medical and health institutions, encompassing practitioners, assistant practitioners, registered nurses, lab technicians, and health supervisors, and excluding managerial staff; the number of practitioners and assistant practitioners per 1000 population, pinpointing qualified physicians engaged in direct medical or preventive care, again excluding managerial staff per 1000 population; the number of registered nurses per 1000 population, indicating the count of certified nursing personnel per 1000 population; the number of other health technical personnel (for specific types of specialized practitioners and public health practitioners, the numbers are generally calculated per 10,000 population, such as the number of mental health practitioners per 10,000 population and the number of pediatricians per 10,000 population); the composition and dispersion of the health workforce, mirroring the caliber and rationality of human workforce allocation, with health resource planning necessitating criteria for professional mix, educational attainment, and hierarchical titles.

Similarly, targets of bed allocation in medical and health institutions incorporate both quantitive and structural targets. Key targets encompass the number of beds in medical and health institutions per 1000 population (allocation targets of total number of beds in medical and health institutions in one region) and the bed allocation structure and distribution. According to the current situation and existing problems of bed distribution in medical and health institutions in one region, supplementary targets may be introduced to meet the special needs, such as dedicated beds for rehabilitation, mental health, or pediatrics, either per 1000 population or as a percentage of total beds. For instance, to invigorate social medical services, the "13th Five-Year Plan on Health and Wellness" targeted over 30% of hospital beds in social hospitals by 2020. To bolster primary health undertakings, the health resource planning may delineate bed capacities for medical and health institutions at various tiers (Table 8.1).

Health expenditure allocation targets are similarly composed of both quantitative and structural targets. Quantitative targets shed light on the magnitude and directional shifts in health spending, exemplified by the total health expenditure. Conversely, structural targets delve into the allocation and utilization patterns of health expenditure, along with the equity in health service provision, as illustrated by the proportion of government health expenditure within the total health expenditure (Table 8.2).

Furthermore, the ambit of health resources extends to encompass elements such as facilities, equipment, information, and technological advancements. In China, governments at all levels customarily undertake the planning of substantial medical equipment, exemplified by stipulating the allocation of advanced apparatuses like electronic computed tomography scanners and magnetic resonance imaging machines on a per 10,000 population basis within a given region. In 2019, a pivotal initiative was launched by the National Health Commission and the National Administration of Traditional Chinese Medicine, unveiling the "National Standards and Norms for the Informatization Construction of Primary Medical and Health Institutions (Trial)." This comprehensive framework outlined a meticulous structure comprising 4 primary, 58 secondary, and 212 tertiary targets, including the target that primary medical and health institutions should provide internet-based medical and health services, and have eight functions such as appointment, payment, diagnosis and treatment suggestions, and doctor-patient communication.

8.2.2 Formulation Process of China's Health Resource Planning

In the formulation of the health resource planning by Chinese governments at various levels, a holistic approach is imperative, necessitating the thorough examination of both intrinsic and extraneous determinants. Health resource allocation targets must stem from an appraisal of the population's health service necessities, with a clear

Table 8.1 The level of targets related to China's health resource planning in 2025

Main targets	Current situation in 2020	Goals for 2025	Target attribute
Number of beds in medical and health institutions per 1000 population	6.46	7.40–7.50	Guided
Including: municipal-level and above public hospitals	1.78	1.90–2.00	Guided
County-level public hospitals and primary medical and health institutions	2.96	3.50	Guided
Number of beds in public hospitals specialized in TCM per 1000 population	0.68	0.85	Guided
Number of practitioners and assistant practitioners per 1000 population	2.90	3.20	Anticipated
Number of practitioners and assistant practitioners of TCM per 1000 population	0.48	0.62	Anticipated
Number of registered nurses per 1000 population	3.34	3.80	Anticipated
Number of pharmacists per 1000 population	0.35	0.54	Anticipated
Doctor to nurse ratio	1:1.15	1:1.20	Anticipated
Bed to health personnel ratio	1:1.48	1:1.62	Anticipated
Proportion of second-level and above general hospitals with geriatric medicine departments (%)	–	$\geq$60.00	Anticipated
Suitable bed number for county-level general hospitals	–	600–1000	Guided
Suitable bed number for municipal-level general hospitals	–	1000–1500	Guided
Suitable bed number for provincial-level and above general hospitals	–	1500–3000	Guided

Notes [a]Hospital beds include beds in the same level of maternal and child health care hospitals and specialized disease prevention and treatment centers (institutes)

[b]"Provincial-level hospitals" include those held by provinces, autonomous regions, and municipalities directly under the central government; "municipal-level and above hospitals" includes provincial-level and above hospitals and municipal-level hospitals, among which "municipal-level hospitals" include those held by prefecture-level cities, regions, prefectures, and leagues; "county-level hospitals" include those held by counties, county-level cities, municipal districts, and banners

[c]Suitable bed number refers to the bed number of a single practice point in a general hospital

Source National Health Commission

demarcation of the discrepancy between present conditions and anticipated objectives, guiding subsequent planning endeavors. The process initiates with a diagnostic phase of issues, succeeded by the drafting of a strategic blueprint. Upon approval, the establishment of steering and working committees follows, with defined roles, team training, and financial provisions set in place.

Table 8.2 Main targets for the development of national medical security in China during the 14th Five-Year Plan period

Category	Main targets	2020	2025	Target attribute
Insurance coverage	Basic medical insurance coverage rate (%)	>95	>95[a]	Obligatory
Fund security	Basic medical insurance (including maternity insurance) fund income (trillion yuan)	2.5	Income scale is more in line with the level of economic and social development	Anticipated
	Basic medical insurance (including maternity insurance) fund expenditure (trillion yuan)	2.1	Expenditure scale is more in line with the level of economic and social development, as well as the basic medical needs of the people	Anticipated
Guarantee level	Proportion of hospitalization expenses within the scope of basic medical insurance for urban employees (%)	85.2	Maintain stability	Anticipated
	Proportion of hospitalization expenses within the scope of basic medical insurance for rural and non-working urban residents (%)	70	Maintain stability	Anticipated
	Proportion of hospitalization medical expenses assistance for key beneficiaries meeting the regulations (%)	70	70	Anticipated
	Proportion of personal health expenditure to total health expenditure (%)	27.7	27	Obligatory
Fine management	Proportion of hospitalization expenses based on disease diagnosis related groups and diagnosis related groups to total hospitalization expenses (%)	–	70	Anticipated
	Proportion of the amount of drugs purchased by public medical institutions through provincial-level centralized procurement platforms to the total amount of drugs (excluding TCM decoction pieces) purchased (%)	Around 75	90	Anticipated

(continued)

Table 8.2 (continued)

Category	Main targets	2020	2025	Target attribute
Fine management	Proportion of the amount of high-value medical consumables purchased by public medical institutions through provincial-level centralized procurement platforms to the total amount of high-value medical consumables purchased (%)	–	80	Anticipated
	Drugs procured through centralized volume-based purchasing (variety)	112	>500[b]	Anticipated
	High-value medical consumables procured through centralized volume-based purchasing (category)	1	>5[c]	Anticipated
High quality service	Direct settlement rate of hospitalization expenses across provinces[d] (%)	>50	>70	Anticipated
	Online availability rate of medical security government services (%)	–	80	Anticipated
	Availability rate of government service windows for medical security (%)	–	100	Obligatory

Notes [a]Refers to the basic medical insurance coverage rate maintained at over 95% annually during the 14th Five-Year Plan period

[b]Refers to the centralized volume-based procurement of over 500 varieties of drugs at the national and provincial levels in various provinces (autonomous regions, municipalities directly under the central government) by 2025.

[c]Refers to the centralized volume-based procurement of high-value medical consumables at the national and provincial levels in various provinces (autonomous regions, municipalities directly under the central government) by 2025, with a quantity of 5 or more categories.

[d]Refers to the proportion of hospitalization expenses directly settled across provinces to the total number of inpatients seeking medical treatment across provinces and regions.

Source General Office of the State Council of the People's Republic of China

Phase I: comprehensive health situation analysis. Initiating health resource planning necessitates an exhaustive examination of the health landscape, encompassing political, economic, social, and environmental dynamics. This analysis transcends the immediate health system, embracing the broader health industry evolution. It also goes beyond the immediate situation, including both past and future contexts. Data gathering could employ techniques like surveys, existing literature reviews, health record audits, and stakeholder symposia for a dynamic, multi-faceted analysis.

The Chinese health administrative departments' health situation analysis encompasses four dimensions: the present status analysis from natural, political, social, and economic perspectives, usually being carried out by common methods such as issue ranking, trend projection, standard analysis, and expert evaluation; retrospective analysis on population, disease, health service needs and demands, health resource utilization and so on; prospective analysis, that is, forward-looking forecasts on economic, demographic, and epidemiological trends; major obstacles analysis, namely, identification of barriers impeding health issue resolutions and industry progress to formulate targeted policies and measures.

The six commonly used analytical methodologies underpin this analysis process are as follows: descriptive analysis detailing the distribution and change pattern of health services or health events in a social population; factor analysis to identify issues and influencing factors in population health and health services via single-factor analysis and multiple-factor analysis; mathematical modeling analysis to elucidate functional relationships between health services and relevant influencing factors; systematic analysis treating health challenges as interconnected systems to analyze system elements, diagnose the issues, reveal the cause of the issues, and put forward the feasible solution to the issues; input–output analysis, including cost–benefit and cost-effectiveness analyses, to explain the relationship between health service input (health resources) and output (health service utilization); composite evaluation analysis to research on the correlations among population health status, health service needs, health resources, and health service utilization.

Phase II: defining population health objectives. Objective-setting for health resource planning embodies the strategic intent of health administrative departments. The three-stage process adopted by health administrative departments when setting objectives includes outlining the thematic focus (the overall direction), pinpointing priority sectors and putting forward strategic initiatives and specific measures, and establishing core targets (qualitative and quantitative targets) that serve as a basis for post-evaluation according to the baseline level. Therefore, the objectives of health resource planning are hierarchical, forming a system composed of overarching objectives, specific objectives, and targets. The overarching objectives define the long-term orientation and development direction, reflecting the expected health outcomes for the population to be achieved during the planning period. Specific objectives include the characteristics, quality, quantity, time frames, and the population and regions involved. Targets are the concrete embodiment of the objectives and serve as the measures by which the achievement of the objectives are evaluated.

Phase III: assessing health resource needs and setting planning objectives. This step entails understanding the type, volume, timing, and allocation of required resources. When formulating health resource planning, it is necessary to draw from principles like efficiency-driven investment and economically scaled planning, prioritizing existing resources before considering additional allocations, taking into account financial feasibility, respecting the opinions of financial personnel, and developing flexible planning. Then the health resource planning objectives should be determined based on the above assessment. Commonly used calculation methods include health service demand method, health need method, service objective method, and health resources to population ratio method. The 2020 document "National Health Commission Planning Management Measures (Trial)" specifies that the formulation of health and wellness plans should involve fundamental work such as conducting current situation surveys, gathering information, and conducting research studies. It emphasizes the importance of thoroughly investigating major issues, setting priority objectives, proposing significant projects and action measures, and conducting comprehensive evaluations. Preliminary foundational research is crucial for planning, while the development positioning of the planning is a prerequisite for its overall approach.

Phase IV: crafting resource development strategies and implementation steps. Four core strategies—self-reliance, social resource mobilization, financial channel broadening, and optimization of the allocation of existing health resources—are adopted. Implementation measures must detail content, rationale, scope, responsible entities, and timelines.

Phase V: supervision and assessment framework. This phase outlines four key steps: establishing planning implementation and evaluation bodies, defining roles and responsibilities, devising detailed execution plans, and creating assessment and monitoring mechanisms inclusive of defining the content, methodology, timelines, and responsible personnel for the implementation of the health resource planning.

Phase VI: budget presentation. The main considerations for preparing the budget for China's health resource planning are as follows: prioritizing key areas to ensure major objectives and health strategies are met; aligning the budget with local economic development levels, ensuring it does not exceed fiscal and individual payment capacities; conducting cost–benefit and cost-effectiveness analyses, directing more funds towards disease response activities and reserving funds for health resource distribution adjustments; for one-time investment budgets, conducting feasibility studies and considering maintenance costs and personnel salary increases; identifying funding sources, including self-owned funds; developing annual rolling budgets due to the long planning period.

Phase VII: feasibility assessment. After the draft plan for regional health resource planning is formed, it is necessary to organize relevant departments and experts from within and outside the region to review, discuss, and provide feedback on the draft plan. It is also important to communicate the core ideas of the draft plan to the public. A set of feasibility assessment targets should be established to provide experts participating in the evaluation with comparable information. The planning staff should avoid influencing or guiding the experts' opinions as much as possible. The draft plan should be revised, supplemented, and improved based on experts' feedback. If conditions permit, it is advisable to use computer simulations to test the feasibility of the draft plan before making further modifications to form the final draft plan for approval.

Phase VIII: legislative approval. The planning concludes with adherence to legal protocols to have legal effect, which means the draft plan should be passed by the health resource planning leading group, validated by the people's government, and considered and adopted by the standing committees of the people's congresses.

The process underscores the government's accountability, collaborative governance, health sector stewardship, societal engagement, and legal safeguards.

Case Study: The 14th Five-Year Plan for the Construction of China's Health Talent Team

Throughout the duration of the 13th Five-Year Plan, China witnessed a notable rise in both the aggregate and per capita numbers of its health personnel. By the conclusion of 2020, the country was home to 13.48 million health personnel, comprising 4.09 million practitioners and assistant practitioners and 4.71 million registered nurses. To bolster this momentum and reinforce the health talent pipeline, thereby furnishing robust human capital for the Healthy China Initiative, the National Health Commission unveiled the "14th Five-Year Plan for Health Talent Development" in August 2022. The overarching ambition for this plan is threefold: to propel enhancements in talent service capabilities alongside a more balanced talent structure, to refine talent management systems and mechanisms, and to foster a nurturing ecosystem conducive to talent growth. Main planning targets for health talent development during this strategic interval are encapsulated within Table 8.3.

Table 8.3 Main planning targets for health talent development in China during the 14th Five-Year Plan period

Main targets	Unit	2020	2025
Total number of personnel	10,000 people	1347.5	1600
Practitioners and assistant practitioners	People/1000 population	2.90	3.20
Practitioners and assistant practitioners of TCM	People/1000 population	0.48	0.62
Registered nurses	People/1000 population	3.34	3.80
Pharmacists	People/1000 population	0.35	0.54
General practitioners	People/10000 population	2.90	3.93
Professional public health institution personnel	10,000 people	92.5	120

1. **Talent Allocation**

Strengthen the development of health technical professionals. Focusing on the allocation of practitioners and nurses, personnel numbers and composition are calibrated based on health service demands and practitioner workload standards. Expand practitioner ranks to reach 4.5 million practitioners and assistant practitioners by 2025. Reinforce nursing staff to achieve 5.5 million registered nurses by 2025. Elevate pharmacist allocation and training to reach 770,000 pharmacists in medical and health institutions. Bolster technical expertise in medical imaging, laboratory, pathology, etc., and define allocation norms, roles, competencies, and professional standards.

Strengthen the development of public health workforce. By 2025, the number of personnel in professional public health institutions should reach 1.2 million, with 250,000 in disease control and prevention institutions. Set up public health positions scientifically, adjust the structure of senior, intermediate, and junior positions in public health institutions, increase the proportion of intermediate and senior positions, and improve the compensation and benefits of personnel.

Strengthen the development of primary health workforce. Accelerate the training of general practitioners, aiming to reach 550,000 general practitioners by 2025, with 3.93 general practitioners per 10,000 population. Strengthen the development of village clinic workforce, promote the transition of village doctors to practitioners and assistant practitioners, and by 2025, have approximately 45% of village doctors as practitioners or assistant practitioners.

Strengthen the development of TCM workforce. By 2025, the number of practitioners and assistant practitioners of TCM should reach 0.62 per 1000 population, with 150,000 TCM pharmacists nationwide. Establish a talent training model that aligns with the characteristics of TCM, promote TCM talent development through major projects, and implement the TCM Special Talent Training Program (Qihuang Program).

Strengthen the development of workforce to address population aging. Actively respond to population aging and changes in population policy, and meet the health service needs of key groups such as the elderly, pregnant women, and infants. Coordinate the allocation of various talent resources for prevention, medical care, nursing, rehabilitation, and palliative care. Strengthen the development of talent for elderly health services, childcare services, and maternal and child health services.

2. **Talent Cultivation**

Develop a clinical medicine talent training system with "5 + 3" as the main structure and "3 + 2" as the supplement. Improve the on-the-job training system and encourage village doctors to participate in formal education. Increase support for higher medical schools in central and western regions, and reduce disparities in training levels between regions, institutions, and disciplines.

Implement a high-level medical talent program to focus on cultivating a group of leading clinical medicine professionals who work on the front lines of medical care, possess excellent medical skills, and are capable of successfully diagnosing and treating difficult and critical conditions. Additionally, these professionals should have significant scientific value, notable social benefits, substantial social impact, and be recognized by peers. By 2025, the full-time equivalent of 180,000 medical research and development personnel in the health system should reach 180,000 annually. Utilize national high-level young talent programs, medical science and technology innovation platforms, and science and technology projects to foster high-level, innovative, and multi-disciplinary clinical talents and build outstanding young innovation teams. Continue to improve the selection of young and middle-aged experts with outstanding contributions, and categorize high-level talents effectively.

Adapt to changes in disease spectrum and medical service needs by focusing on enhancing the training and development of clinical specialists in critical care, oncology, cardiovascular and cerebrovascular diseases, and other key areas. Prioritize support for diseases with high provincial mortality rates and high referral rates by enhancing technical and talent support from national-level high-quality hospitals to provincial-level hospitals, addressing gaps in specialized disciplines, and improving diagnostic and treatment capabilities at the provincial level. Strengthen the talent development in county-level medical institutions, with a focus on building specialist teams in oncology, cardiovascular, and cerebrovascular fields.

3. **Talent Utilization**

Improve the personnel mechanism for public institutions, and implement open recruitment and competitive appointments. Deepen the reform of the income distribution system in public hospitals, implementing a performance-based approach where more effort leads to more rewards and higher performance results in better compensation. Innovate the management model for public medical and health institutions' staffing, reasonably determine the total number of personnel, and make dynamic adjustments. Explore various personnel mechanisms and government service purchase methods.

Enhance the three-stage medical talent training system, including college education, post-graduate education, and continuing education, with organic connections and standardized norms. Improve medical education quality based on industry demand to balance the supply and demand of medical talents.

Reasonably develop personnel staffing standards for public medical and health institutions and establish a dynamic evaluation and adjustment mechanism. Strengthen talent collaboration between hospitals, primary medical and health institutions, and professional public health institutions. Improve professional title evaluation standards, enhance title management and service methods, adhere to the principle of demand-based use, refine job settings, and clarify job responsibilities, qualification requirements, and competency standards. Expand the autonomy of medical and health institutions in job settings and personnel hiring, optimize the job structure, and increase the proportion of intermediate and senior professional and technical positions.

Establish a sound compensation system suited to the characteristics of the medical and health industry. Improve the income and expenditure structure of public hospitals, increasing the proportion of personnel expenses. Optimize the compensation structure for medical staff, raising the level of guaranteed wages.

Allow public health institutions to exceed current salary control levels for public institutions. Implement performance-based salary policies for primary medical and health institutions to improve the income levels of primary health personnel.

Chapter 9
Health Financing and Total Health Expenditure in China

The contradiction between limited health resources and people's increasing need for health services will always exist. Health financing is not merely about raising funds but also effectively allocating and utilizing them. Securing adequate funds and their effective allocation and utilization is crucial for the efficient operation of the health service system and maximizing its functional effectiveness. Based on its developmental history and current state, China has adopted a government-led, multi-source collaborative financing strategy. According to the *China Health Statistical Yearbook 2022*, in 2021, Chinese total health expenditure was 7684.5 billion yuan, accounting for 6.72% of the GDP. Personal health expenditure accounted for 27.60%, which is below the global average with per capita health expenditure at 5440.0 yuan.

This chapter covers three major areas: health financing in China, allocation and utilization of health funds in China, and total health expenditure.

9.1 Health Financing in China

As previously mentioned, health resources encompass the aggregate of various elements utilized or consumed in the provision of health services, including health human resources and health material resources. Health funds are the monetary expression of health resources, which flows into the health field in monetary form and then achieves its consumption and compensation through various forms of health services, thus flowing out of the health sector and producing the improvement of the health of the population. This process is known as the movement of health funds. In a sense, studying health financing involves examining the patterns of fund movements within the health sector.

Z. Feng et al. (eds.), *China's Health System*, Introduction to China's S&T Innovation,
https://doi.org/10.1007/978-981-95-1205-8_9

9.1.1 Overview of Health Financing

9.1.1.1 The Concept of Health Financing

The World Health Organization defines health financing activities as the total activities of raising, allocating, and utilizing funds for health in a way that is adequate, fair, and efficient. This includes four aspects: how funds are raised for health services, how funds are allocated and how services are organized, how the efficiency of fund utilization is enhanced, and how to control the unreasonable increase of health expenditure. Health financing entails the activities of raising funds for health services and studying the collection, reasonable allocation, and effective utilization of funds within a certain period and social context. It involves fund-raising, risk-sharing, and service purchasing functions. Evaluation of health financing mainly focuses on assessing different financing methods.

9.1.1.2 Objectives of Health Financing

The World Health Organization and United Nations Children's Fund proposed the primary health care (PHC) strategy in the "Declaration of Alma-Ata" in 1978, urging countries to provide their residents with the most basic, universally accessible, socially equitable, and affordable for both the public and the government health care services. The objectives of health financing include both intermediate objectives and ultimate objectives. The intermediate objectives focus on equity, efficiency, risk sharing, and sustainability of health financing, while the ultimate objectives include improving health status, financial risk protection, and patient satisfaction.

9.1.2 Raising of Health Funds in China

9.1.2.1 Health Financing Sources in China

Internationally, sources of health financing are divided into two major categories: public health expenditure and private health expenditure. The former, also known as broad government health expenditure, can be further subdivided into government budget (tax revenue) and social health insurance expenditure, reflecting the role of government organizations and institutions as funding entities in health financing. Private health expenditure refers to funds raised by individuals or their employers through voluntary health insurance or community insurance (not government-sponsored or mandatory), including commercial health insurance expenditure and personal health expenditure; costs incurred by non-governmental health institutions are also included in private health expenditure.

	Category		Specific content	Category	
International health financing sources	Public health expenditure (broad government health expenditure)	Government budget (tax revenue)	Government expenditure on medical services, public health services, health surveillance, etc.	Government health expenditure	Health financing sources in China
		Social health insurance expenditure	Government subsidies for social health insurance1		
			Social health insurance premiums paid by individuals (and their employers)	Social health expenditure	
	Private health expenditure	Commercial health insurance expenditure	Commercial health insurance premiums		
		Other non-governmental organization expenditure	Non- governmental organization health expenditures and social donations, etc.		
		Personal health expenditure	Residents' cash payments when receiving medical and health services	Personal health expenditure	

Fig. 9.1 Comparison of health financing sources in China with international health financing sources. *Note* 1 refers to basic medical insurance for urban employees and basic medical insurance for rural and non-working urban residents. *Source Health Systems in Transition* by Meng et al., 2015

In China, government health expenditure, social health expenditure, and personal health expenditure are the three main sources of total health expenditure. Government health expenditure includes expenses at all government levels for medical and health services (including medical services and public health services), medical insurance administrative affairs, and other government investments in the medical and health sector. Social health expenditure refers to contributions to health from all sectors of society excluding government spending, including social medical security payments (excluding government subsidies), commercial health insurance premiums, social donations, fees from privately-run medical institutions, and administrative and public service fee revenue. Personal health expenditure refers to cash payments made by residents when receiving various medical and health services. Fig. 9.1 shows a comparison of health financing sources in China with international health financing sources, and Fig. 9.2 illustrates changes in the structure of health financing in China from 2000 to 2021.

9.1.2.2 Chinese Statutory Health Financing System

Chinese statutory health financing system covers basic medical insurance, medical assistance and disease emergency assistance systems, public health systems, and major illness insurance for urban and rural residents. Among them, basic medical

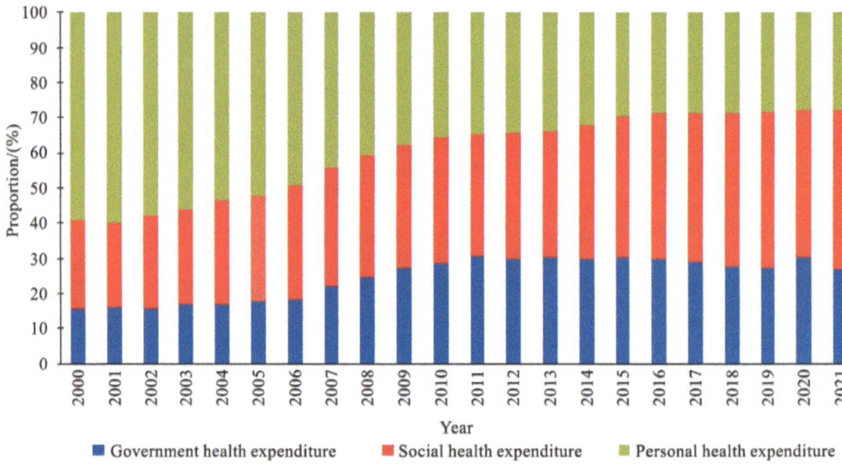

Fig. 9.2 Changes in the structure of health financing in China from 2000 to 2021. Source China Health Statistical Yearbook 2022

insurance and the medical assistance system together form the basic medical security system covering both urban and rural residents. Specifically, employees in urban areas are covered by basic medical insurance for urban employees, while non-working urban residents and rural residents are covered by basic medical insurance for rural and non-working urban residents. The medical assistance and disease emergency assistance systems act as a safety net for impoverished populations in urban and rural areas, subsidizing the cost of basic medical insurance and providing further aid for medical expenses not covered by basic medical insurance after reimbursement. The public health systems are primarily funded by the governments and offer basic public health services free of charge to all residents. The major illness insurance for urban and rural residents is an institutional arrangement that provides further protection against high medical costs incurred by patients with serious illnesses. Table 9.1 provides an overview of Chinese statutory health financing system.

9.2 Allocation and Utilization of Health Funds in China

Once health funds have been mobilized, the next task is how they are utilized and for whom, which determines who has access to health services, what type of health services are accessed, and the quantity and quality of health services. Governments need to consider in which institutions to invest, and for which services within an institution they should invest. The question of how to fulfil the functions of health financing to promote effective service delivery in the health service system and the improvement of the overall health of the population is not only a question in the field of economics, but also, to a large extent, a political, social and ethical one.

Table 9.1 Overview of Chinese statutory health financing system

System		Coverage			Financing		Utilization of funds	
		Scope (population)	Breadth (services)[a]	Depth (costs)[b]	Government health expenditure	Social insurance fees	Fiscal transfer payments	Health insurance funds[a]
Basic medical insurance	Basic medical insurance for urban employees	Urban employees	Inpatient, outpatient, and retail drug costs at designated institutions	There are starting payment criteria, co-payment and maximum payment limits for eligible fees listed on the insurance medicines / medical service/ diagnostic and treatment items catalog		Individuals and employers jointly bear at least 2% and 6% of employee wages, respectively		Individual accounts + social pooling funds
	Basic medical insurance for rural and non-working urban residents[b]	Non-working urban residents (including students) and rural residents	Mainly inpatient, whereas outpatient services are also covered in eligible areas		√	Premiums paid by individuals and government subsidies	√	Social pooling funds
Medical assistance and disease emergency assistance systems		Impoverished population			√		√	
Public health systems		All residents			√		√	
Major illness insurance for urban and rural residents						√		Major illness insurance social pooling funds

Notes [a]Indicates differences exist between regions and medical insurance systems
[b]Is managed and subsidized by central and local governments. Despite its voluntary nature, it is essentially considered a public or social insurance, hence included under social health expenditure
Source: *Health Systems in Transition* by Meng et al., 2015

9.2.1 *Overview of Allocation and Utilization of Health Funds*

The allocation of health funds involves scientifically and rationally optimizing the allocation of health funds through government macro-control and market regulation, ultimately directing them towards various sectors of the health service system. The structure of health fund allocation describes where health resources ultimately flow, including which institutions, projects, or regions. The main users of health funds include hospitals, community health institutions, and public health institutions, which are both payees of health funds and providers of health services. Expenditures take various forms, such as diagnostic and treatment fees, inspection fees, medication fees, health education fees, preventive care fees, and construction fees of public health emergency response institutions.

9.2.2 *Structure of Health Fund Allocation in China*

9.2.2.1 Integration of Health Funds in China

1. Fiscal Transfer Payments

In 1994, China established a tax-sharing fiscal management system and a corresponding transfer payment system. There are two basic types of transfer payments: general transfer payments and special transfer payments. The Central Committee of the Communist Party of China issues general transfer payments to ensure funding for welfare sectors like education and social security. Special transfer payments are allocated by the Central Committee of the Communist Party of China to achieve specific policy goals and development strategies, or to compensate local governments for delegated tasks, with local finances required to utilize the funds according to specified purposes.

2. Medical Insurance Funds

China manages its two major basic medical insurance funds separately, settling accounts with medical institutions within designated pooling areas. These funds are centrally managed by medical insurance administrative institutions and are uniformly adjusted to cover expenses such as medication fees, surgery fees, nursing fees, and basic diagnostic fees for insured individuals. Medical insurance management departments in these pooling areas annually prepare budget forecasts for revenue and expenditure. Revenue budgets consider factors such as local economic development, wage levels, insurance coverage, and financing ratios. Expenditure budgets take into account the age structure of the insured, disease spectrum, growth in medical costs, benefit coverage, security levels, and fund balances.

The basic medical insurance for urban employees implements the management of designated medical institutions and retail pharmacies. Individual accounts can be used to cover the individual's share of general outpatient expenses and hospitalization costs, and drugs purchased at designated retail pharmacies. They may also be used to cover eligible medical expenses for family members who have been linked through the family pooling system. The social pooling funds pay for inpatient medical expenses, outpatient treatment for serious illnesses that comply with regulations, and gradually included general outpatient expenses. Medical expenses below the deductible are paid from individual accounts or out-of-pocket; costs above the deductible and below the maximum payment limit are primarily paid by social pooling funds, with the individual bearing a certain percentage. The specific deductible, maximum payment limit, and the individual's share of expenses between these thresholds of social pooling funds are determined by the pooling area. In China, there are different provisions for different levels of medical institutions in the setting of the deductible. Typically, first-level hospitals have the lowest deductibles, followed by second-level hospitals, with third-level hospitals having the highest. A similar trend exists for co-payment ratios, with first-level hospitals having the lowest co-payment rates (highest reimbursement rates), thus encouraging patients to seek treatment at appropriate levels and utilize health resources efficiently.

The national basic medical insurance drug catalog, diagnosis and treatment item catalog, and medical service facility catalog, along with respective management methods, define the scope and standards for basic medical services. The national basic medical insurance drug catalog is divided into Class A and Class B. Class A drugs, which are uniformly standardized across China, are included in the basic medical insurance fund's payment scope and are reimbursed according to the payment standards of the basic medical insurance. Class B drugs, where the insurance fund covers part of the cost, require the patient to pay a certain proportion of the expenses before being included in the insurance fund's payment scope and reimbursed according to the payment standards of the basic medical insurance. The "National Basic Medical Insurance, Work Injury Insurance, and Maternity Insurance Drug List (2022)" includes a total of 2967 drugs, consisting of 1586 Western medicines and 1381 Chinese patent medicines.

3. Medical Assistance Fund

Medical assistance is financed through government appropriations and social donations, catering to the different medical needs of the assisted individuals. Medical assistance includes subsidizing the individual contribution to basic medical insurance for rural and non-working urban residents and further subsidizing unaffordable out-of-pocket expenses for individuals and their families that remain after payments from basic medical insurance, major illness insurance, and other supplementary insurance. Members of urban and rural low-income households, households enjoying "five guarantees" and other registered impoverished residents automatically qualify for medical assistance. Using relevant documentation, they only need to pay the out-of-pocket part at designated medical institutions, with the rest covered by medical assistance fund and settled immediately with the institutions. Unregistered eligible beneficiaries must initially pay the full medical costs and later apply for reimbursement from civil affairs departments.

4. Disease Emergency Assistance Fund

Since 2013, provincial-level and municipal-level governments in China have been establishing disease emergency assistance fund at their respective levels, encouraging contributions from all sectors of society. The fund aids patients within China suffering from acute, severe illnesses or injuries who need emergency care but cannot pay and whose identities may be unknown. For eligible emergency treatment expenses, medical institutions can apply for subsidies from the disease emergency assistance fund, which implements direct payment. Fund management institutions review and summarize payment applications from medical institutions before submitting them to the corresponding financial departments for disbursement from social security funds directly to the medical institutions.

9.2.2.2 Services Purchased with Health Funds in China

1. Basic Medical Services

According to the regulations of basic medical insurance, patients can only receive reimbursements from the medical insurance fund when they seek treatment at designated medical institutions or pharmacies. Patients use their social security cards to directly claim reimbursements from the fund. At non-designated institutions or pharmacies, insured individuals can receive medical services at their own expense.

Basic medical insurance involves setting deductibles, co-payment ratios, and maximum payment limits to share medical costs with patients. For service providers, medical insurance institutions implement prior approvals, concurrent reviews, and post-use audits to reduce unnecessary services provided by medical institutions. Some regions have experimented with payment methods such as service unit, capitation, and total budget control to grant medical institutions greater financial autonomy. Medical insurance administrative institutions manage designated medical institutions and retail pharmacies through the establishment and implementation of designated service agreements. These agreements regulate the management of designated medical institutions and retail pharmacies and clarify the rights and obligations of these institutions and pharmacies and the medical insurance administrative agencies.

2. Public Health Services

Government and community-driven medical and health institutions that meet certain standards and requirements and have the requisite service capabilities can apply to provide public health services. To ensure that residents in the same area have access to essentially equal public health services, local governments and relevant departments determine the public health services for their jurisdiction as the content of government service purchase based on local economic and social development, fiscal payment capacity, and residents' basic public health needs. Individual public health services, such as immunization plans, may be funded by calculating the per capita cost of service recipients to determine fixed subsidies per unit. Group public health services, such as health education, may have their comprehensive costs

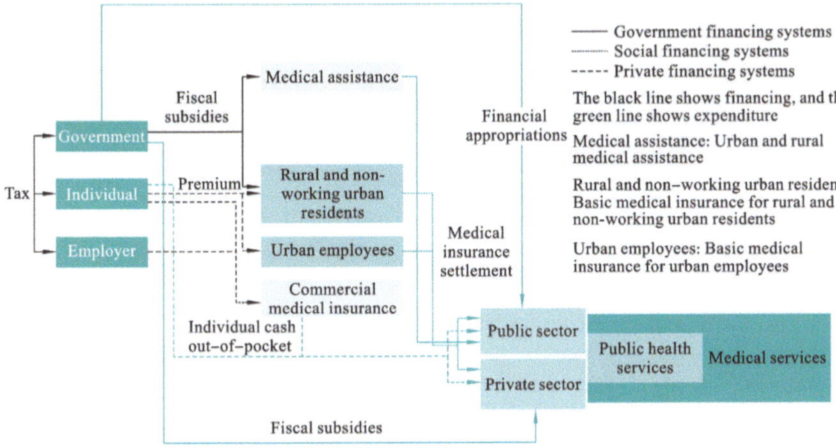

Fig. 9.3 The flow of health funds in China

calculated to set comprehensive project subsidies or package all public health service projects into a single comprehensive project subsidy.

The flow of health funds in China is illustrated in Fig. 9.3.

9.2.3 Main Users of Health Funds in China

9.2.3.1 Medical Institutions

In China, the financing of public health services is primarily through fiscal appropriations from local health departments, which are distributed based on capitation. Some paid service items are directly charged to the users (such as flu vaccines, which are not included in the national basic public health services). For some primary health care services and emergency services, public medical institutions may receive partial budget allocations from local health departments and charge patients based on service items. If the patient is insured, local medical insurance funds settle accounts with the institutions using mixed payment methods. In terms of medical cost settlement, the service recipient (patient) pays according to service items, and this payment method is also applied to basic medical insurance fund payments, as shown in Table 9.2.

In 2011, the Ministry of Human Resources and Social Security released the "Opinions of the Ministry of Human Resources and Social Security on Further Advancing the Reform of Medical Insurance Payment Methods," which outlined the current objectives of the payment method reform as follows: to enhance total budget control through the management of fund budgets and to explore the payment method of globe budget. Building on this foundation, the reform seeks to explore capitation in conjunction with the implementation of outpatient pooling, and DRGs in conjunction

Table 9.2 Payment mechanisms for providers

Provider	Payer				
	Local government	Local social medical insurance fund[a]	Private/ commercial medical insurance	Cost sharing	Direct payment
Primary public medical institutions	Subsidy	Mixed payment[b] (globe budget, capitation, fixed quota, fee-for-service, etc.)	Fee-for-service	Fee-for-service	Fee-for-service
Second-level and third-level public medical institutions	Subsidy	Mixed payment[b] (globe budget, fee-for-service, etc.)	Fee-for-service	Fee-for-service	Fee-for-service
Private medical institutions	None	Mixed payment[b]/none	Fee-for-service	Fee-for-service	Fee-for-service
Retail pharmacies	None	Fee-for-service	None	Fee-for-service	Fee-for-service
Public health service institutions or medical institutions providing preventive services	Subsidy	None/ fee-for-service	None/ fee-for-service	None/ Fee-for-service	Fee-for-service for paid services

Notes [a]Typically includes capitation for outpatient services, service unit for inpatient services, with both globe budget and fee-for-service applicable to both outpatient and inpatient services
[b]Refers to the use of mixed payment methods for different service types under a medical insurance system (e.g., capitation for outpatient services, globe budget for inpatient services)
Source: *Health System in Transition* by Meng et al., 2015

with the security offered for major diseases in both inpatient and outpatient settings. The plan involves establishing and improving the negotiation and consultation mechanisms between medical insurance administrative institutions and medical institutions, along with risk-sharing mechanisms, to gradually develop a payment system that aligns with the evolution of the basic medical insurance system, emphasizing both incentives and constraints.

9.2.3.2 Medical Staff

In China, medical staff, as employees of hospitals, have their salaries and benefits closely tied to the medical institutions they work for, with human resource costs primarily compensated through service revenues. Beyond the basic salary, workload has historically been a major criterion for assessing medical staff's bonus income. Theoretically, performance metrics, patient satisfaction, and the completion rate of medical insurance indicators have been progressively included in evaluations, significantly impacting the bonus income of medical staff. With the advancement of health system reforms, the "Opinions of the Central Committee of the Communist Party of China and the State Council on Deepening the Reforms of the Medical and Health System" proposed implementing a comprehensive performance appraisal and job performance wage system focusing primarily on service quality and workload to effectively motivate medical staff.

Starting from October 1, 2009, public health institutions and primary medical and health institutions in China began implementing performance wage reforms, with the full implementation of the performance wage system by 2010. Central and local governments provide fiscal subsidies for the reform of the performance wage system. Performance wages are divided into two parts: basic performance wages and bonus performance wages. Basic performance wages, constituting about 60% to 70% of the total performance wages, reflect factors such as regional economic development, price levels, and job responsibilities, and are generally issued monthly. Bonus performance wages primarily reflect workload and actual contributions and are disbursed based on assessment results, allowing for flexible distribution methods and approaches. Depending on the circumstances, performance wages may include position allowances and comprehensive goal assessment rewards. Over the long term, the setting of performance wages helps to curb excessive prescribing and other irrational medical behaviors, enhancing efficiency, service quality, and patient satisfaction. However, the negative effects of performance wages cannot be overlooked, as it could erode trust between colleagues and weaken team cohesion.

9.3 Total Health Expenditure

9.3.1 Overview of Total Health Expenditure

Total health expenditure is a comprehensive monetary measure used to reflect the total amount of financial resources raised by the whole society for health services within a specific period (typically one year) in a country or region. It includes recurrent health expenditures and fixed capital formation costs. Recurrent health expenditures represent the monetary value of all medical and health products and services ultimately consumed by residents within the accounting period. Fixed capital formation costs refer to the value of assets acquired by health service providers (net of the disposal value of similar assets) within the accounting period, which are repeatedly used or have a useful life of more than one year in the provision of health services.

Total health expenditure is a societal concept, encapsulating all health care spending by the whole society, including internal expenditures within the health sector as well as those by other units and individuals. It also includes gratuitous aid and donations to the health sector from various community groups and international organizations. Total health expenditure serves as an informational tool capable of effectively analyzing and evaluating the equity and efficiency of a nation's or health system's performance, providing crucial information and objective evidence for government health policy decisions.

9.3.2 Health Expenditure Accounting

The System of Health Accounts (SHA) aligns with the principles and systems of national economic accounting, targeting the entire health system to establish health expenditure accounting indicators and an accounting framework, specifically to study the financial operations within the health system. SHA allows for the calculation of a country or region's health expenditures and guides the accounting of sub-accounts in health, such as disease expenditures, expenditures by different age groups, public health expenditures, and pharmaceutical expenditures.

SHA divides the dimensions of health expenditure accounting into core and extended dimensions based on the funding, production, and consumption phases of medical and health services. Core dimensions include service functions, service providers, and financing schemes, addressing three fundamental questions: what types of medical and health products and services are consumed, which health service providers deliver these products and services, and which financing schemes compensate for these products and services. The funding phase of the extended dimensions further clarifies where the funds for the funding schemes originate and how they are raised. The production phase addresses the resource costs and capital investments consumed by health service providers in producing medical and health products and services, while the consumption phase answers who consumes the medical and health products and services, including the distribution of health expenditures by disease, age, gender, region, and economic status. Health expenditure accounting methods include source-based method, institution-based method, function-based method, expenditure-based method, and matrix balancing accounting method, with adjustments made by countries based on their existing systems and health policy analysis needs. The SHA2011 accounting framework is shown in Fig. 9.4.

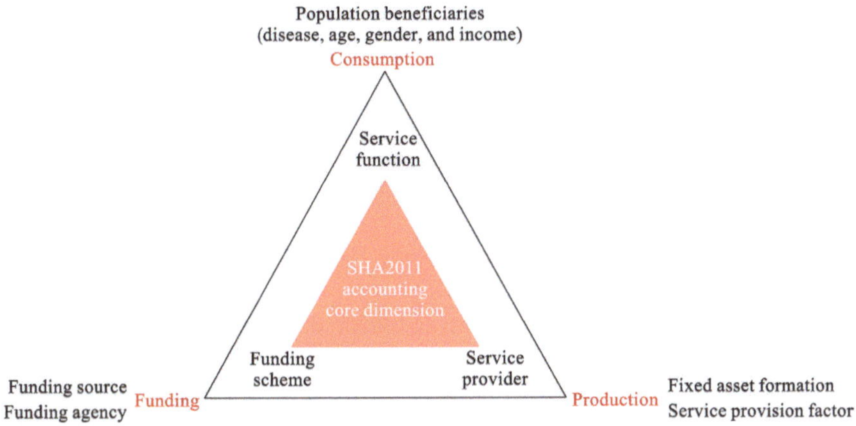

Fig. 9.4 The SHA2011 accounting framework

9.3.3 Total Health Expenditure in China

In 2021, the total funding for health expenditure in China reached 7684.5 billion yuan, accounting for 6.72% of the GDP. The per capita health expenditure was 5440.0 yuan. According to the classification of financing, in 2021, the government health expenditure was 2067.6 billion yuan, accounting for 26.91% of the total health expenditure; social health expenditure was 3496.33 billion yuan, accounting for 45.50% of the total health expenditure; personal health expenditure reached 2120.57 billion yuan, making up 27.60% of the total health expenditure.

From 1980 to 2021, the average annual growth rate of Chinese total health expenditure was 16.57%; the proportion of total health expenditure relative to GDP increased from 3.15% to 6.72%, with an average annual growth rate of 1.87%.

Over the same period, the share of government health expenditure in total health expenditure decreased from 36.24% to 26.91%; social health expenditure's share increased from 42.57% to 45.50%; personal health expenditure's share rose from 21.19% to 27.60%.

The basic information of Chinese total health expenditure from 1980 to 2021 is shown in Table 9.3.

Table 9.3 Chinese total health expenditure from 1980 to 2021

Year	Total health expenditure (100 million yuan)				Composition of total health expenditure (%)			Urban and rural health expenditure (100 million yuan)		Per capita health expenditure (yuan)			Total health expenditure as a percentage of GDP (%)
	Total	Government health expenditure	Social health expenditure	Personal health expenditure	Government health expenditure	Social health expenditure	Personal health expenditure	Urban	Rural	Total	Urban	Rural	
1980	143.23	51.91	60.97	30.35	36.24	42.57	21.19			14.5			3.15
1985	279.00	107.65	91.96	79.39	38.58	32.96	28.46			26.4			3.09
1990	747.39	187.28	293.10	267.01	25.06	39.22	35.73	396.00	351.39	65.4	158.8	38.8	3.96
1995	2155.13	387.34	767.81	999.98	17.97	35.63	46.40	1239.50	915.63	177.9	401.3	112.9	3.51
2000	4586.63	709.52	1171.94	2705.17	15.47	25.55	58.98	2624.24	1962.39	361.9	813.7	214.7	4.57
2005	8659.91	1552.53	2586.41	4520.98	17.93	29.87	52.21	6305.57	2354.34	662.3	1126.4	315.8	4.62
2006	9843.34	1778.86	3210.92	4853.56	18.07	32.62	49.31	7174.73	2668.61	748.8	1248.3	361.9	4.49
2007	11,573.97	2581.58	3893.72	5098.66	22.31	33.64	44.05	8968.70	2605.27	876.0	1516.3	358.1	4.29
2008	14,535.40	3593.94	5065.60	5875.86	24.73	34.85	40.42	11,251.90	3283.50	1094.5	1861.8	455.2	4.55
2009	17,541.92	4816.26	6154.49	6571.16	27.46	35.08	37.46	13,535.61	4006.31	1314.3	2176.6	562.0	5.03
2010	19,980.39	5732.49	7196.61	7051.29	28.69	36.02	35.29	15,508.62	4471.77	1490.1	2315.5	666.3	4.85
2011	24,345.91	7464.18	8416.45	8465.28	30.66	34.57	34.80	18,571.87	5774.04	1804.5	2697.5	879.4	4.99
2012	28,119.00	8431.98	10,030.70	9656.32	29.99	35.67	34.34	21,280.46	6838.54	2068.8	2999.3	1064.8	5.22
2013	31,668.95	9545.81	11,393.79	10,729.34	30.10	36.00	33.90	23,644.95	8024.00	2316.2	3234.1	1274.4	5.34
2014	35,312.40	10,579.23	13,437.75	11,295.41	29.96	38.05	31.99	26,575.60	8736.80	2565.5	3558.3	1412.2	5.49
2015	40,974.64	12,475.28	16,506.71	11,992.65	30.45	40.29	29.27	31,297.85	9676.79	2962.2	4058.5	1603.6	5.95
2016	46,344.88	13,910.31	19,096.68	13,337.90	30.01	41.21	28.78	35,458.01	10,886.87	3328.6	4471.5	1846.1	6.21
2017	52,598.28	15,205.87	22,258.81	15,133.60	28.91	42.32	28.77			3756.7			6.32

(continued)

Table 9.3 (continued)

Year	Total health expenditure (100 million yuan)				Composition of total health expenditure (%)			Urban and rural health expenditure (100 million yuan)		Per capita health expenditure (yuan)			Total health expenditure as a percentage of GDP (%)
	Total	Government health expenditure	Social health expenditure	Personal health expenditure	Government health expenditure	Social health expenditure	Personal health expenditure	Urban	Rural	Total	Urban	Rural	
2018	59,121.91	16,399.13	25,810.78	16,911.99	27.74	43.66	28.61			4206.7			6.43
2019	65,841.39	18,016.95	29,150.57	18,673.87	27.36	44.27	28.36			4669.3			6.67
2020	72,175.00	21,941.90	30,273.67	19,959.43	30.40	41.94	27.65			5111.1			7.12
2021	76,844.99	20,676.06	34,963.26	21,205.67	26.91	45.50	27.60			5440.0			6.72

Notes [a]This table shows accounting figures, and figures of 2021 are the preliminary accounting figures
[b]The figures are calculated on the prices of the indicated years
[c]Since 2001, the total health expenditure does not include funds for higher medical education, and since 2006, it includes funds for urban and rural medical assistance
Source: *China Health Statistical Yearbook 2022*

Chapter 10
Legal System and Supervision of Medicine and Health in China

Medical and health services are closely related to the health of billions of people and the well-being of countless households, making themselves a significant issue of people's livelihood. Deepening the medical and health system reform, accelerating the development of medical and health services, strengthening the construction of the legal system and supervision of medicine and health, adapting to the growing medicine and health demand of the people, and continuously improving the health quality of the people are inevitable requirements for implementing the Scientific Outlook on Development and promoting comprehensive, balanced, and sustainable economic and social development. They are also crucial measures to safeguard social fairness and justice, and enhance people's quality of life, and an important task in building a moderately prosperous society in all respects and a harmonious socialist society.

10.1 Overview of China's Legal System for Medicine and Health

10.1.1 Concept and Characteristics of China's Legal System for Medicine and Health

The legal system for medicine and health in China refers to the total of legal norms that regulate various social relationships arising from citizens' health affairs. As an important component of China's legal system, it has the general properties of laws, such as normativity, state compulsion, state will, universality, and justifiability, as well as its own unique characteristics.

Z. Feng et al. (eds.), *China's Health System*, Introduction to China's S&T Innovation,
https://doi.org/10.1007/978-981-95-1205-8_10

10.1.1.1 Legislative Characteristics of China's Legal System for Medicine and Health

As China's health legal system gradually improves, the country's legal system for medicine and health has gradually become an essential component of the socialist legal system. First, China's legal system for medicine and health is constantly being refined and perfected around the core content of citizens' health rights and interests, demonstrating strong professionalism, scientific rigor, and technical expertise. Second, problem-oriented system improvement has become a new characteristic of China's legal system for medicine and health. As the systems at the level of health laws and administrative regulations tend to stabilize, the implementation of China's legal system for medicine and health and the issues arising from its implementation, as well as the revisions and even legislation driven by the feedback of implementation effects, have become the main topics in the construction of China's legal system for medicine and health. Additionally, significant progress has been made in the legal construction of TCM in China, elevating it to the level of a national development strategy and moving towards modernization.

10.1.1.2 Enforcement Characteristics of China's Legal System for Medicine and Health

First, the implementation of China's legal system for medicine and health are distinctly policy-oriented. Various specific measures are issued in the form of policies, and overall planning and special actions are implemented through policy methods. Second, the implementation of this system is grounded in the standard system. As an essential component of China's legal system for medicine and health, medical and health standards provide guidance for the implementation of this system. Third, the legal construction of China's drug regulatory system has been steadily advancing, and the overall objectives of it are gradually being implemented. Fourth, anti-monopoly efforts in China's pharmaceutical sector continue to escalate. The National Development and Reform Commission has gradually increased its law enforcement efforts against horizontal monopoly issues in the medicine and health sector. Fifth, China is actively building a working mechanism to connect drug administrative law enforcement with criminal justice, aiming to combat drug-related crimes and violations.

10.1.1.3 Judicial Characteristics of China's Legal System for Medicine and Health

First, judicial interpretations enhance the guidance of relevant laws. Second, judicial authorities severely combat drug-related crimes and offenses, establish institutionalized and normalized accountability mechanisms, and accelerate the construction of medical dispute early warning and response mechanisms. Third, judicial authorities attach great importance to the guiding role of typical case judgments. Guiding cases, typical cases, and others are published for reference in related cases, thus providing judicial guidance for the law enforcement and supervision of the legal system for medicine and health.

10.1.2 Basic Principles of China's Legal System for Medicine and Health

The basic principles of China's legal system for medicine and health are the overarching rules that guide and regulate the development of medicine and health law, including legislation, law enforcement, and judicial activities. Even when the law does not regulate certain health affairs, it should also play a role in guiding, regulating, and restricting such affairs. The basic principles of China's legal system for medicine and health include the following three aspects.

10.1.2.1 Safeguarding Citizens' Health

The purpose of medical and health laws and regulations across different departments and levels is to safeguard citizens' health. The right to health is one of the fundamental human rights, recognized and protected by the Constitution of China. The constitutional right to health can be specified through legislation on basic medical health and health promotion into citizens' rights to access public health service resources and basic medical service guarantees. Its manifestations include the right to basic medical services, the right to medical security, the right to medical assistance, and the right to emergency medical treatment.

10.1.2.2 Government Leadership

China's Constitution clearly states the government's basic obligation to provide medical and health services. The Law of the People's Republic of China on Basic Medical and Health Care and the Promotion of Health released in 2019 clarifies the overall government's leadership responsibility, mainly manifested in the government's investment in the establishment of public hospitals at all levels, the development of medical education, the establishment of social medical insurance system, the free provision of basic public health services and the provision of medical assistance to needy people. However, government leadership does not mean that the government shoulders everything. China adheres to the principle of combining government leadership and market-oriented mechanisms.

10.1.2.3 Putting Disease Prevention First

In accordance with the law of disease development and to improve the efficiency of the utilization of medical and health resources, China adheres to the principle of putting disease prevention first and combining prevention with treatment in the field of health. Its connotation includes national health investment tilted towards health care, emphasizing pre-risk control and prevention, establishing a sensitive mechanism for disease risk prediction, control and prevention, and so on.

10.1.3 Origin and Development of China's Legal System for Medicine and Health

It is widely believed that the earliest recorded evidence of ancient Chinese medicine and health law can be traced back to the Yin and Shang dynasties. In books such as *Han Fei Zi*, *The Book of Change*, *Spring and Autumn Annals*, *Rites of Zhou*, and *Zuo's Commentary*, there are ancient records of the importance placed on healthy descendants. *Rites of Zhou* extensively records medical management systems, including the organizations managing medicine, medical record-keeping, and physician assessment systems. Since the Tang and Song dynasties, health legislation has become more detailed. The *Tang Code* contains many provisions related to medicine and health, with criminal legal provisions for medical malpractice, fraud, dispensing errors, and harm caused by medicine, as well as regulations in the areas of food hygiene and health management. During the Song Dynasty, a specialized pharmaceutical agency was established to manage pharmaceutical affairs within and outside the palace, and a national pharmacy bureau was opened. In the period of the Republic of China, health legislation became specialized and specific, with regulations such as the "Regulations on the Prevention of Infectious Diseases" and the Medical Practitioners Law. After the founding of the People's Republic of China, the development of China's legal system for medicine and health went through four phases.

The first phase: from the founding of the People's Republic of China to the promulgation of the first Constitution in 1954. China attached great importance to the construction of health undertakings and the health legal system. Many health regulations were established to promote the development of medical and health services and safeguard the physical health of citizens. Apart from the "Common Program of the Chinese People's Political Consultative Conference," which served as a temporary constitution, a series of laws and regulations were issued, including the "Regulations on Health Organizations of the Central People's Government," the "Interim Measures for Inoculation," the "Provisional Regulations on the Management of Narcotic Drugs," and the "Interim Measures for Traffic Quarantine," marking the beginning of the development of China's legal system for medicine and health.

The second phase: from the promulgation of the first Constitution of China in 1954 to the eve of the reform and opening-up in 1978. Under the guidance of the

Constitution, China successively promulgated a large number of laws and regulations related to medicine and health, such as the "Interim Measures for the Health and Epidemic Prevention Stations and Organizational Structure Regulations for Health and Epidemic Prevention Stations at All Levels" issued by the Ministry of Health in 1954, the "Management Measures for Infectious Diseases" issued by the Ministry of Health in 1955, the "Safety and Health Regulations for Factories" issued by the State Council in 1956, the "Frontier Health and Quarantine Regulations of the People's Republic of China" issued by the Standing Committee of the National People's Congress in 1957, the "Some Provisions on Strengthening Drug Administration" jointly issued by the Ministry of Health and other ministries in 1963, and the "Provisional Regulations on the Management of Poisonous Drugs and Restriction of Highly Toxic Drugs" jointly issued by the Ministry of Health and other ministries in 1964.

The third phase: from the beginning of the reform and opening-up in 1978 to 2013. The Constitution of the People's Republic of China in 1982 explicitly stipulated "developing medical and health services" and "protecting the health of the people," providing a constitutional basis for the legal system of medicine and health. Since then, the Standing Committee of the National People's Congress had successively enacted laws such as the Drug Administration Law of the People's Republic of China, the Frontier Health and Quarantine Law of the People's Republic of China, and the Food Hygiene Law of the People's Republic of China. At the same time, there were a lot of health administrative regulations approved and issued by the State Council, such as the "Measures for the Control of Narcotic Drugs," the "Measures for the Control of Psychotropic Drugs," and the "Regulations on the Handling of Medical Accidents." During this period, the health administrative departments formulated and issued thousands of health regulations and normative documents. Local health legislation was also relatively common.

The fourth phase: from 2014 to the present. The legislation in this phase is a deepened development of the third phase and a proactive adjustment made under the guiding ideology of comprehensively promoting the construction of a healthy and law-based China. The focus of legislation is to strengthen the legal construction in health, while ensuring traditional medical and health services, and enhance the legal construction and supervision in the field of medical devices. In 2019, the Standing Committee of the National People's Congress enacted the Law of the People's Republic of China on Basic Medical and Health Care and the Promotion of Health, ending the situation in which the development of medical and health care and the guarantee of basic medical and health care services for citizens had no legal basis, giving the health sector of China its own "basic law."

10.2 Main Components of China's Legal System for Medicine and Health

Due to China's vast territory and varying levels of development across different regions, coupled with the extensive and complex nature of health activities, the adjustment of health legal relations relies not only on laws but also on administrative regulations, departmental rules, local laws and other normative documents. Even at specific implementation levels, a large number of normative documents are needed as supplements. These documents vary in rank and have different effects. The legal system for medicine and health in China is centered on the right to health and can be divided into three parts based on different objects: public health legal system, medical legal system, and medical security legal system. These laws, regulations, and normative documents basically cover all aspects involved in the development of China's health undertakings, including public health, disease prevention and treatment, medical administration, pharmaceutical administration, and other fields.

10.2.1 Public Health Legal System

10.2.1.1 Legal System for Prevention and Treatment of Infectious Diseases

The law on the prevention and treatment of infectious diseases is formulated and promulgated by the state, and its implementation is guaranteed by the state's coercive power. It regulates the various social relations arising from the efforts of the state, government, social organizations and citizens in the prevention, control, and elimination of the occurrence and prevalence of infectious diseases, as well as the protection of human health and public health activities. In February 1989, China promulgated the Law of the People's Republic of China on Prevention and Treatment of Infectious Diseases. This law was revised in August 2004, providing clear and specific provisions on the policies and principles for the prevention and treatment of infectious diseases, prevention of infectious diseases, epidemic reporting, notification and announcement, epidemic control, medical treatment, supervision and management, safeguard measures, and legal responsibilities. It serves as an important legal basis and fundamental guideline for standardizing and institutionalizing the control and prevention of infectious diseases.

10.2.1.2 Legal System for Public Health Emergency Response

The public health emergencies refer to the unexpected and sudden public health events that cause or may cause significant harm to the health of the general public. These events include major infectious disease outbreaks, outbreaks of diseases of unknown origin, severe food poisoning and occupational poisoning, and other public health incidents that severely affect the physical and mental health of the public. In May 2003, the State Council issued the "Regulations on Preparedness for and Response to Public Health emergencies." It summarizes the lessons learned from the prevention and treatment of SARS and establishes institutional arrangements for the scope and specific content of public health emergency management. It further institutionalizes the rapid response mechanism for dealing with public health emergencies from a legal perspective and strengthens corresponding responsibilities. In August 2007, the 29th Session of the Standing Committee of the 10th National People's Congress passed the Emergency Response Law of the People's Republic of China, which provides clear provisions on prevention, emergency preparedness, monitoring and early warning, emergency response and rescue, post-incident recovery and reconstruction, and other activities related to the response to emergencies. This law, together with the "Regulation on Preparedness for and Response to Public Health emergencies" and relevant departmental regulations, constitutes a relatively comprehensive legislative system for dealing with public health emergencies in China.

10.2.1.3 Legal System for Mental Health

In China, the definition of mental health has both narrow and broad senses. Narrowly speaking, mental health specifically refers to the prevention, diagnosis, treatment, and rehabilitation of mental disorders. Broadly speaking, in addition to the above-mentioned activities, it also includes the promotion of mental health and corresponding safeguard measures. In October 2012, the 29th Session of the Standing Committee of the 11th National People's Congress passed the Mental Health Law of the People's Republic of China. This law is a legal instrument that regulates the treatment of patients with mental disorders, safeguards their legitimate rights and interests, and promotes their recovery. It is a compilation of legal norms that govern the various social relations arising from the efforts of the state, government, social organizations, and citizens in maintaining and enhancing mental health, preventing and treating mental disorders, promoting the recovery of patients with mental disorders, and safeguarding human health. It was officially implemented in May 2013.

10.2.2 Medical Legal System

10.2.2.1 Legal System for Medical Institution Management

Currently, in terms of medical institution management in China, there are two main legislative models: specialized legislation and comprehensive legislation. Specialized legislation primarily involves formulating administrative regulations, rules, and other normative documents, such as the "Regulations on the Administration of Medical Institutions" and the "Implementation Details of the Regulations on the Administration of Medical Institutions," which clearly stipulate matters related to the nature, purpose, planning and approval, registration, practice, and supervision of medical institutions. These two documents are the core legal documents governing the management of medical institutions. The regulations on medical institution management are not only supported by specialized legislative documents, but also scattered throughout other comprehensive legislative documents, such as the Drug Administration Law of the People's Republic of China and the Law of the People's Republic of China on the Prevention and Treatment of Occupational Diseases, which contain relevant legal provisions concerning the management of medical institutions.

10.2.2.2 Legal System for Medical Practice Management

Medical practice refers to the services provided by medical professionals utilizing their specialized medical knowledge and skills to patients, including diagnosis, treatment, nursing, prevention, rehabilitation, and other services aimed at safeguarding physical health and life safety. In terms of the management of medical practice, Chinese legal documents cover a wide range, from laws to administrative regulations, to local laws and regulations, and even include relevant diagnosis and treatment norms and guidelines as supplements, basically forming a complete management system. There are specific management regulations governing everything from professional practice management to facility management, as well as pharmaceuticals, medical devices, emergency rescue, and specific diagnosis and treatment practices.

10.2.2.3 Legal System for the Management of Health Professionals

The law of medical practitioners is a compilation of legal norms that govern the various social relations arising from the physician qualification examination, practice registration, and medical practice activities. The Law of the People's Republic of China on Medical Practitioners was passed by the 3rd Session of the Standing Committee of the 9th National People's Congress in June 1998 and came into effect in May 1999. It applies to professional medical staff who work in medical, preventive, and health care institutions, have legally obtained the qualification of medical practitioners or assistant medical practitioners, have obtained a physician practice license through registration, and engage in corresponding medical, preventive, and health care services. This includes medical practitioners in family planning technical service institutions and foreign medical practitioners who temporarily practice medicine in China.

A nurse refers to a health professional who has obtained a nurse practice license through registration, engages in nursing activities in accordance with regulations, and fulfills the responsibilities of protecting life, alleviating pain, and promoting health. Currently, China's legislation on nursing work is still not perfect, the implementation of some legitimate rights and interests of nurses is insufficient, and the quality of nursing in some primary medical and health institutions is not good. Although the ratio of doctors to nurses has been optimized, some medical and health institutions prioritize medical treatment while neglecting nursing, and there is still a phenomenon of reducing the number of nurses, which poses many potential hazards to medical safety and makes it imperative to improve the legislation for nurse management. The relevant departments of the State Council, people's governments at all levels, and their relevant departments should take measures to improve nurses' working conditions, guarantee their compensation, strengthen the construction of the nursing team, and promote the healthy development of the nursing industry. The relevant departments of the State Council and local people's governments at or above the county level should take measures to encourage nurses to work in urban and rural primary medical and health institutions.

Rural doctors refer to health personnel who have not yet obtained the qualification of medical practitioners or assistant medical practitioners but have obtained the rural doctor practice license issued by the local health administrative agencies. They are registered to engage in preventive, health care, and general medical services in rural medical and health institutions. In August 2003, the State Council promulgated the "Regulations on the Practice of Rural Doctors," marking the entry, education, training, and management of rural doctors onto a legal track. This file stipulates that the country implements a rural doctor practice registration system, and the health administrative departments of the people's government at the county level is responsible for the registration of rural doctors.

A licensed pharmacist refers to a pharmaceutical technician who has passed the national unified examination, obtained the certified pharmacist license, and has been registered and certified. Licensed pharmacists engage in professional activities in drug production, distribution, use and other units. Currently, China implements a registration system for licensed pharmacists, only and other those who are registered can practice. Those who are not registered are not allowed to practice as licensed pharmacists. The NMPA is the administrative body responsible for the qualification registration of licensed pharmacists nationwide, while the drug regulatory agencies of various provinces (autonomous regions, municipalities directly under the central government) are the registration agencies for licensed pharmacists within their respective jurisdictions. To apply for registration, one must obtain the certified pharmacist license, abide by laws and regulations, adhere to the professional ethics of pharmacists, be physically healthy and able to persevere in working as a licensed pharmacist, and obtain the approval of the unit where they work.

10.2.2.4 Legal System for Pharmaceutical Affairs Management in Medical Institutions

The relevant laws and regulations on pharmaceutical affairs management in China are centered on the Drug Administration Law of the People's Republic of China and the "Regulations for the Implementation of the Drug Administration Law of the People's Republic of China." They supervise and manage drugs throughout the drugs' entire lifecycle, including research and development, production, distribution, and use, to ensure drug quality and medication safety. The Drug Administration Law of the People's Republic of China is formulated to strengthen drug management, guarantee drug quality, safeguard the public's medication safety and legitimate rights and interests, and protect and promote public health. All units or individuals engaged in drug research and development, production, distribution, use, and supervision and management activities within the territory of China must abide by this law.

10.2.3 Medical Security Legal System

10.2.3.1 Basic Medical Insurance System for Urban Employees

The basic medical insurance system for urban employees refers to a social medical insurance system implemented through national legislation, targeting all employers and their employees as well as flexible employment personnel. Its funding is primarily raised through contributions from both employers and in-service employees, as well as individual contributions from flexible employment personnel, to ensure the basic medical needs of insured individuals. The basic medical insurance system for urban employees is a significant component of China's basic medical insurance system. In December 1998, after summarizing the pilot experience from various localities, the State Council issued "The Decision of the State Council on Setting up Basic Medical Insurance System for Urban Employees," which proposed to initiate the establishment of the basic medical insurance system for urban employees nationwide from early 1999. This marked the gradual replacement of the government-funded and labor protection medical systems, which had been implemented in urban areas in China for nearly half a century, with the new medical insurance system for employees. In October 2010, the Social Insurance Law of the People's Republic of China, passed by the 17th Session of the Standing Committee of the 11th National People's Congress of China, listed "basic medical insurance for employees" as one of the specific types of basic medical insurance.

10.2.3.2 Basic Medical Insurance System for Rural and Non-working Urban Residents

The basic medical insurance system for rural and non-working urban residents refers to a social insurance legal system under which the state provides basic medical care to rural and non-working urban residents in need of treatment due to illness or non-work-related injuries. Based on the principles of comprehensive coverage, basic protection, multiple levels, and sustainability, China has established a basic medical insurance fund for rural and non-working urban residents through diversified financing methods such as government subsidies and individual contributions, aiming to achieve social mutual assistance and safeguard the medical insurance rights and interests of rural and non-working urban residents. The basic medical insurance system for rural and non-working urban residents in China originated from the basic medical insurance system for non-working urban residents and the new rural cooperative medical care system. In 2016, the State Council integrated the two systems and established a unified basic medical insurance system for rural and non-working urban residents.

For a long time, China's medical and health sector has involved numerous departments, and poor coordination between them has been a significant bottleneck hindering the deepening of medical reform. In 2018, the State Council conducted institutional reform and established the National Health Commission, upholding the concept of comprehensive hygiene and comprehensive health, initiating a new round of super-department reform. This concept aligns with the advocacy of a legal perspective in China's health sector, as it can clarify responsible entities, reduce internal frictions and resistances in medical reform, smoothen coordination, and assist the government in playing a stronger leadership role in actively promoting reform. China attaches great importance to the connection between health legalization and deepening reform, actively promotes the revision and improvement of laws and regulations, and implements the Law of the People's Republic of China on Basic Medical and Health Care and the Promotion of Health to safeguard the development of the medical and health industry.

10.3 Medicine and Health Supervision and Management in China

10.3.1 Overview of Medicine and Health Supervision in China

10.3.1.1 Concept, Function, and Role of Medicine and Health Supervision

Medicine and health supervision is an important guarantee for safeguarding the life and health rights of all citizens. It refers to the administrative law enforcement activities conducted by relevant government administrative departments in accordance with health laws and regulations, including the supervision and inspection of individuals, legal persons, and organizations engaged in health-related administrative permit matters and their implementation of health laws and regulations, as well as the handling of their behaviors.

The function of medicine and health supervision refers to the effectiveness that medicine and health supervision possesses or should exert, including regulatory, restrictive, preventive, and promotional functions. The regulatory function refers to the role of medicine and health supervision in standardizing people's behaviors, indicating what behaviors are legal or must be enforced by law through recognition of law-abiding individuals and punishment of violators. The restrictive function refers to the limitation of relevant rights and constraints on specific behaviors imposed by the supervisory actions of medicine and health supervision entities on the counterparts. The preventive function is the embodiment of the health policy of putting disease prevention first, which is a system that enforces and standardizes social health affairs or behaviors to prevent potential problems. Medicine and health supervision is not a passive and reactive activity, but an active and proactive involvement or integration into the entire operation process of the supervised entities, aiming to identify and eliminate potential health hazards in advance. The promotional function refers to the fact that medicine and health supervision can significantly promote the continuous improvement of various aspects, links, and fields of the social system, especially those related to health activities, effectively protecting people's health and continuously improving the level of productivity.

The role of medicine and health supervision is multifaceted. First, it promotes the modernization of the national governance system and governance capabilities. The medical and health system is a crucial component of modern national system, and the management in the field of medicine and health reflects a country's administrative governance capabilities and level. As the foundation and guarantee for the overall operation of the medicine and health management system, the medicine and health supervision system can effectively ensure the scientific development of the health undertakings on a legal track. It is one of the important means to standardize and maintain the medical and health system, and promote the development of the national governance system and socialist modernization. Second, it safeguards people's health rights and upholds the strategic position of national health. People's health is a significant indicator of national prosperity and strength. Optimizing health services, creating a healthy ecosystem, and providing comprehensive and lifelong health protection for the people serve as a solid foundation for enhancing people's well-being and achieving national rejuvenation. Medicine and health supervision is an important carrier and implementation means for national administrative departments to oversee and manage the development of the health undertakings and safeguard the health of the people. Third, it maintains the environment of the medical and health industry. Since the reform and opening-up, significant changes have occurred in the internal and external environments of China's medicine, health, and health care service supply markets. Market mechanisms inevitably have inherent drawbacks such as blindness, spontaneity, and profit-seeking tendencies. The purpose of medicine and health supervision and management is to correct market failures caused by improper market incentives. Regulating the behavior of various entities in the medical and health industry not only relies on self-moral constraints, industry rules, and social supervision, but also requires a combination of market regulation and government supervision to intervene in the economic operation and resource allocation of the medical and health service market, maintain public order, and ensure the quality of health services.

10.3.1.2 Principles of Medicine and Health Supervision

In China, the supervision of medicine and health follows the principle that "laws must be established, laws must be followed, law enforcement must be strict, and violations of the laws must be punished" in addition to the following principles.

1. The Principle of Legality

The principle of legality is a fundamental requirement for law enforcement in modern countries and governments governed by law. It primarily includes the following aspects: the establishment of medicine and health supervision entities must be lawful, the possession of medicine and health supervision powers must be lawful, the exercise of medicine and health supervision powers must be lawful, and those who unlawfully exercise their supervision powers shall bear legal responsibilities.

2. The Principle of Rationality

The principle of rationality refers to the necessity of ensuring that the establishment of medicine and health supervision entities, the possession of supervision powers, the exercise of supervision powers, the accountability of illegal acts, and the implementation of administrative relief are all just, objective, and appropriate. Specifically, it comprises two main aspects. First, the principle of fairness and justice requires equal treatment of all parties concerned without discrimination. Second, the principle of proportionality stipulates that medicine and health supervision entities should take into account both the achievement of supervisory objectives and the protection of the legal rights and interests of the supervised parties when carrying out their supervisory duties.

3. The Principle of Due Legal Process

The principle of due legal process refers to the necessity for medicine and health supervision entities to follow proper legal procedures when conducting supervisory actions that affect the rights and interests of the supervised parties. This includes informing the supervised parties beforehand, explaining the basis and rationale for the actions, listening to their statements and defenses, and providing appropriate relief channels for the supervised parties afterwards.

4. The Principle of Reliance Protection

The fundamental meaning of the principle of reliance protection is that medicine and health supervision entities should uphold their credibility in their actions or commitments, and should not change them arbitrarily or act inconsistently.

10.3.1.3 The Medicine and Health Supervision Entities

The medicine and health supervision entities serve as the organizational foundation for the state to exercise its functions of health supervision and management, and to achieve the objectives of health legislation. They are organizations that enjoy the power of national health supervision, can conduct health supervision activities in their own name, and independently bear legal responsibilities for the consequences of their actions. According to Chinese medicine and health laws and regulations, the medicine and health supervision entities in China consist of two main categories: health supervision administrative agencies and organizations authorized by laws and regulations.

Health supervision administrative agencies refer to state organs that are established in accordance with national laws to exercise the functions of national health supervision and management, including the health administrative departments of people's governments at all levels, drug regulatory agencies, and other health supervision agencies. Health administrative departments generally refer to the departments within governments at all levels that are responsible for medical and health administrative work, primarily overseeing policy formulation and environmental protection in the field of medical and health care. Specific law enforcement and operational work is carried out by subordinate institutions such as health supervision bureaus (offices) responsible for administrative law enforcement, centers for disease control and prevention responsible for the control and prevention of infectious diseases and chronic diseases, maternal and child health care hospitals responsible for maternal and child health, as well as hospitals at all levels and township health centers. Currently, drug supervision and management in China is primarily handled by the NMPA. Its responsibilities mainly include:

First, to supervise the safety of drugs (including TCMs and ethnic medicines, the same below), medical devices and cosmetics; to draw up regulatory policy plans, organize the drafting of laws and regulations, formulate departmental regulations, and supervise the implementation thereof; to research and formulate regulatory and service-related policies that encourage new technologies and new products for drugs, medical devices and cosmetics.

Second, to undertake standard management for drugs, medical devices and cosmetics; to organize the formulation and publication of the Chinese Pharmacopoeia and other drug and medical device standards, organize the drafting of cosmetic standards, organize the formulation of the classification management system, and supervise the implementation thereof; to participate in formulating the National Essential Medicine List, and assist in the implementation of the national essential medicine system.

Third, to regulate the registration of drugs, medical devices and cosmetics; to develop the registration system, conduct strict review and approval for marketing, improve measures to facilitate the review and approval process, and organize the implementation thereof.

Fourth, to undertake the quality management for drugs, medical devices and cosmetics; to formulate quality management standards for research and development and supervise the implementation thereof; to formulate production quality management standards and supervise the implementation thereof in line with NMPA's responsibilities; to formulate quality management standards for distribution and usage and guide the implementation thereof.

Fifth, to undertake post-market risk management for drugs, medical devices and cosmetics; to organize the monitoring, evaluation, and handling of drug adverse reactions, medical device adverse events, and cosmetic adverse reactions; to undertake emergency response management for drugs, medical devices and cosmetics in accordance with law.

Sixth, to undertake management of qualifications for licensed pharmacists; to formulate regulations of qualifications for licensed pharmacists, and guide and supervise the registration of licensed pharmacists.

Seventh, to organize and guide the supervision and inspection of drugs, medical devices and cosmetics; to develop the inspection system, investigate and punish illegal activities during the registration process for drugs, medical devices and cosmetics in accordance with law, and organize and guide the investigation and punishment of illegal activities during the manufacturing process in line with NMPA's responsibilities.

Eighth, to engage in international exchange and cooperation in the regulation of drugs, medical devices and cosmetics, and participate in developing relevant international regulatory rules and standards.

Ninth, to guide the work of drug regulatory departments of all provinces, autonomous regions, and municipalities directly under the central government.

Tenth, to complete other tasks assigned by the Central Committee of the Communist Party of China and the State Council.

The organizations authorized by laws and regulations to carry out medicine and health supervision and management refer to organizations other than administrative organs that are authorized by laws and regulations to exercise specific administrative functions in their own name, including social organizations, social groups, enterprises, and public institutions.

10.3.2 Main Content of Medicine and Health Supervision and Management in China

10.3.2.1 Supervision and Management of Medical Institutions

Supervision of medical institutions generally encompasses oversight of their establishment and practice, referring to the administrative law enforcement activities where the health supervision entities conduct inspections on whether the establishment approval, licensing of practice grades, and practice activities of medical institutions are lawful in accordance with relevant laws and regulations, and handle any illegal or improper acts during the establishment and practice of medical institutions. To ensure the quality and safety of medical care and protect the health of citizens, China has continuously strengthened the management of medical institutions and regulated the order of the medical service market. Since 1994, China has promulgated and implemented various laws and regulations related to the supervision of medical institutions, such as the "Regulations on the Administration of Medical Institutions," the "Implementation Details of the Regulations on the Administration of Medical Institutions," the "Measures for the Administration of Medical Cosmetology Services," and the "Measures for the Administration of Prescriptions," and has now formed a relatively complete legal and regulatory system for the supervision of medical institutions.

The establishment and approval process of medical institutions consists of three parts: planning for the establishment of medical institutions, approval for the establishment of medical institutions, and medical institution practice registration and related management such as cancellation, change registration and verification. First, the planning for the establishment of medical institutions is primarily the responsibility of the health administrative departments of local people's governments at or above the county level. The planning is based on the current situation of population, medical resources, medical needs, and distribution of medical institutions within the administrative area. Second, the approval for the establishment of medical institutions is premised on compliance with the planning layout and medical institution establishment plan within the administrative area. Any unit or individual wishing to establish a medical institution must obtain the approval of the health administrative department at or above the county level in the locality. After obtaining the Approval Certificate for the Establishment of a Medical Institution, they can proceed with other procedures at relevant departments. Finally, the practice registration of medical institutions mainly examines whether the medical institutions applying for practice possess the statutory qualifications for operations.

The supervision of medical institutions' practice generally refers to the oversight conducted by health administrative departments to ensure the legality of medical institutions' practice activities. It comprises three main aspects: supervision of practice licenses, supervision of practice activities, and supervision of practice norms, duties, and obligations. First, supervision of practice licenses includes both the supervision of practice access and the use of stamps and names. The former requires medical institutions to obtain the Practicing License of Medical Institution before conducting any medical activities, while the latter involves ensuring that the stamps, bank accounts, plaques, and names used in medical documents are identical to the approved and registered name of the medical institutions. Second, supervision of practice activities includes oversight of the scope of diagnosis and treatment, practicing medical personnel, and medical diagnostic and treatment activities. Lastly, supervision of practice norms, duties, and obligations requires medical institutions to adhere to relevant clinical diagnosis and treatment norms in their practice and fulfill related obligations such as providing preventive health care and medical support for sudden health events.

10.3.2.2 Supervision and Management of Health Professionals

Supervision of health professionals refers to the administrative law enforcement activities conducted by medicine and health supervision entities in accordance with health management laws and regulations to oversee and inspect health professionals, and to pursue the responsibilities of those who violate the law. Health professionals refer to those engaged in health technical work, specifically, professionals who have acquired medical and health knowledge through higher or secondary medical and health education or training, passed the review of health administrative departments, and are engaged in medical treatment, prevention, pharmacy, nursing, or other health technical work.

The supervision of health professionals primarily focuses on professional qualifications, qualifications for specialized technical services, and diagnostic and treatment practices of the health professionals.

First, the supervision of health professionals' professional qualifications primarily involves overseeing and managing their acquisition of corresponding qualifications. These qualifications refer to the knowledge, skills, abilities, and status qualifications that personnel providing specific health technical services to the public should possess. Health professionals often need to go through a series of rigorous review procedures to obtain these qualifications. Generally, the acquisition process begins with examinations or assessments, such as the medical practitioner qualification examination, the nurse licensing examination, and the licensed pharmacist qualification examination, and ends with registration in the health administrative department.

Second, the supervision of health professionals' qualifications for specialized technical services refers to the qualifications they further obtain under legal circumstances to perform specific specialized health technical services after registration or assessment, due to the numerous health service projects in a certain field and the different risk and complexity of each project.

Third, the supervision of health professionals' diagnostic and treatment practices directly affects the level of diagnostic and treatment practices and patients' health. Therefore, various countries and governments implement strict regulatory measures to standardize their practices. The primary means of regulation is the implementation of qualification licensing, which involves strict management of industry access, even down to the access of specific diagnostic and treatment practices. After health professionals obtain general industry access qualifications, the focus of health supervision lies in their specific behaviors, including their scope of practice and other areas.

10.3.2.3 Drug Supervision and Management

Drug supervision and management refers to the oversight and inspection activities conducted by drug regulatory agencies in accordance with their statutory authorities, covering various aspects of drug research and development, production, sales, use, pricing, and advertising. In China, the NMPA is in charge of drug supervision and management. The legal basis for drug supervision and management includes the Drug Administration Law of the People's Republic of China, the "Good Laboratory Practice for Non-Clinical Laboratory Studies," the "Good Clinical Practice," and the "Good Manufacturing Practice (Revised in 2010)," among others.

The main content of drug supervision and management includes drug management, licensed pharmacist management, and drug supervision and inspection, all conducted in accordance with relevant laws and regulations. These laws and regulations are normative documents formulated and issued in accordance with the law, covering issues such as national drug standards. Drug management primarily involves the supervision and management of drug market access, the production, circulation, and use of drugs, and drug quality, the investigation and handling of illegal drugs, and the supervision and management of market exit, etc. Licensed pharmacist management mainly involves the supervision and management of the professional access, professional conduct, and professional exit of pharmaceutical technicians practicing in key pharmaceutical technology professions. Drug supervision and inspection refers to the oversight and inspection conducted by drug regulatory authorities on drug research and development, production, distribution, and use activities in accordance with laws and regulations.

10.3.2.4 Supervision of Infectious Disease Prevention and Treatment

Supervision of infectious disease prevention and treatment refers to the administrative law enforcement activities carried out by the government's health administrative departments in accordance with health laws and regulations, including granting permits to individuals, legal persons, and organizations engaged in matters related to infectious diseases, overseeing and inspecting the implementation of laws and regulations for infectious disease prevention and treatment, and taking actions against any violations. The purpose of this supervision is to effectively prevent, control, and eliminate the occurrence and prevalence of infectious diseases, safeguard people's health, and uphold the unity and dignity of the national health legal system.

According to the Law of the People's Republic of China on Prevention and Treatment of Infectious Diseases, the health administrative department of the State Council is responsible for the prevention, treatment, and supervision of infectious diseases nationwide, and the health administrative departments of local people's governments at or above the county level are responsible for the prevention, treatment, and supervision of infectious diseases within their respective administrative regions. The supervision of infectious disease prevention and treatment generally includes prevention supervision, control supervision, and other aspects.

Case Study: The Promulgation of the Law of the People's Republic of China on Basic Medical and Health Care and the Promotion of Health

The Law of the People's Republic of China on Basic Medical and Health Care and the Promotion of Health was passed by the 15th Session of the Standing Committee of the 13th National People's Congress on December 28, 2019. The law includes the basic elements necessary for national health legislation, while also embodying new concepts such as "comprehensive hygiene," "comprehensive health," and "integrating health into all policies." The law came into effect on June 1, 2020.

The establishment of the Law of the People's Republic of China on Basic Medical and Health Care and the Promotion of Health is accompanied by the continuous deepening of the health system reform of China. With the gradual establishment of the basic medical and health system with Chinese characteristics, many fundamental and principled issues in the development of China's health undertakings urgently need to be regulated by a basic and comprehensive law. At the same time, the task of promptly elevating proven effective practices and specific systems to the level of law had emerged.

In terms of legislative objectives, the law primarily focuses on the following: first, implementing the provisions in the Constitution of the People's Republic of China on the state's development of medical and health undertakings and the protection of people's health; second, guiding the overall reform and development of China's medical and health services; third, promoting and ensuring the effective implementation of the construction of a healthy China. Under the guidance of the legislative approach that upholds government leadership, ensures basic services, strengthens grassroots-level services, and establishes mechanisms, the law makes macro legal norms and institutional designs in areas such as actively ensuring government investment, mobilizing participation from the entire society, comprehensively safeguarding people's health throughout their lives, significantly improving people's health levels, and significantly improving health equity. It fully plays the important role of law in leading, promoting medicine and health system reforms, and ensuring the construction of a healthy China.

This law is China's first fundamental and comprehensive law in the field of medical and health sector, reflecting the concept shift from "treating illnesses as the center" to "putting people's health at the center," providing legal guarantees for the reform and development of the medical and health undertakings. To date, the health rule of law has developed well as a comprehensive legal field involving multiple traditional legal departments, and the legal system of medicine and health composed of constitutional provisions, laws and regulations, regulatory documents, and standard guidelines has basically taken shape.

Chapter 11
China's Medical and Health Information System

In the information era, the information construction in the medical and health industry has become a crucial national development strategy. As the core of medical and health informatization, the construction of information systems has a profound impact on improving the quality and efficiency of medical services, optimizing the allocation and utilization of medical resources, promoting the management and supervision of the medical and health, and enhancing the intelligent governance capabilities of public health. With the continuous progress and application of information technology, the construction of medical and health informatization in China has made great progress, but it is still necessary to continuously strengthen the construction and application of information systems, and improve the integration and innovative capabilities of information technology with the medical and health industry to promote sustainable and healthy development of medical and health undertakings. This chapter will discuss the importance of the medical and health information system, the development status of medical and health informatization in China, and the medical and health information management system in China, to provide insights into the current status, issues, and future directions of medical and health informatization in China.

11.1 The Importance of the Medical and Health Information System

11.1.1 Macro Level

With the establishment of a socialist market economy, the construction of medical and health information infrastructure is crucial for the development of the medical and health undertakings. Building a practical and shared medical and health information

Z. Feng et al. (eds.), *China's Health System*, Introduction to China's S&T Innovation,
https://doi.org/10.1007/978-981-95-1205-8_11

system can help authorities and researchers to access reliable information promptly, provide efficient medical and health management services and comprehensively improve medical and health quality, capacity, and management levels. Recently, many urban areas in China have advanced the construction of the medical and health information system. The "14th Five-Year Plan for National Health Informatization" highlights that during the 13th Five-Year Plan period, significant efforts were made to integrate the strategies of Healthy China and Digital China, fully implement the 13th Five-Year Plan for national health informatization development, and accelerate the normative application of healthcare big data and innovative development of "Internet + Healthcare." This integration played a vital role in supporting the high-quality development of health undertakings. On a macro level, the importance of the construction of medical and health information system to the development of the medical and health undertakings is reflected in several aspects.

First, enhancing the spread of healthcare services and the rational allocation of resources. In the drive for medical reform and informatization, healthcare services in China are poised for deeper transformation. Although public hospitals remain the mainstay of medical and health service system in China, the key to promoting the upgrading of medical and health services is to address regional disparities in medical resources, and form a new pattern of medical treatment of "minor diseases at the grassroots level, major diseases to the hospital, and rehabilitation back to the community" by implementing measures such as hierarchical diagnosis and treatment and telemedicine. Among them, the hierarchical diagnosis and treatment information system, which leverages big data, cloud computing, mobile internet, and the Internet of Things is one of the very important construction content. This system can interconnect with the information system of various medical and health institutions, providing unified referral information services, optimizing workflows in medical institutions, encouraging residents to develop better medical-seeking habits, and enhancing the orderliness, accessibility, fairness, and cost-effectiveness of medical services, thereby optimizing regional health resource allocation.

Second, strengthening medical and health management and supervision. According to the requirements of the "Code of Practice for the Recording of the Entire Process of Administrative Law Enforcement in Healthcare" issued by the National Health Commission, establishing a sound health supervision system, accelerating the promotion of the "Internet + Transparent Supervision" model in health supervision, striving to build a comprehensive management service platform of smart health supervision, optimizing the law enforcement process, improving the efficiency of law enforcement, and truly achieving a leap from traditional to modern law enforcement modes, are crucial for safeguarding public health. By supervising and evaluating the behavior of medical institutions and health professionals, medical services can be standardized and normalized, to increase patient satisfaction. Achieving data-driven collaboration in public health management and data-supported intelligent decision-making applications can effectively support refined management of health supervision and enhance comprehensive supervision and enforcement capabilities. With the growing demand for internet-based medical services, the focus on China's smart health supervision is shifting towards comprehensive supervision. The use of big data for detailed analysis, the discovery of violations and timely investigation, and the efforts to achieve the transformation of supervision channels from offline to online, play an important role in the realization of the whole process of supervision.

Third, enhancing the capability of intelligent public health governance. The application of cutting-edge technologies such as block chain and artificial intelligence significantly boosts the resilience of public health information systems and shapes the future direction of health governance. Public health, fundamentally a process of social governance centered around "groups," requires distributed group participation to achieve the resilience of information systems. Intelligent public health governance represents an innovative form of public health management, relying on the informatization process of institutional structures and system reform and leveraging professional and independent knowledge for scientific and efficient public health governance. This approach is crucial for timely responses to major diseases and public health emergencies. In the future, public health information systems will become integral to smart cities, coordinated through smart city command centers, enabling intelligent city-wide management and offering efficient services across economic and social domains, including public health.

Fourth, facilitating the advancement and transformation of the medical and health industry. As the government continues to promote the reform of the medical and health system and the digital transformation of the medical and health industry, the medical information industry is undergoing significant upgrades and shifts. It is transitioning from focusing solely on medical service informatization to rapid development in health insurance informatization and pharmaceutical informatization, progressing towards integrated and collaborative informatization across the entire life-health industry chain. During this transformation, platforms based on cloud computing and big data, adopting middle platform thinking for digital transformation, are being rapidly deployed to support the construction and operation of core systems in medical treatment, medical insurance, and pharmaceuticals. These platforms also support the development and operation of various innovative medical applications. The digital transformation platform is expanding its services from independent medical or medical insurance departments to the entire industry chain, presenting both opportunities and challenges for upgrading and transforming the medical and health industry.

11.1.2 Micro Level

In May 2020, the General Office of the National Health Commission issued the "Notice of the General Office of the National Health Commission on Further Improving the Appointment Diagnosis and Treatment System and Strengthening the Construction of Smart Hospitals," calling for speeding up the establishment and improvement of the appointment diagnosis and treatment system, innovating and building the smart hospital systems, and vigorously promoting the development of internet-based diagnosis and treatment as well as internet hospitals, which prompted many hospitals to focus on their information system construction and accelerate the pace of informatization. Hospital informatization construction has become an essential means for hospitals to implement refined management, reduce operational costs, and reform medical treatment processes. During the 13th Five-Year Plan period, many hospitals aligned their informatization efforts with the national medical informatization development plan, using third-party platforms to integrate medical data, strengthen information management levels, and promote the informatization and paperless operation in various functional departments. On a micro level, the importance of medical and health information system construction for hospital management is evident in the following aspects:

First, optimizing medical-seeking processes and reducing waiting times. By implementing self-service registration and payment systems and outpatient queuing systems, hospitals can optimize outpatient medical-seeking processes, addressing the "Three Long, One Short" (long queues for registration, consultation, and payment, and short consultation times) problem. The introduction of intelligent medical devices like automatic diagnostic equipment and smart medicine cabinets allows patients to self-check and retrieve medications, thus reducing the workload on medical staff and enhancing efficiency. Online consultations and appointment registration via internet hospitals can further facilitate convenient medical-seeking access for patients, avoiding the traditional congestion and crowding in outpatient settings, and significantly improving medical-seeking efficiency and patient experience.

Second, establishing and implementing electronic medical record (EMR) to improve the quality of medical records. Establishing EMR is central to integrating data from various hospital function systems, such as hospital information system, laboratory information system, and picture archiving and communication system. EMR is at the core of hospital informatization construction. As EMR evolves, hospital informatization construction is shifting focus from billing processes to clinical workflows. EMR plays a crucial role in structuring clinical data, helping to integrate and analyze data comprehensively, showcasing patients' diagnosis and treatment processes, and providing essential data support for the management and control of personnel (personnel management and performance evaluation), finance (budget management and cost accounting), and materials (medication and supply management). Establishing and implementing EMR not only improves the quality of medical records but also aids doctors in accurate diagnosis and treatment, facilitating automated and intelligent hospital management, including unified management of medical records quality and personnel.

Third, promoting clinical informatization construction to enhance diagnostic and treatment quality and efficiency. Clinical informatization construction focuses more on patients than hospital informatization construction. At its core is the establishment of clinical information system centered around EMR, covering nursing, imaging, laboratory testing, and more. Its primary goal is to assist doctors in providing rapid and accurate diagnosis and treatment, improving work efficiency while ensuring the quality and traceability of medical records. Currently, third-level hospitals in China lead in clinical informatization construction, particularly in clinical laboratory information management and medical imaging information management, with the highest penetration rates. In the future, clinical information systems will integrate new technologies such as big data and artificial intelligence, advancing from speeding up and improving informatization management to data integration and intelligent analysis, addressing core issues of medical resource shortages.

Given the growing emphasis on the development of medical and health undertakings in China, advancing health insurance informatization has been included in the "Outline of the 14th Five-Year Plan (2021–2025) for National Economic and Social Development and the Long-Range Objectives Through the Year 2035." This provides a broader and more robust foundation for strengthening information system construction and application, enhancing the integration and innovation capabilities of information technology with the medical and health industry, and achieving high-quality development in medical and health undertakings, thereby improving public health and well-being.

11.2 Development Status of Medical and Health Informatization in China

11.2.1 Policy Planning and Development Requirements for Medical and Health Informatization in China

11.2.1.1 Policy Planning

At the national level, China has continuously promoted the development of the information industry and progressively strengthened informatization construction in the medical and health sector. From the 10th Five-Year Plan to the 14th Five-Year Plan periods, China has clearly outlined the need to enhance information system construction in medical and health sector and issued policies to support and regulate the development of medical informatization. Key documents, such as the "Opinions of the Central Committee of the Communist Party of China and the State Council on Deepening the Reform of the Medical and Health System" and the "Outline of the 12th Five-Year Plan for the National Economic and Social Development of the People's Republic of China," have actively promoted the development of medical and health informatization, telemedicine systems, and the informatization of public hospitals. In recent years, medical and health informatization layout in China has accelerated, reflecting the government's strong emphasis on medical and health informatization. Through ongoing policy improvements and increased investment, sustained progress in medical and health informatization has been achieved.

At the policy level, China has introduced a series of guiding documents to support the development of medical and health informatization, including the "14th Five-Year Plan for National Informatization," as shown in Table 11.1. These documents demonstrate the government's focus and support for the development of medical and health informatization, providing policy guidance for the industry's development.

Practically, China actively promotes the construction and application of medical and health informatization infrastructure, strengthens data standardization and sharing, and fosters deep integration of medical and health informatization with other industries and fields, such as artificial intelligence, big data, and cloud computing. Additionally, China is enhancing legal frameworks to ensure the security and effectiveness of medical and health information.

Overall, from the 10th Five-Year Plan to the 14th Five-Year Plan periods, the implementation of medical and health informatization policies in China has achieved significant success, laying a solid foundation for the modernization of medical services. Future efforts will be needed to focus on enhancing technological innovation and practical exploration to improve the coverage and quality of medical and health informatization.

11.2.1.2 Development Requirements

The development requirements for medical and health informatization in China can be summarized as follows:

First, the informatization construction of medical institutions. The informatization construction of medical institutions has to meet the needs of medical quality management, pharmaceutical management, medical record management, patient management, and physician scheduling, ensuring the stable and reliable operation of the information platform. Additionally, medical institutions must comply with information security management requirements, strengthening data backup and recovery management to ensure data integrity, confidentiality, and availability.

Second, the informatization construction of pharmaceutical manufacturing enterprises. The informatization construction of pharmaceutical manufacturing enterprises requires establishing a comprehensive, efficient, and digital information management system to support the research and development, production, sales, and quality management of pharmaceuticals. The information platform for pharmaceutical manufacturing enterprises must meet accuracy, real-time, and security requirements and interface with regulatory authorities at various levels to ensure lawful and compliant operations.

Third, the informatization construction of pharmaceutical distribution and retail enterprises. The informatization construction of pharmaceutical distribution and retail enterprises requires creating an end-to-end information management chain to meet the needs of supply chain, inventory management, and business processing. Additionally, establishing e-commerce portals and mobile applications to provide online purchasing and payment services can meet the diverse needs of consumers.

Fourth, the informatization construction of medical insurance. The informatization construction of medical insurance involves advancing the informatization of medical insurance management, data statistics, fund settlement, and medical insurance card management, establishing a national medical security system to achieve information management and unified supervision. This requires building

Table 11.1 Examples of policy planning for China's medical and health informatization

Release date	Issuing department	Document title	Interpretation of the key content	Policy attribute
September 2020	National Health Commission, National Development and Reform Commission, Ministry of Education, Ministry of Industry and Information Technology, Ministry of Public Security, Ministry of Human Resources and Social Security, Ministry of Transport, Ministry of Emergency Management, National Healthcare Security Administration	Guiding Opinions on Further Improving Pre-Hospital Emergency Medical Services	Enhancing the informatization level of pre-hospital emergency infrastructure and supporting facilities	Normative
November 2020	General Office of the Ministry of Industry and Information Technology, General Office of the National Health Commission	Notice of the General Office of the Ministry of Industry and Information Technology and the General Office of the National Health Commission on Organizing the APPLICATION for 5G+ Healthcare Application Pilot Projects	Pilot promotion: promoting the pilot of replicable and scalable 5G smart healthcare new products, new formats, and new models	Supportive
September 2021	General Office of the State Council	14th Five-Year Plan for National Healthcare Security	Achieving breakthroughs in healthcare security informatization and standardization, promoting the coding standards for medical insurance business and the application of electronic medical insurance credentials	Supportive

(continued)

Table 11.1 (continued)

Release date	Issuing department	Document title	Interpretation of the key content	Policy attribute
September 2021	National Health Commission, National Administration of Traditional Chinese Medicine	Action Plan to Promote High-Quality Development of Public Hospitals (2021–2025)	Building three-pronged smart hospitals and promoting the standardization and normalization of hospital information construction	Supportive
December 2021	Central Cyberspace Affairs Commission	14th Five-Year Plan for National Informatization	Actively exploring the use of informatization to optimize medical service processes, constructing major medical infrastructure platforms, accelerating the construction of dedicated medical clouds, promoting data sharing and mutual recognition and business collaboration across various levels of medical and health institutions, and building an authoritative, unified, and shared national health information platform at all levels	Supportive

a robust medical insurance information platform to protect patient privacy security and information security.

Fifth, the informatization construction of medical device enterprises. The informatization construction of medical device enterprises necessitates developing comprehensive information management platforms for digital management of product research and development, production, and sales processes. At the same time, it is necessary to meet the requirements of the "Compliance with Medical Device Safety Management" to ensure product quality.

Sixth, the informatization construction of medical institution evaluation standards. The informatization construction of medical institution evaluation standards must comply with national medical institution evaluation standards and related regulations on medical quality management and accident management, ensuring the usability, safety, and reliability of information systems, thereby improving medical service quality and patient satisfaction.

In summary, the development of medical and health informatization should focus on enhancing the level of information technology, continuously strengthening talent development and technological innovation, promoting the application of information technology in medical and health sector, establishing a sound information security system, guiding the medical and health sector to gradually form scientific and standardized information application models, and improving medical service levels and the medical environment. The government should formulate policies and regulations that align with national conditions, providing policy support and security for the development of medical and health informatization, promoting the application of medical and health informatization standards, providing technical support for the interaction and interoperability of the medical and health information system, and facilitating the integration and optimization of the medical and health information system.

11.2.2 Development of Medical and Health Informatization in China

The development of medical and health informatization in China dates back to the early 1980s. At that time, China began to engage with computer technology, with some hospitals attempting to use it to improve medical service quality and management levels. However, the integration of computer technology with medical services was not mature, and its application was limited. In the 1990s, as information technology continued to advance and spread, medical and health informatization entered a rapid development phase. This period saw a focus on hospital informatization construction, with hospitals at various levels implementing hospital information systems and clinical information systems, applying them to areas like EMR, medical quality control, medical resource management, and medical insurance management. Meanwhile, China also introduced a series of policies to support the development of medical and health informatization, fostering its widespread adoption and application. With the advent of new technologies like mobile internet, cloud computing, and artificial intelligence, medical and health informatization is moving towards more intelligent, digital, and universal directions. Nowadays, China has made significant strides in the construction of medical and health informatization, with continued innovation and development in hospital informatization, digital medical treatment, and telemedicine. Future advancements in information technology and its application scenarios will make medical and health information system a crucial support for medical services and research.

11.2.3 Current Status of Medical and Health Informatization in China

With the arrival of the information age, the construction of medical and health informatization in China has become a significant issue. Although China has established a relatively complete medical and health informatization infrastructure, the application of new medical reform models still faces severe challenges. The primary issues in regional medical and health informatization construction in China include information silos, lack of standardized workflows, insufficient funding, and a shortage of skilled personnel. In terms of building residents' electronic health records, China has made substantial progress, with nearly half of the provinces achieving an archiving rate of over 90% for residents' electronic health records, indicating potential for further advancement. In clinical informatization, China actively promotes the use of EMR and advances the application of informatization in medical imaging, laboratory testing, and teleconsultation. Despite common issues of mismatched output and input, the scaling up of medical and health institutions and increasing demands for national policies have led to gradual increases in staffing and funding for EMR systems, which are crucial for enhancing medical quality and efficiency.

11.3 Medical and Health Information Management System in China

11.3.1 Structure of Medical and Health Information Management System in China

In 2010, the Ministry of Health proposed the "3521 Project" overall framework for health informatization during the 12th Five-Year Plan period. In 2013, this project evolved into the "4631-2 Project," which serves as the top-level design for the development of medical and health informatization in China. The "4631-2 Project" aims to integrate health resources and establish a comprehensive, multidimensional national medical and health information management system to enhance the quality and efficiency of health services. The "4631-2 Project" includes four levels of population health information platforms, six business applications, three basic databases, one converged network covering all types of medical institutions (including TCM institutions), and two standard systems. Fig. 11.1 illustrates the overall framework of the "4631-2 Project" in China.

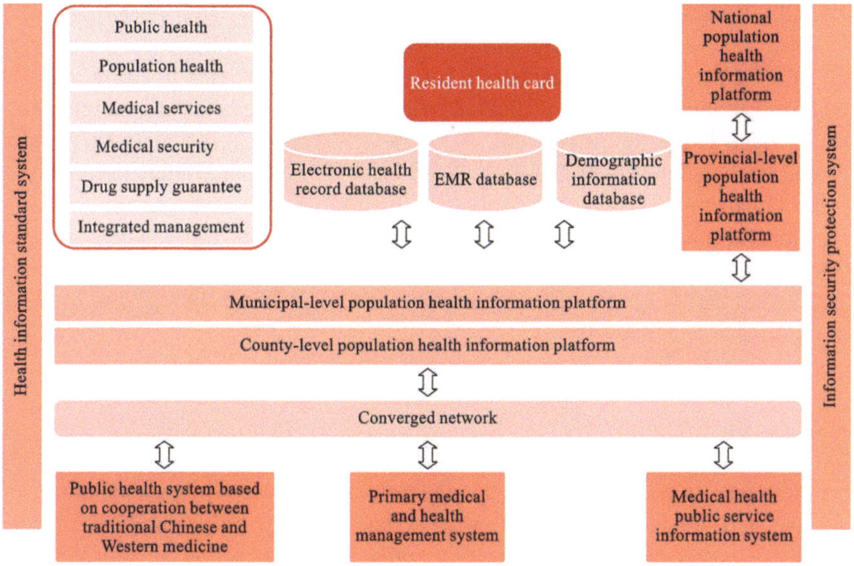

Fig. 11.1 Overall framework of the "4631-2 Project" in China

11.3.1.1 Regional Population Health Information Platforms

Regional medical informatization construction involves integrating information systems across various medical institutions within a specific region through the use of information technology and platforms, achieving information interconnectivity and collaborative operations. This is an important part of China's medical and health informatization construction, and one of the important measures to advance the medical and health system reform and improve medical service quality and efficiency.

To promote regional medical informatization construction, China has introduced significant initiatives for building regional population health information platforms. According to the "Guiding Opinions on Accelerating the Construction of Population Health Informatization," there should be comprehensive development of interlinked and interconnected four levels of population health information platforms, among which the regional population health information platforms are the most important and basic platforms to realize China's health modernization. The construction of regional population health information platforms will help improve the quality and efficiency of medical services, promote the popularization and application of medical information, and realize the goal of national health and medical and health modernization.

11.3.1.2 Business Applications

The "4631-2 Project" encompasses six business applications: public health, population health, medical services, medical security, drug supply guarantee, and integrated management. These applications fall within the scope of the implementation plan for medical and health informatization construction in China. Coordinating the construction and deepening of six key business application systems covering various areas of health and achieving interoperability among these systems can enhance the level of medical services, promote the improvement of the medical security system, standardize drug management, strengthen population health management, and improve medical management levels.

11.3.1.3 Basic Databases

The three basic databases include the electronic health record database, the EMR database, and the demographic information database. The electronic health record database is based on electronic health records, with data primarily sourced from various regional medical and health institutions' operational systems, including EMR system. The EMR database is based on EMR, storing structured lifelong electronic information about patients' health and medical conditions in numerous data tables after segmenting the medical record template according to business norms, to enable data storage and retrieval. The demographic information database is designed for population management, incorporating fields for household registration, residence, and management location (management location refers to specific management services for population monitoring and family development). These fields categorize information on household registration, residence, and management location, respectively, for statistical purposes, providing data on registered, permanent, and managed populations.

11.3.1.4 Converged Network

Following regional health planning requirements and localized management principles, the construction of a regional public health information network platform at the city level integrates various health administrative departments, disease control departments, and medical and health institutions into a unified network connected to the national public data network, forming a regional health information network.

11.3.1.5 Standard Systems

The standard systems within the "4631-2 Project" overall framework includes the health information standard system and the information security protection system. The health information standard system is a crucial part of the top-level design

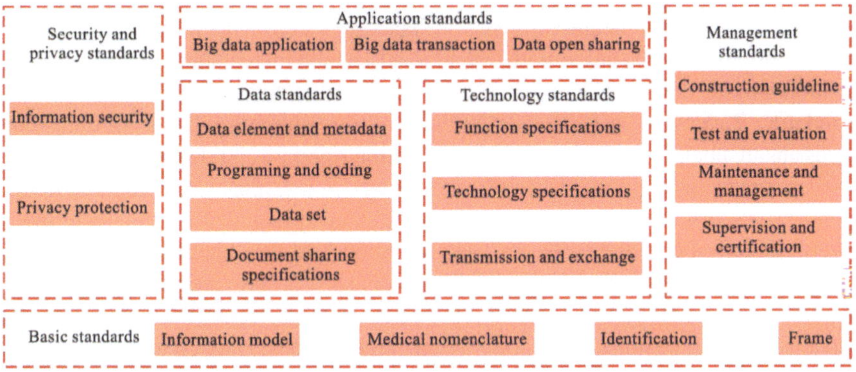

Fig. 11.2 Framework of health information standard system in China

for health informatization. Health information standard system in China currently encompasses six categories: basic, data, application, technology, management, and security and privacy standards, as shown in Fig. 11.2. The information security protection system ensures the security of medical data during generation, transmission, and integration processes. It was established in response to emerging issues such as the lack of medical information security standards, unreasonable network structures in medical institutions, information leakage led by network collaboration, and breaches of patient privacy.

11.3.2 Operation Mechanisms of Medical and Health Information Management System in China

Based on the "4631-2 Project," the "14th Five-Year Plan for National Informatization" in 2021 proposed to actively explore the use of informatization to optimize medical service processes, accelerate the construction of dedicated medical clouds, promote data sharing and business collaboration across information systems of various medical and health institutions, and build authoritative, unified, and interconnected national health information platforms. Accordingly, the operation mechanisms of medical and health information management system can be categorized as follows.

11.3.2.1 Health Data Governance

Health data governance is a core and most complex aspect of health information management, involving the construction of health information standard system, data collection and integration, data security and privacy protection, etc.

The construction of health information standard system is the foundation of health data governance. China has initially established a health information standard system, including basic, data, application, technology, management, and security and privacy standards. Basic standards provide guidance and overarching direction; data standards ensure unambiguous semantics; application standards guide data provision and application; technology standards set requirements for business application systems' technical levels and information network security and privacy protection technology levels; management standards are used to guide business application systems to reasonably apply relevant standards and to evaluate, supervise and manage the application of standards; and security and privacy standards regulate data security and privacy issues in health-related applications and services. Data collection and integration are critical components of health data governance. The health information management system collects and integrates relevant data through various information systems, such as EMR system and residents' health record system. China has established standardized residents' health records, including personal basic information, health check-up records, key population health management records, and other medical and health service records. Data security and privacy protection are also essential aspects of health data governance. The health information management system must establish robust data security and privacy protection mechanisms to safeguard the privacy and data security of patients and health service providers. China places a high priority on cybersecurity and, in terms of information security, is able to guide information sharing and network security development through relevant legal documents. Classifying the security levels of regional health information platforms and implementing platform rectifications are helpful to protect individual privacy and data security.

11.3.2.2 Construction of Health Information Platforms

The health information management system requires an open data-sharing and communication platform to enable data interconnectivity and sharing among various health institutions and service providers. This facilitates efficient and high-quality health services and provides comprehensive and accurate data support for decision-makers. The population health information platform is central to the "4631-2 Project," with municipal-level population health information platforms playing a crucial role in bridging and coordinating data sharing and interconnectivity between higher and lower levels. The construction of regional health information platforms must adhere to the "four unifications" principle: unified standards, unified deployment, unified special network, and unified platform. Unified standards require adherence to national information standard norms, strengthening the application and implementation of standards to achieve horizontal data integration and sharing among higher and lower units. Unified deployment involves centralized management of the regional health information platform project by the city health information center. Unified special network demands the unified operation of special networks across city, county, township, and village levels to facilitate interconnectivity and data sharing. Unified platform necessitates the development of interfaces for existing information systems in subordinate medical and health institutions, enabling regional health information interoperability and sharing.

11.3.2.3 Construction of Health Informatization Talent Team

To effectively promote the construction of health informatization talent team, the Office of the Ministry of Health successively issued the "Implementation Opinions on the Development of National Health Statistics and Informatization Talents" and the "Opinions on Strengthening the Construction of Health Statistics and Informatization Talent Teams" in 2011 and 2012. These documents set clear standards for staffing health informatization personnel in health administrative departments, hospitals above the second level, and public health institutions. In August 2022, the National Health Commission issued the "14th Five-Year Plan for Health Talent Development," aiming to improve talent management systems and mechanisms and create a conducive environment for talent development. Stakeholders in health information management include demand-side entities (health administrative departments, and medical and health institutions), supply-side entities (information technology companies), and maintenance entities, each with specific needs for health informatization talents. Therefore, China first adopts a demand-oriented mechanism for the cultivation and utilization of health informatization talents, with clear cultivation objectives and top-level planning for talent development. Additionally, a unified curriculum system is built to broaden the horizons of health informatization talents. Finally, a multi-level and multi-angle comprehensive practice training system is established to meet the need for cultivating versatile and application-oriented talents.

11.3.2.4 Promoting the Adoption of Health Informatization Application

Promoting the adoption of the application of health informatization is vital for improving health service quality and efficiency. Efforts should focus on building hardware facilities in primary medical and health institutions, enhancing their informatization levels to achieve comprehensive coverage of basic health services. In 2017, China issued the "Guiding Opinions of the General Office of the State Council on Promoting the Construction and Development of Medical Consortiums," advocating for the establishment of county-level medical communities and the concentrated construction of provincial-level, municipal-level, and county-level basic health data centers to achieve health information interconnectivity. These measures support the availability and reliability of information systems, providing robust support for the promotion of health informatization. Beyond hardware facilities, the imbalance in the talent workforce is a significant barrier to the widespread application of health informatization. Therefore, China has implemented various measures, such as formulating guidance on reforming training and promotion mechanisms for health information management talents and encouraging the transition of health informatization talents. These measures help enhance the capabilities of health informatization talents, advancing the construction and adoption of health informatization.

In China, health informatization application has become widespread, with the "Healthy Hubei" public service platform being a successful example. This platform aims to create a unified online health public service platform across Hubei province, integrating resources from hospitals at all levels into a single platform, offering functions such as appointment registration, outpatient payment, report inquiries, online consultations, and health monitoring. Users can conveniently access one-stop medical treatment and health services through a single platform. After several years of upgrades, the platform, building on the original "One-Stop Consultation," relies on the Hubei Provincial Health Medical Big Data Center to integrate advantageous medical and health resources across the province, create a people-centered smart health service system, provide comprehensive health services for convenience and public benefit and refined management throughout the life cycle, and promote "one-net" and "one-stop" medical treatment and health services to create a unified, province-wide health public service platform with a single entry point. As of December 2022, it has already brought together hundreds of medical institutions above the second level and thousands of registered doctors in Hubei province, with nearly 5 million registered users and over 20 million services provided (including more than 13 million pandemic-related services). Additionally, more than 5 million electronic health cards have been issued through the platform.

References

1. Overview of China's Health System

General Office of the State Council. (2021, September 29). *Notice of the General Office of the State Council on issuing the "14th Five-Year Plan for National Medical Security"*. https://www.gov.cn/zhengce/content/2021-09/29/content_5639967.htm

National Bureau of Statistics. (2022). *China statistical yearbook 2022*. China Statistics Press.

National Health Commission. (2020). *China health statistical yearbook 2020*. Peking Union Medical College Press.

National Health Commission of the People's Republic of China. (2022). *Statistical bulletin on China's health development in 2021*. https://www.gov.cn/xinwen/2022-07/12/content_5700670.htm

3. China's Medical Service System

General Office of the State Council. (2017, April 26). *Guiding opinions of the General Office of the State Council on promoting the construction and development of medical consortiums*. https://www.gov.cn/zhengce/content/2017-04/26/content_5189071.htm

General Office of the State Council. (2022, March 29). *Notice of the General Office of the State Council on issuing the "14th Five-Year Plan for the Development of Traditional Chinese Medicine"*. https://www.gov.cn/zhengce/content/2022-03/29/content_5682255.htm

General Office of the State Council. (2022, May 20). *Notice of the General Office of the State Council on issuing the "14th Five-Year Plan for National Health"*. https://www.gov.cn/zhengce/content/2022-05/20/content_5691424.htm

Li, Z. F. (2020, October 29). "13th Five-Year" period sees 7.5% annual growth in fiscal health expenditure. *China Financial and Economic News*. https://114.118.9.73/epaper/index.html?guid=1732742846168956931

National Bureau of Statistics. (2022). *China statistical yearbook 2022*. China Statistics Press.

National Health Commission. (2020). *China health statistical yearbook 2020*. Peking Union Medical College Press.

National Health Commission of the People's Republic of China. (2022). *Statistical bulletin on China's health development in 2021*. https://www.gov.cn/xinwen/2022-07/12/content_5700670.htm

Z. Feng et al. (eds.), *China's Health System*, Introduction to China's S&T Innovation, https://doi.org/10.1007/978-981-95-1205-8

5. China's Medical Security System

Chen, X. Z., & Yu, Y. Y. (2010). Construction of supplementary medical insurance system and its path selection. *Health Economics Research, 1*, 34–36.

Cheng, X. Y. (2010). *Health insurance* (2nd ed.). Fudan University Press.

Diao, X. H., & Tan, X. Y. (2010). The construction sequence and system integration of China's medical security system. *Finance & Economics, 3*, 77–84.

Gu, H., & Wu, D. (2021). The basic connotation and strategic conception of high-quality development of basic medical security system during the "14th Five-Year Plan" period. *Management World, 9*, 158–167.

Gu, X. (2017). The fragmentation of China's medical security system and its governance. *Academia Bimestris, 1*, 126–133.

Jia, H. B., & Yang, Y. N. (2013). The development of China's supplementary medical insurance: Achievements, problems and solutions. *China Soft Science, 1*, 81–92.

Jia, W. Z. (2008). Research on the current situation and countermeasures of urban medical assistance system in China. *Population & Economics, 1*, 61–66.

Lei, X. S., & Cui, F. (2016). Integration and improvement of basic medical insurance system for rural and non-working urban residents. *Journal of Northwest a&f University (Social Science Edition), 16*(5), 1–7.

Li, X. W., & Wu, H. Z. (2009). Historical development and current situation of medical assistance system. *Chinese Health Economics, 28*(12), 32–35.

Li, Z. (2007). *Social security theory* (2nd ed.). China Labor and Social Security Publishing House.

Liang, H., Qu, D. W., & Zhao, D. Y. (2007). The concept and institutional design of medical assistance for urban poor in China. *Chinese Health Resources, 10*(6), 290–292.

Liu, L. L. (2006). Social medical assistance systems in various countries and their enlightenment to establishing social medical assistance for urban poor in China. *Population & Economics, 1*, 65–70.

Liu, Y. L., Cheng, X. Y., Meng, Q. Y., Tian, J., Zhou, C. H., & Ding, G. W. (2003). Design of basic service package for medical assistance to poor and vulnerable groups. *Chinese Health Economics, 22*(6), 14–15.

Lu, Z. X. (2003). *Social medical insurance.* People's Medical Publishing House.

Lyu, Z. Y., & Wang, X. (2013). Research on the coupling and coordinated development of commercial health insurance and social medical insurance system. *Insurance Studies, 9*, 31–42.

Meng, Q. Y., Yang, H. W., Chen, W., Sun, Q., & Liu, X. Y. (2015). *Health system in transition.* World Health Organization.

Peng, H. R., & Yue, J. L. (2020). The integration of China's basic medical insurance system: Theoretical debates, practical progress and future prospects. *Academic Monthly, 52*(11), 55–65.

Qiu, Y. L., & Wang, Z. Q. (2018). Analysis on the integrated development of basic medical insurance system for urban and rural residents. *China Health Insurance, 2*, 16–20.

Qiu, Y. L., Zhai, S. G., & Hao, J. (2011). Research on the integrated development of urban and rural medical security: Theory, evidence and countermeasures. *China Soft Science, 4*, 75–87.

Sun, Q. X., Zhu, J. S., Zheng, W., & Li, M. Q. (2007). Reform of China's medical security system: Three-pillar framework of universal coverage. *Economic Science, 5*, 8–17.

Wang, B. Z. (2005). *Medical security.* People's Medical Publishing House.

Wang, C. Q. (2018). Integration of basic medical insurance system for rural and non-working urban residents: Based on policy comparison of 28 provinces. *Dongyue Tribune, 39*(11), 83–92.

Wang, H. F. (2011). *Medical security.* China Renmin University Press.

Wang, J. H. (2009). Comparative study on the convergence models of urban and rural basic medical insurance systems. *Journal of Soochow University (Philosophy & Social Science Edition), 6*, 21–24.

Xia, Y. Q., Jing, X. L., & Duan, Q. J. (2010). Current situation, problems and suggestions on the convergence of basic medical insurance system for rural and non-working urban residents in China. *Chinese Journal of Health Policy, 3*(1), 43–48.

Yao, L., & Xiong, X. J. (2013). *Medical security*. People's Medical Publishing House.
Zhang, T. X. (2001). On the current reform of medical insurance system in China. *Theory Monthly, 3*, 63–64.
Zhao, M. (2009). Review and prospect of China's medical insurance system reform. *Hubei Social Sciences, 7*, 60–63.
Zhu, K., Zhang, X. J., & Zhu, D. W. (2018). Analysis of financing policies for integrated basic medical insurance system for rural and non-working urban residents: Based on equity perspective. *Chinese Journal of Health Policy, 11*(3), 46–50.

6. China's Drug Supply Guarantee System

Yang, S. M. (2016). *Pharmacy administration* (6th ed.). People's Medical Publishing House.
Zhang, X. P., & Liu, L. R. (2023). *Drug management* (2nd ed.). People's Medical Publishing House.
Zhang, Z. Q. (2018). *Hospital pharmacy management*. People's Medical Publishing House.

7. TCM Services and Management

Jia, E. P., Xiong, J. Y., Li, X. L., Peng, Y. Y., Jiang, M. Z., Shen, X., Ren, Y., Yu, H. Y., & Zhang, L. (2020). Research on the current situation and improvement path of traditional Chinese medicine health services in China. *Chinese Hospitals, 24*(3), 25–27.
National Health Commission. (2021). *China health statistical yearbook 2021*. Peking Union Medical College Press.
Xiong, J. Y. (2020). *Research on strategies and mechanisms for improving the development of traditional Chinese medicine*. Science Press.
Zeqiao Doctor. (2022, March 8). *Antimalarial drug—Artemisinin*. https://baijiahao.baidu.com/s?id=1726716997318769683
Zhang, Y., Li, J., & Wang, L. (2024). Current situation, problems and countermeasures of traditional Chinese medicine services in China. *Soft Science of Health, 38*(3), 53–57.

8. China's Health Resource Planning

Li, X. M., & Yin, J. Z. (2017). *Formulation and practice of health planning*. Science Press.
Song, W. K. (1998). Working procedures for regional health planning. *Chinese Health Economics, 17*(1), 26–27.
Wang, S. P., Huang, E. D., & Gan, G. (2021). Thoughts and discussions on the planning ideas and development orientation of the medical and health service system during the "14th Five-Year Plan" period. *Chinese Health Economics, 40*(5), 8–11.
Yan, X. L., Mao, A. Y., Hu, G. Y., Meng, Y. L., & Qiu, W. Q. (2017). The development process, existing problems and prospects of health and family planning planning in China. *Soft Science of Health, 31*(12), 40–43.
Zheng, Y., Dai, T., & Li, L. (2015). Experiences and enlightenment of medical and health service system planning in some countries. *Chinese Journal of Health Policy, 8*(5), 8–12.

9. Health Financing and Total Health Expenditure in China

Chen, W. (2017). *Health economics* (4th ed.). People's Medical Publishing House.

World Health Organization. (2003). *Guide to producing national health accounts: With special applications for low-income and middle-income countries*. World Health Organization.

World Health Organization. (2010). *Health systems financing: The path to universal coverage*. World Health Organization.

World Health Organization & The World Bank. (2021). *Global monitoring report on financial protection in health 2021*. https://iris.who.int/bitstream/handle/10665/350240/9789240040953-eng.pdf?sequence=1

10. Legal System and Supervision of Medicine and Health in China

Chen, Y. L. (2019). *Health law*. Higher Education Press.

Fan, L. H. (2013). *Health supervision* (2nd ed.). People's Medical Publishing House.

Le, H., & Zhao, M. (2020). *Research on the development of health law in China*. Huazhong University of Science and Technology Press.

Yuan, J., Ding, W., & Zhao, N. (2020). *Interpretation of the Law of the People's Republic of China on Basic Medical and Health Care and the Promotion of Health*. China Democracy and Legal System Publishing House.

Zhang, J., & Zhao, M. (2014). *Health law*. Tsinghua University Press.

11. China's Medical and Health Information System

Central Cyberspace Affairs Commission. (2021, December 28). *The Central Cyberspace Affairs Commission released the "14th Five-Year Plan for National Informatization"*. https://www.gov.cn/xinwen/2021-12/28/content_5664872.htm

General Office of the State Council. (2017, April 23). *Guiding opinions of the General Office of the State Council on promoting the construction and development of medical consortiums*. https://www.gov.cn/gongbao/content/2017/content_5191699.htm

Health Commission of Hubei Province. (2022, December 10). *"Healthy Hubei" WeChat public platform and Alipay dual platform serving citizens*. https://wjw.hubei.gov.cn/bmdt/dtyw/202212/t20221210_4450300.shtml

Hu, H. P., Qin, P. P., Lei, X. Y., Gao, X., Wang, Y., & Wan, Y. L. (2019). Development history and prospects of national health informatization in China. *Journal of Medical Informatics, 40*(7), 2–6.

Ma, J. D., & Nan, J. H. (2022). Training path for interdisciplinary health information talents in China under digital transformation. *Journal of Medical Informatics, 43*(3), 9–14.

National Health and Family Planning Commission of the People's Republic of China & National Administration of Traditional Chinese Medicine. (2014, February 20). *Guiding opinions of the National Health and Family Planning Commission of the People's Republic of China and the National Administration of Traditional Chinese Medicine on accelerating the construction of population health informatization*. https://www.gov.cn/gongbao/content/2014/content_2600086.htm

National Health Commission of the People's Republic of China. (2019, January 9). *Notice of the National Health Commission of the People's Republic of China on issuing the work specification for whole-process recording of health administrative law enforcement*. http://www.nhc.gov.cn/zhjcj/s5863/201901/e4f459fc8ce94021b0683679d78f0e0e.shtml

National Health Commission of the People's Republic of China, National Administration of Traditional Chinese Medicine, & National Disease Control and Prevention Administration. (2022, November 9). *Notice on issuing the "14th Five-Year Plan for national health informatization"*. http://www.nhc.gov.cn/cms-search/xxgk/getManuscriptXxgk.htm?id=49eb570ca79a42f688f9efac42e3c0f1

Office of the National Health Commission of the People's Republic of China. (2020, May 21). *Notice of the Office of the National Health Commission of the People's Republic of China on further improving the appointment system and strengthening the construction of smart hospitals*. http://www.nhc.gov.cn/yzygj/s3594q/202005/b2adae99376d4af0834fd8d43c5ddb4f.shtml

Wang, Q. L., Wang, Z., & Qu, Q. (2020). Construction of new national public health information system: Thoughts on improving system resilience. *Reform, 4*, 17–27.

Wang, S., & Su, W. (2010). Current situation, problems and countermeasures of regional medical informatization development in China. *Modern Preventive Medicine, 37*(22), 4241–4243.

Zhou, G. H., Xu, X. D., & Hu, J. P. (2019). Development history, characteristics and prospects from health informatization to national health informatization. *Chinese Journal of Health Informatics and Management, 16*(4), 384–388, 394.